ON COURSE:

Strategies for Creating Success in College and in Life

A GUIDED JOURNAL APPROACH

ON COURSE:

Strategies for Creating Success in College and in Life

A GUIDED JOURNAL APPROACH

SKIP DOWNING
BALTIMORE CITY COMMUNITY COLLEGE

HOUGHTON MIFFLIN COMPANY BOSTON TORONTO
Geneva, Illinois Palo Alto Princeton, New Jersey

To Jocelyn, Jill, and Guy

Sponsoring Editor: Bill Webber
Assistant Editor: Melissa Plumb
Project Editor: Nicole Ng
Senior Production/Design Coordinator: Jill Haber
Senior Manufacturing Coordinator: Marie Barnes

Cover Design & Image: Karen Lehman

We would like to acknowledge and thank the following sources for permission to reprint material from their work:

TEXT: p. 36: "We Real Cool," by Gwendolyn Brooks © 1991 from her book "BLACKS," published by Third World Press, Chicago, 1991; **p. 150:** "Summer Words for a Sister Addict," from *I've Been A Woman*, Third World Press, Chicago, Ill. © 1978 by Sonia Sanchez; **p. 168:** "Piano" by D. H. Lawrence, from THE COMPLETE POEMS OF D. H. LAWRENCE by D. H. Lawrence, edited by V. de Sola Pinto & F. W. Roberts. Copyright © 1964, 1971 by Angelo Ravagli and C. M. Weekley, Executors of the Estate of Frieda Lawrence Ravagli. Used by permission of Viking Penguin, a division of Penguin Books USA Inc.; **p. 177:** "Harlem (A Dream Deferred)," from THE PANTHER AND THE LASH by Langston Hughes. Copyright © 1951 by Langston Hughes. Reprinted by permission of Alfred A. Knopf, Inc.

(Credits continued on p. 225)

Printed in the U.S.A.

Library of Congress Catalog Number: 95-76934

ISBN: 0-395-73878-4

123456789—B—99 98 97 96 95

Contents

Preface

On Course is the result of my own quest to live a rich, personally fulfilling life and my strong desire to pass on what I've learned to my students. As such, *On Course* is a very personal book. In it, I invite readers to explore in depth their personal world: their successes and failures, their strengths and weaknesses, their thoughts and actions, their feelings and beliefs, their goals and dreams, their past and present, and, most importantly, their ideal future.

In the past few decades, courses that teach study skills have made an important contribution to student success at many colleges and universities. However, barriers to students' success go far beyond weak study skills. Today, many students find greater obstacles among the complicating forces in their lives — such as jobs, relationships, children, and personal problems — and the resulting challenge of making consistently wise choices. Before students can make full use of a college experience, they need to master their own lives. *On Course* shows students how to make wise choices in every realm of their lives. In their journals, students use their college experience as a personal laboratory for discovering how to live a richer, fuller life.

On Course is intended for college students of any age who want to create success both in college and in life. Its focus on proven success strategies makes *On Course* ideal for use in student success courses, freshman seminars, college orientations, and any "inward-looking" courses of psychology, self-exploration, or personal growth. Its extensive use of guided journals well suits *On Course* for use in college writing classes. *On Course* is intended to help students learn how to write more effectively as they discover how to live more successfully.

Why I Wrote *On Course*

During my first two decades of teaching college English and speech courses, I consistently observed a sad and perplexing puzzle. Each semester I watched students unconsciously sort themselves into two groups. One group achieved varying degrees of academic success: a few of them excelled, others demonstrated competence, and some barely squeaked by. The other group struggled, creating a far less successful outcome: These students withdrew, disappeared, or failed. Now, here is the puzzling part. The unsuccessful students often displayed as much academic potential as their more successful classmates, in some cases more. What, I wondered, caused the vastly different outcomes of these two groups?

And what could I do to help my struggling students achieve greater success?

Somewhere around my twentieth year of teaching, I experienced a series of crises in both my personal and professional life. In a word, I was struggling. After a period of feeling sorry for myself, I embarked on a quest to improve the quality of my life. I read, I took seminars and workshops, I talked with wise friends and acquaintances, I kept an in-depth journal, I saw a counselor, I even returned to graduate school for a masters degree in applied psychology. I was seriously motivated to change my life for the better.

If I were to condense all that I learned into one sentence, it would be this: Successful, happy people consistently make wiser choices than do struggling, unhappy people. I came to see that the quality of my life was essentially the result of all of my previous choices. I saw how the wisdom (or lack of wisdom) of my choices influenced every aspect of my life. The same, of course, was true of my struggling students. Both my students and I could change our lives for the better if we learned how to make wiser choices and make them more often.

For the past decade, I have continued my quest to identify the choices that support success both in college and in life. As a result of what I learned (and continue to learn), I created and teach a course at Baltimore City Community College called the College Success Seminar. This course teaches students how to make the essential choices that empower us all to achieve more of what we want in life. I teach this course in part because it has the power to change my students' lives for the better. I teach it for another, more personal reason. I teach the College Success Seminar and I wrote *On Course* because both activities keep me conscious of the wise choices I must consistently make to live a richer, more personally fulfilling life. Now that much of my life is back on course, I don't want to forget how I got here!

Intended Outcomes of *On Course*

Through readings and guided journals, *On Course* shows students how to make wise choices that can dramatically change the outcomes of their lives. The choices they learn to make will empower them to experience greater . . .

Self-Responsibility.   *On Course* shows students how to take charge of their lives, gaining greater personal control over the outcomes that they create both in college and in life. (Chapter 2: "Accepting Personal Responsibility")

Self-Motivation.   *On Course* assists students to create greater inner motivation by discovering their own personally meaningful goals and dreams. (Chapter 3: "Discovering a Meaningful Purpose")

Self-Management.   *On Course* offers students numerous strategies for taking control of their time and energy, allowing them to move more effectively and efficiently toward accomplishing their goals and dreams. (Chapter 4: "Taking Purposeful Actions")

Interdependence.   *On Course* assists students to move beyond dependence, co-dependence, and rigid independence to develop interdependent relationships that support both parties to achieve their goals and dreams. (Chapter 5: "Developing Mutually Supportive Relationships")

Inner Awareness. *On Course* assists students to understand and revise their self-defeating patterns of behavior, thought, and emotion as well as their unconscious limiting beliefs. (Chapter 6: "Succeeding from the Inside Out")

Active and Life-Long Learning. *On Course* shows students a powerful process of learning that moves them from being passive recipients of their education to being active seekers of personally relevant knowledge. (Chapter 7: "Maximizing Your Learning")

Optimism, Happiness, and Inner Peace. *On Course* offers students effective strategies for improving their positive experience of life and their sense of emotional well-being. (Chapter 8: "Creating a Positive Experience of Life")

Self-Esteem. *On Course* helps students develop self-acceptance, self-confidence, self-respect, self-love, and unconditional self-worth. (Chapter 9: Believing in Yourself")

Writing Skills. *On Course* assists students to improve their writing skills through the extensive writing practice offered by guided journal entries.

Creative and Critical Thinking Skills. *On Course* emphasizes the thinking skills essential for analyzing and solving problems in students' academic, professional, and personal lives.

Features of the Text

Articles on Success: *On Course* presents forty-two short articles, each explaining proven strategies for creating success in college and in life. Each strategy is based upon the ideas of respected figures in psychology, philosophy, business, sports, politics, literature, and personal and professional effectiveness.

Guided Journal Entries: Following each article, a guided journal entry gives students an immediate opportunity to apply the success strategies to their lives and to practice effective writing skills. The journal entries are designed not only to teach students about success strategies but also to teach them writing strategies used by accomplished writers.

Personal Assessment Questionnaires: *On Course* begins and ends with a personal assessment questionnaire. By completing the initial one, students can see what areas of growth need their focused attention. By completing the concluding questionnaire, students can see their semester's growth in developing new attitudes and behaviors that will support their success.

Focus Questions: Each journal section begins with focus questions that encourage students to read the articles with the purpose of finding personally valuable answers. This feature assists students to improve their reading skills by encouraging them to formulate questions before reading and to seek answers while they read. Focus questions are also useful for initiating class discussions or free-writing activities.

Quotations: Each text section features quotations expressing the wisdom of famous and not-so-famous people regarding the success strategies under consideration. These quotations can function either as prompts for class discussion or additional free-writing experiences.

Poems & Cartoons: Poems and cartoons throughout the book are thematically linked with the success strategies being explored and provide additional prompts for class discussion or free-writing.

Exercises: The instructor's resource manual includes numerous in-class exercises that encourage active exploration of the success strategies presented in the students' journals. These exercises include role playing, learning games, dialogues, demonstrations, metaphors, mind-mappings, brainstorms, questionnaires, drawings, skits, scavenger hunts, and many others. These exercises offer dynamic prompts for class discussion or free-writing.

Support for the Instructor

Instructor's Resource Manual: This resource manual offers specific suggestions for using *On Course* in various kinds of courses (including step-by-step directions for leading the exercises mentioned above). Additionally, the manual endeavors to answer questions that instructors might have about using *On Course* to support their students' success.

Instructor Trainings: The author conducts faculty development workshops for educators who wish to learn strategies for assisting students to be successful in both college and in life. These workshops are ideal for, but not limited to, college instructors who wish to learn effective ways of using *On Course* with their students. For information, please contact the author through the Houghton Mifflin Faculty Development Programs at 1-800-856-5727.

"Roundtable Discussions" Videotapes: These two videotapes (the 35-minute "Study Strategies" videotape covers notetaking, reading, memory, and test-taking; the 25-minute "Life Skills" videotape covers goal setting, time management, and stress management) feature five college students who discuss and seek solutions to the problems they face in college and in life. Each videotape is also available in a closed-captioned version. Call 1-800-733-1717 or contact your Houghton Mifflin representative for more information.

Acknowledgements

This book would not exist without the assistance of an extraordinary group of people. I can only hope that I have returned (or will return) their wonderful support in kind.

At Houghton Mifflin I would like to thank Alison Zetterquist for her faith in a book that chose a road less traveled, and Melissa Plumb for her meticulous word-crafting and persistent, gentle guidance. And especially Daryl Peterson — mentor and friend — thanks for sharing the vision.

At Baltimore City Community College, my thanks go to president Jim Tschechtelin for his enthusiastic support of the College Success Seminar. Also, I acknowledge the extraordinary work of my colleagues, the teachers of the College Success Seminar: Tessie Black, Paul Blaisdell, Joan Cobb, James Coleman, Carolyn Dabirsiaghi, Mona Hartz, Doug Holt, Synethia Jones, Lynn Kerr, Angela Lawler, Audrey Lawson, Jon Mangana, Stanley Mazer, Art Mueller, Elliott Oppenheim, Asnah Perlman, Anita Read, Ann Ritter, Robert Selby, Almeta Sly, Alfred Sutton, Eric Wakefield, Mardi Walker, and Jerry Wood, all of whom made my job a treat. Eric Hallengren's constant encouragement picked me up and got me back on course more times than he will ever know — thanks, bud.

To Anita Read and Eric Wakefield, what would I have done without your wisdom, love, and unflagging support? To Tom Maze, Rich Rosen, John McDaniel, and Roxanne MacDougal, thanks for your active listening, your guidance, and most of all, your friendships.

Additionally, I'd like to thank Dave Ellis for inspiring me to make different choices as a teacher, Ron and Mary Hulnick and Norm Frye of the University of Santa Monica for creating the learning environment in which I could discover how to make wiser choices, and Pauline Signor and her colleagues at Harrisburg Area Community College for believing in my dream even before I did, and supporting me to make it come true.

A number of wise and caring reviewers have made valuable contributions to this book, and I thank them for their guidance:

Kathy Carpenter
University of Nebraska—Kearney

Dora Mae Estey
Pearl River Community College

Lori Kanitz
Oral Roberts University

Leslie Kaufman
Burlington County College

Joanne O'Neill
Austin Community College—Pinnacle Campus

Peter J. Quinn, Sr.
Commonwealth College

Susan J. Rossbottom
Johnson and Wales University

Adelaida Santana
Northern Arizona University

James Tschechtelin
Baltimore City Community College

Finally, my deep gratitude goes out to the students who over the years have had the courage to explore and change their thoughts, actions, feelings, and beliefs. I hope, as a result, you have all lived richer, more personally fulfilling lives. I know I have.

S.D.

Chapter 1
■■■■■■■■■

GETTING ON COURSE
TO YOUR SUCCESS ■■■■■■■■■■■

focus questions If you were totally successful, what would you **have,** what would you be **doing,** what kind of person would you **be**? How will college help you achieve success as you define it?

■ ■ ■ ■ 1. Taking the First Step

Congratulations on choosing to attend college! With this choice, you've begun a journey that can lead to a future of great personal and professional success.

Have you decided yet what "success" means to you? Do you know how you'll decide years from now if you've achieved success in college and in life?

I've asked many college graduates what success meant to them while they were undergraduates. Here are some typical answers.

When I was in college, success to me was . . .

. . . getting all A's and B's while working a full-time job.

. . . making two free throws to win the conference basketball championships.

. . . improving my grade point average every semester.

. . . having a great social life.

. . . parenting two great kids and still making the dean's list.

. . . being the first person in my family to earn a college degree.

. . . graduating with honors.

College is a place where a student ought to learn not so much how to make a living, but how to live.
Dr. William A. Nolen

Notice that the emphasis here is on *outer success*: high grades, social popularity, sports victories, college degrees. These successes are public. They are the visible achievements that allow the world to judge one's abilities, one's value, one's worth.

I've also asked college graduates, "If you could do your college years over, what would you do differently?" Here are some typical answers:

If I got a second chance at college, I would . . .

. . . focus on learning instead of getting good grades.

. . . major in engineering, the career I really wanted.

. . . constantly ask myself how I could use the information or the skill of each course to enhance my life.

. . . have someone teach me how to take care of myself in a more support-ive and nurturing way.

. . . be more diligent about setting and obtaining my goals.

. . . spend more time experiencing my feelings and get more involved with issues on campus for which I had strong feelings.

. . . learn more about the world I live in and more about myself . . . espe-cially more about myself!

Notice that the focus some years after graduation is on *inner success*: enjoy-ing learning more, believing in themselves, following their true interests, focus-ing on their own values, applying what they have learned to create more fulfilling lives.

These successes are private. They are the invisible inner accomplishments that other people can *not* see, let alone judge. These victories give us a deep sense of personal contentment, happiness, and self-worth.

None of this is to suggest that outer success is not important. It is. But inner satisfaction is also important, and it is inner success that is often overlooked until too late in life. Only with hindsight do most college graduates realize that, to be completely satisfying, success must occur both in the visible world *and* in the invisible spaces of our minds and hearts.

As a college teacher, I have seen thousands of students arrive on campus with a dream, then struggle, fail, and fade away. I've seen thousands more come to college with a dream, pass their courses, then graduate having done little more than cram thousands of new facts into their brains. Sure, they've earned a de-gree, but as thinking, feeling, acting human beings, they remained virtually un-changed.

This book, then, is about how to achieve both outer *and* inner success in col-lege and in life. It is about how to achieve success in the world while becoming more aware of and happy with who you really are.

To that end, I suggest the following definition of success for your consideration:

Success is staying on course to your greatest dreams, while creating wisdom, happiness, and unconditional self-worth along the way.

Our primary responsibility in life, I believe, is to perfect the incredible po-tential with which each of us is born. All of our experiences — including col-lege — merely serve (or fail to serve) the creation of our best selves.

On Course will show you how to use your college experience as a laboratory experiment. In this laboratory you'll search for methods that will support you to create a rich, personally fulfilling life. Chapters two through five offer you specific strategies for staying on course to your greatest dreams in the outer world — college degrees, loving relationships, great jobs, valued possessions, world travel, and the like. Chapters six through ten suggest specific strategies for creating important inner experiences — greater wisdom, happiness, and unconditional self-worth, for example. Your job is to experiment with all of these strategies and pick the ones that work for you.

Getting on course to your success

Here is a curious puzzle: Two students enter a college class on the first day of the semester. Both appear to have similar intelligence and abilities. The weeks slide by. Before you know it, the semester ends. Now look at this: One student has passed, the other failed. One soared, the other stumbled. One fulfilled his potential, the other fell short. Why the difference?

More important . . . which one of these students is you?

Teachers observe this puzzle in every class. I know you've seen it, too . . . not only in school, but also in sports, in business, in politics, in relationships . . . every place where two or more people gather. Some folks have a knack for creating success in their lives. Others wander about dazed, confused, and often bitter at life, unable to create the success they say they want.

What, then, *are* the essential human ingredients for creating success?

The cycle of success

The quality of our lives is determined by the quality of the choices we make on a daily basis. **Successful people stay on course to their destinations by *choosing beliefs and behaviors* that less successful people don't choose.**

Like the chicken and the egg, it's hard to say which came first, the beliefs or the behaviors. Some psychologists argue that beliefs cause behaviors. Other psychologists argue that behaviors create the beliefs.

This much is clear: Once you adopt a positive belief or an effective behavior, you usually find yourself getting on course to success. Positive beliefs lead to effective behaviors. Effective behaviors foster additional positive beliefs. You're now in a cycle of success. Thus, it matters little which comes first, beliefs or behaviors. What matters is this:

> **When you create a habit of choosing effective behaviors and empowering beliefs, you maximize your chances of staying on course to success.**

Here are a few examples that illustrate how the choice of beliefs and behaviors affects the outcomes in our lives. Until 1954, most track and field experts believed that it was physically impossible for a human being to run a mile in less than four minutes. On May 6, 1954, however, Roger Bannister erased this limiting belief by running a mile in the world-record time of 3:59.4. Once Bannister had proven that running a sub-four-minute mile was possible, within months, many other runners also broke the "impossible" four-minute barrier. In other words, once runners chose a new belief (*a sub-four-minute mile is possible*), they pushed their physical abilities to perform new behaviors, and suddenly the impossible became possible.

Our actions affect our attitudes, and our attitudes affect our actions.
Shad Helmstetter

Here's another example. Students often slip off course when they don't do as well on a test as they had hoped or expected. After a disappointing test score, struggling students often express their negative belief with a judgment like, *Well, I knew I couldn't do college math!* That belief will likely lead to negative behaviors such as missing classes and not doing assignments. These self-defeating behaviors lead to even lower test scores and further negative beliefs. The student is now so far off course that passing math seems impossible. This illustrates the cycle of failure. In that same class, however, someone with no better math ability is passing the course. Why? Because this second student has chosen beliefs and behaviors that keep her on course to maximizing, rather than minimizing, the abilities with which she was born. This student believes, "*I* **can** *pass college math.*" She chooses positive behaviors such as doing all assignments, getting a tutor, and asking the teacher for assistance. Her grades go up and her empowering belief is confirmed. This student is on course to success in math. She has created her own cycle of success.

Someone once said, "If you keep doing what you've been doing, you'll keep getting what you've been getting." That's why if you want to improve your life (and why else would you have come to college?) you'll need to change some of your beliefs and behaviors. In this course, you will have an opportunity to learn many beliefs and behaviors that have assisted people in all walks of life to achieve success.

A well-written life is almost as rare as a well-spent one.
Thomas Carlyle

By experimenting with some new beliefs and behaviors, you'll learn which success strategies will make a positive contribution to your life. Once the choice of these new beliefs and behaviors becomes a habit in your life, you, too, will be in the cycle of success. You will be on course to creating your dreams in college . . . and in life.

Write your life

College is the perfect place to design the life you want to live. A time-tested tool for this purpose is a journal, a written record of your thoughts and feelings about your past, present, and future.

Journal writing is an opportunity to turn your mental focus inward to the center of who you are, who you used to be, and who you are becoming. In your journal for this course, you'll write the script that will keep you on course to your greatest goals and dreams. Along the way, you'll also explore and discover your unique "self."

Journal work is an excellent approach to uncovering hidden truths about ourselves, and I heartily recommend keeping an autobiographical, private log of both triumphs and tribulations along this path.
Marsha Sinetar

Because you will be writing about your life and your success (important stuff!), I urge you to purchase a special journal book. You can buy an inexpensive composition book, or you can splurge and purchase a fancy journal book. Either way, your journal will become a valued record of your growing wisdom about your life.

Many people who keep journals do what is called "free writing." They simply write whatever thoughts come to mind. This approach can be extremely valuable for exploring issues that are present in one's mind at that moment. Think of free writing like being on a journey in which you can explore whatever points of interest you happen upon.

In using *On Course*, however, you will write a different kind of journal — a guided journal. A guided journal is like going on a journey with an experienced mentor. Your guide takes you places and shows you sights that you might never have discovered on your own. What you give up in spontaneity you get back manyfold in the depth of learning available through the experience of your guide.

In each journal article, you'll read about success strategies that have made a major impact on the lives of others. Then, in the guided journal entry that follows, you'll be invited to take three steps: 1) relax, 2) think, and 3) write.

The first two steps — relaxing and thinking — are crucial. Our first thoughts about any issue are often what we believe we *should* think, rather than an expression of our own personal experience and truth. Our initial thoughts may merely be tape recordings of ideas we've heard from influential adults in our lives. To find your own voice, it's important to relax and focus on what **you** really think.

After relaxing and thinking, begin writing your thoughts (guided by the journal directions) as fast as they come. Imagine that your thoughts are liquid and you are pouring them into your journal without pausing to edit or rewrite. The more you practice writing, the easier your ideas will flow! There will be plenty of time afterwards to polish what you write.

Here are five suggestions to help you create a meaningful journal:

- *Be spontaneous*: Write whatever comes into your mind in response to the directions. Don't concern yourself with what is "right" or "wrong."
- *Write for yourself*: Imagine that you'll find your journal ten, twenty, or even thirty years from now. Write for that older, wiser you.
- *Be honest*: Tell yourself the absolute truth; therein lies the route to your most significant discoveries.
- *Be creative*: Use words, use drawings, use poems. Add color. Add photographs. Add pictures from magazines. This is your journal. Express your best "self."
- *Dive deep*: When you think you have exhausted a topic, write more. Your most valuable ideas and discoveries will often take the longest to surface from the recesses of your unconscious mind. So, most of all — DIVE DEEP!!

After you have written a number of journal entries, you will likely find that you have mastered a technique for discovering your creative thoughts, for breaking through mental blocks, and for increasing the depth and quality of your thinking and writing. Most significant, in your journal you will very likely make discoveries about yourself and initiate changes that will dramatically alter the outcome of your life for the better.

Relax

Before you write each journal entry, you will be invited to take a few moments to *RELAX*. You might be tempted to rush past this suggestion. Resist the urge. The few moments it takes you to relax in the special way we will discuss will pay you back many times over in benefits.

Many experiments have shown that relaxation before a learning session greatly improves the results. Here's why. During a normal day, your brain is continually firing electrical waves at fourteen or more cycles per second. These waves, known as *beta* waves, are great for getting daily tasks done, but they're less efficient for learning something new.

Research clearly shows that a short period of relaxation prior to a problem-solving session significantly enhances your mental ability.
David Lewis & James Green

When you take a few minutes to relax deeply, your brain waves slow down. These slower waves, called *alpha* waves, occur at between seven and fourteen cycles per second. Studies worldwide have compared the impact of various types of brain waves on learning. The evidence is clear: *Alpha waves increase learning capacity*.

When we experience *alpha* waves, our mind is better able to focus on learning because it is less distracted by muscle tension in our body or by irrelevant thoughts in our conscious mind. Additionally, in the *alpha* level, our conscious mind seems able to retrieve information held in our unconscious mind, information that would otherwise be unavailable to us. Relaxation also appears to allow the two sides of our brain — the logical and linear left brain and the creative and holistic right brain — to work together. All in all, *alpha* waves seem to tune up our brain for increased mental performance.

As if the mental benefits weren't enough, relaxation aids us physically as well. Medical studies of people who do daily relaxation sessions reveal physical benefits that include lowered blood pressure, increased energy, relief from inner tension and stress, improved physical health, and strengthened immune systems. Furthermore, people who relax regularly benefit with improved emotional health, an increased sense of well-being, and, often, enhanced self-esteem.

*Physiological research also shows this calmed state of the body facilitates mental functioning and learning. The body uses **less** energy, so there's more for the mind.*
Sheila Ostrander & Lynn Schroeder

To achieve relaxation, only four elements are required: 1) a quiet place; 2) a comfortable physical position; 3) a passive attitude; and 4) something on which to focus your mind.

Any quiet place where you will be undisturbed is appropriate for deep relaxation. Many people use music to assist them in achieving relaxation. The music should have a slow beat (sixty beats per minute is ideal) and no words to distract you. Some people find it relaxing to listen to tapes of environmental sounds like the ocean, a bubbling stream, or gently falling rain. Listening with earphones is an effective way to shut out all other distractions.

Various positions are appropriate for relaxation, but one that many people like is simply sitting in a comfortable chair with your feet flat on the floor, toes pointing somewhat outward. Rest your arms and hands in your lap. Find a comfortable position for your head, probably tipped slightly forward. When you close your eyes, imagine that you are looking at the tip of your nose. If you decide to relax while lying on a bed, couch, or carpeted floor, find a similarly comfortable position, but be sure to stay awake.

Many ways to achieve deep relaxation have been discovered. Two effective approaches are described below. The first method is a more physical approach, and the second a more mental approach to relaxation. Experiment and decide which works better for you. If you already have a relaxation process that works for you, stick with it.

You may wish to tape record the directions to your preferred relaxation method over soothing music or environmental sounds. Then you can simply sit back, pull on your earphones, and the tape player does the rest. Tape recording the directions is unnecessary, however. The directions are easy to remember, and after a few sessions, you will be able to follow them easily from memory.

Mastery of some sort of relaxation techniques may conceivably become a regular part of a child's educational experience.

Allyn Prichard & Jean Taylor

Relaxation Method #1: Find a comfortable position in your chair and close your eyes. Breathing deeply through your nose, feel your stomach expand with the air filling and refreshing you. Hold your breath for a count of five. Now expel the air with a loud sigh.

Breathing deeply through your nose, take another deep breath and tighten the muscles in your *feet*. Hold your breath and keep your muscles tight for a count of five. Now expel the air with a loud sigh and let your feet relax fully.

Breathing deeply through your nose, take another deep breath and tighten the muscles in your *calves*. Hold your breath and keep your muscles tight for a count of five. . . . Now expel the air with a loud sigh and let your calves relax fully.

Keep doing this progressive relaxation as you move up your body. Breathe deeply, then (one at a time) tighten and relax the muscles in your thighs, buttocks, lower back and abdomen, upper back and chest, shoulders and neck, then your face and scalp.

Finally, taking one more deep breath, tighten all of the muscles of your body. Hold your breath and keep all of your muscles tight for a count of five. Now expel the air with a loud sigh and let your whole body relax fully.

Enjoy the feeling of being fully relaxed. And when you are ready, slowly open your eyes feeling supremely relaxed and completely refreshed.

For fast-acting relief, try slowing down.

Lily Tomlin

Relaxation Method #2: Find a comfortable position in your chair and close your eyes. Breathing slowly and deeply through your nose, feel your stomach expand with the air filling you and refreshing you. Hold your breath for a count of five. Now gently release your breath.

Continue to breathe slowly and deeply through your nose, focusing your attention on the tip of your nose. Be aware of the air each time it passes in and out.

If thoughts wander into your mind, simply release the distracting ideas and bring your attention back to the tip of your nose once more. Again, become totally conscious of the air going in and out as it passes the tip of your nose.

Become especially aware of how each breath is slightly different from all others.

At first you will probably find that holding this alert mental focus on your breath is a challenge. You may, therefore, wish to begin with a very short session (a minute or two), slowly adding time to your sessions. Some practitioners of

No matter what you want to
learn — from guitar playing
to real-estate law — you'll do
better if you know how to
relax.

Sheila Ostrander
& Lynn Schroeder

this meditation technique can focus on their breath for many hours. For our purposes, five minutes will probably give the refreshed, mentally heightened focus that will benefit your thinking and writing.

One caution: Don't expect to gain total control of your thoughts. Your mind will wander from thought to thought. This is natural. Don't criticize either yourself or your mind for leaping about. When your mind entertains thoughts other than your breathing, gently remind yourself that you are relaxing now; then let go of the thought and return your focus to your breathing.

To achieve its greatest efficiency, your body needs vigorous exercise. Your mind, however, requires quite the opposite. To achieve its greatest efficiency, your mind needs the focused relaxation that creates *alpha* waves. Choosing to relax before your mental workouts will improve the quality of your thoughts, your writing, and your life.

Self-assessment

Before looking at the choices of successful students, take a few minutes to complete a self-assessment questionnaire on the next page. Your discoveries about yourself may suggest areas of your life that could benefit from change. As you write your guided journals over the next few months, you will learn many strategies that will assist you to make these positive changes in your life. At the end of this book, you will have an opportunity to repeat this self-assessment. By comparing your two scores, you will see how you have changed.

This self-assessment is not a test. There are no right or wrong answers. The questions simply give you an opportunity to look at aspects of yourself that will have a significant impact on the kind of future you create. The picture you create of yourself today will only be accurate if you are absolutely honest. Have fun with this activity. This is your first step on a journey that can change the outcome of your life!

The deepest personal defeat
suffered by human beings is
constituted by the difference
between what one was capable of becoming and what one
has in fact become.

Ashley Montagu

Self-assessment

Read the seventy statements below and score each one according to how true or false you believe it is about you. To get an accurate picture of yourself, consider what is currently true about you (not what you want to be true).

Assign each statement a number from zero to ten, as follows:

totally false 0 1 2 3 4 5 6 7 8 9 10 totally true

1.____ I live day to day, without much of a plan for the future.
2.____ I use my time extremely well.
3.____ I prefer working on projects with other people.
4.____ When I think about performing an upcoming challenge (such as a college test), I picture myself doing poorly.
5.____ I lack confidence about learning something new.
6.____ I make wise choices that help me get what I really want in life.
7.____ I'm comfortable expressing my emotions.
8.____ I have important things in my life that I've put off completing for too long.
9.____ I accept myself just as I am, even with my faults and weaknesses.
10.____ I know very few people on whom I can really count for help.
11.____ I have a written list of specific, long-term goals.
12.____ I finish what I start.
13.____ I have learned important lessons from the obstacles in my life.
14.____ Rather than complain, blame others, or make excuses, I look to solve my problems.
15.____ When I encounter a problem, I ask for help.
16.____ I'm not sure what I want to accomplish in the next three to six months.
17.____ I forget to do important things in my life.
18.____ Whether I'm happy or not depends mostly on me.
19.____ When fun activities come up, I often postpone school assignments until later.
20.____ I feel very committed to what I am doing with my life right now.
21.____ The quality of my life is mostly the result of the choices I've made.
22.____ While other people are talking to me, I often think about what I'll say next.
23.____ I find little value in the feedback I get from teachers.
24.____ I often feel bored or anxious.
25.____ I have a network of people in my life whom I can count on for help.
26.____ I have learned valuable lessons from my failures.
27.____ I often think about my positive qualities.
28.____ I feel very uncommitted to what I'm doing in my life right now.
29.____ I make poor choices that keep me from getting what I really want in life.
30.____ I like myself better when I'm a success.
31.____ I waste a lot of time.
32.____ I break promises that I make to myself or to others.
33.____ I don't make the same mistake twice.
34.____ I seldom express my true feelings.
35.____ The quality of my life is mostly the result of things beyond my control.
36.____ I could do better work on my school assignments if I wanted to.
37.____ I'll accept myself more as soon as I get rid of my faults and weaknesses.

totally false 0 1 2 3 4 5 6 7 8 9 10 totally true

38.___ I have a written list of specific goals that I want to accomplish in the next three to six months.
39.___ I often feel happy and fully alive.
40.___ I hold back from telling others what I'm really thinking.
41.___ Whether I'm happy or not depends mostly on what's happened to me lately.
42.___ I'm very aware of why I've made the important choices I have in my life.
43.___ I write lists of the important tasks I need to do each day.
44.___ When I realize I'm not going to be able to achieve a goal that I want, I let it go and move on.
45.___ The feedback I get from most teachers has value for me.
46.___ I have no long-term goals that excite me.
47.___ I prefer working on projects by myself.
48.___ I feel that I'm not as worthwhile as some other people I know.
49.___ I'm confident that I will accomplish my greatest goals and dreams.
50.___ I tend to complain, blame others, or make excuses.
51.___ I do my very best work on school assignments.
52.___ I have trouble finishing what I start.
53.___ I often think about my negative qualities.
54.___ People consider me to be a good listener.
55.___ I tend to hang onto things (people, jobs, dreams) long after they've stopped being good for me.
56.___ I'm not sure I'm capable of achieving my most important goals and dreams.
57.___ My failures have brought me much pain and little value.
58.___ I keep promises that I make to myself or others.
59.___ When I look at important choices I've made, I wonder why I made them.
60.___ I like myself even when I've failed.
61.___ I try to solve my problems by myself.
62.___ I have a written plan that states exactly what I intend to accomplish during my life.
63.___ I tend to repeat my mistakes.
64.___ I forgive people who do or say things I don't like.
65.___ When I think about performing an upcoming challenge (such as a college test), I picture myself doing well.
66.___ When I have important school assignments to do, I postpone fun activities until later.
67.___ I'm good at telling people what I'm thinking in a way that lets them really understand me.
68.___ I believe that I can learn anything I need or want to know.
69.___ Obstacles to my success are a frustration and nothing more.
70.___ I think that I'm just as worthwhile as other people I know.

Transfer your scores to the scoring sheets on page 11. For each of the seven areas, total your scores in columns A and B. Then total your final scores as shown in the sample.

Self-assessment Scoring Sheet

sample			
A		**B**	
6. _3_		19. _8_	
14. _6_		29. _6_	
21. _4_		35. _5_	
42. _4_		50. _6_	
66. _8_		59. _8_	

_25_ + 50 – _33_ = _58_

score #1

A	**B**
6.____	19.____
14.____	29.____
21.____	35.____
42.____	50.____
66.____	59.____

____ + 50 – ____ = ____

score #2

A	**B**
11.____	1.____
20.____	16.____
27.____	28.____
38.____	46.____
62.____	53.____

____ + 50 – ____ = ____

score #3

A	**B**
2.____	4.____
12.____	17.____
43.____	31.____
51.____	36.____
65.____	52.____

____ + 50 – ____ = ____

score #4

A	**B**
3.____	10.____
15.____	22.____
25.____	40.____
54.____	47.____
67.____	61.____

____ + 50 – ____ = ____

score #5

A	**B**
13.____	5.____
26.____	23.____
33.____	57.____
45.____	63.____
68.____	69.____

____ + 50 – ____ = ____

score #6

A	**B**
7.____	8.____
18.____	24.____
39.____	34.____
44.____	41.____
64.____	55.____

____ + 50 – ____ = ____

score #7

A	**B**
9.____	30.____
49.____	32.____
58.____	37.____
60.____	48.____
70.____	56.____

____ + 50 – ____ = ____

Carry these scores to the corresponding boxes in the chart on page 12.

CHOICES OF SUCCESSFUL STUDENTS

Your score	Successful students . . .	Struggling students . . .
Score _____	1. . . .accept **personal responsibility** for creating the quality of their lives.	1. . . .see themselves as victims, believing for the most part that what happens to them is out of their control.
Score _____	2. . . .discover a motivating **purpose,** characterized by personally meaningful goals and dreams.	2. . . .have difficulty choosing a purpose, often experiencing depression and/or resentment about the meaninglessness of their lives.
Score _____	3. . . .consistently plan and take effective **actions** in pursuing their goals and dreams.	3. . . .seldom identify the specific actions needed to accomplish a task. And when they do, they tend to procrastinate.
Score _____	4. . . .build **mutually supportive relationships** that assist them in pursuing their goals and dreams.	4. . . .are solitary, not requesting, even rejecting offers of assistance from legitimate resources.
Score _____	5. . . .**maximize learning** by finding valuable lessons in nearly every experience they have.	5. . . .tend to resist learning new ideas and skills, often viewing learning as drudgery rather than play.
Score _____	6. . . .actively create a **positive experience of life** characterized by optimism, happiness, and peace of mind.	6. . . .experience life negatively, focusing much of their attention on what is disappointing and painful.
Score _____	7. . . .**believe in themselves,** feeling capable, lovable and unconditionally worthy as human beings.	7. . . .doubt their personal value, feeling inadequate to accomplish meaningful tasks and unworthy to be loved by others or by themselves.

Now you can identify your strengths and weaknesses on these important life choices. A score below fifty suggests that, for this choice, you have the beliefs and behaviors of a struggling student. A score between fifty and eighty indicates that your beliefs and behaviors in this realm will sometimes get you off course. A score above eighty suggests that you have developed supportive beliefs and behaviors that will help you keep on course. In the next few months, you will learn how to choose all of these beliefs and behaviors more consistently. If you choose them as your daily habits, you will definitely get on course to achieving success both in college and in life. I wish you a great journey. Let us begin!

Journal #1

In this journal entry, you'll have an opportunity to take an important first step toward your success in college and in life. This first step is a personal inventory of your strengths and weaknesses. You'll do this inventory by analyzing the results of your self-assessment questionnaire. In this way, you'll discover changes that you'll want to make in your behaviors and beliefs, changes that will get you on course to a rich, personally fulfilling life.

1. In your journal, write a paragraph (or more) exploring what you learned about yourself from the self-assessment questionnaire. Consider areas of personal strength, areas of weakness, and discoveries that surprised, disappointed, or pleased you. Your entry might begin, *By doing the self-assessment, I learned that I . . .*

2. Write another paragraph (or more) exploring changes you would like to make in yourself during this course. Consider the saying, "If you keep doing what you've been doing, you'll keep getting what you've been getting." With this thought in mind, identify the specific changes you'd like to make in yourself over the next few months.

As you write, remember the five suggestions mentioned earlier for creating a meaningful journal: 1) **Be spontaneous.** 2) **Write for yourself.** 3) **Be honest.** 4) **Be creative.** 5) **Dive deep.**

If you take a few minutes to relax before writing, you will get much more value from this journal entry. Use either of the relaxation methods you learned in this introduction or any other method that works for you.

Relax, think, and write.

Chapter 2

Accepting Personal Responsibility

I accept responsibility for creating my life as I want it.

Successful Students . . .	**Struggling Students . . .**
1. . . . **adopt the Creator role,** believing that their choices create the outcomes of their lives.	1. . . . accept the Victim role, believing that external forces determine the outcomes of their lives.
2. . . . **live consciously,** keenly aware of their situation and the options available for bettering their lives.	2. . . . live unconsciously, oblivious to the reality of their situation and the ineffectiveness of their choices.
3. . . . **make wise choices,** thus designing the future they want.	3. . . . let the future happen by chance rather than by choice.
4. . . . **master the language of Creators.**	4. . . . use Victim language.
5. . . . **make mature decisions,** accepting short-term pain when necessary to achieve long-term gains.	5. . . . act like children, often choosing immediate pleasure at the expense of long-term gains.

■ ■ ▪ ■ 2. Adopting the Creator Role

I am the master of my fate;
I am the captain of my soul.
William E. Henley

I first met Deborah when she was a student in my English 101 class; she was taking the course for the fourth time. Deborah was in her early thirties and a mother of three. She wanted to be a nurse, but before she could qualify for the nursing program, she had to pass English 101.

"Your writing shows fine potential," I told Deborah after I had read her first essay. "You'll pass English 101 as soon as you eliminate your grammar problems."

"I know," she said. "That's what my other three teachers told me."

"Well, let's make this your last semester in English 101. After each essay, why don't you make an appointment with me to go over any grammar problems."

"Okay."

"And, do you know about the Writing Lab?"

"Oh, sure," she said.

The more we practice the habit of acting from a position of responsibility, the more effective we become as human beings, and the more successful we become as managers of our lives.

Joyce Chapman

"Go to the lab as often as possible. Start by studying verb tense. Let's eliminate one problem at a time."

"I'll go this afternoon!"

But Deborah never found time: *No, really . . . I'll go to the lab just as soon as I . . . .*

Deborah scheduled two conferences with me during the semester. She canceled them both: *I'm so sorry . . . I'll come to see you just as soon as I . . . .*

To pass English 101 at our college, students must pass one of two essays written at the end of the semester. Each essay, identified by social security number only, is graded by two other instructors. At semester's end, Deborah once again did not pass English 101.

"It isn't fair!" Deborah protested. "Those exam graders expect us to be professional writers. This is the only class that's keeping me from becoming a nurse!"

I suggested another possibility: "What if *you* are the only obstacle keeping you from becoming a nurse?"

Deborah didn't like that idea. She wanted to believe that her problem was "out there." The obstacle was her teachers. All her disappointments were their fault. She saw herself as helpless.

I reminded Deborah that it was *she* who had not studied her grammar. It was *she* who had not come to conferences. It was *she* who had not taken the actions that she knew she had to take to pass the course. It was *she* who had not accepted personal responsibility for creating her life the way she wanted it.

"Yes, but, . . ." she said.

Personal responsibility

Many people misunderstand this idea of personal responsibility. To them, *responsibility* is a heavy burden. They picture themselves dragging RE-SPONS-I-BIL-I-TY through life. Add a little chain gang music here, and you'll have the idea.

Quite the contrary, being personally responsible is *not* a burden. In fact, accepting responsibility is the only way to take greater control of your life.

The essence of being personally responsible is responding effectively to all of life's opportunities and challenges.

When responsible people encounter a stimulus — a person, idea, or event, say — they pause for a moment to consider their available choices. They decide which choice is most likely to keep them on course to their success (without hurting others). Then they take action. If they don't get the results they want, they evaluate what went wrong, and then try something different.

When irresponsible people experience a stimulus in their lives, they automatically respond according to old patterns. If the result is undesirable, they blame, complain, excuse, and repeat ineffective behaviors.

When responsible people create the best life possible given their circumstances, they are acting as **Creators**. When irresponsible people allow life to happen to them, they are acting as **Victims**.

When you accept personal responsibility, you accept that you are responsible for creating *everything* in your life. **Everything!** This idea upsets some people. They don't believe for a moment that they created what they have in their life. Accidents happen, they say. Other people treat them badly. Some things just aren't their fault. Sometimes they really are victims of outside circumstances.

This claim, of course, is true. At times, we *are* all affected by circumstances beyond our control. If a hurricane destroys my house, I am a victim (with a small "v"). But if I allow that event to ruin my life, I am a Victim (with a capital "V"). Whether I see them or not, I still have choices.

People who respond to life from Victim consciousness have very little chance of creating a rich, full, satisfying life. If I believe that my parents, or society, or a teacher, or a neighbor, the economy, the government, bad luck, or whatever, is responsible for the results in my life, then most likely I'll sit back and wait for them to change. I'm choosing to be a Victim.

The essential issue is this: Would it improve your life to believe that you are the cause of all that you have in your life? No matter who may *actually* be responsible, would you be better off to assume that *you* create the outcomes in your life?

Answer "YES!" and see how that belief will improve your life. After all, if you believe that someone or something out there causes all of your problems, then it's up to "them" to change. What a wait that can be! How long will Deborah, in our earlier example, have to wait for "those English teachers" to change?

If, however, you believe that *you* create your own results, what happens then? As a Creator, you will choose the behaviors and beliefs necessary to keep you on course to your best possible life.

Psychologist Richard Logan studied people who had survived ordeals such as being imprisoned in concentration camps or lost in the frozen Arctic. Logan found that all of these survivors shared one thing in common. They believed with certainty that their destiny lay in their own hands. They accepted personal responsibility for the outcomes of their lives. When you resist personal responsibility, you're in conflict with outside forces because you blame them for your problems. Whether your challenge is excelling in college or surviving an Arctic blizzard, accepting personal responsibility moves you into cooperation with yourself and with your world. You begin to take the actions necessary to improve your life.

Responsibility and choice

[Y]ou are responsible for the eventual outcome of your life. You have been given the greatest power in the world — the power to choose.

Denis Waitley

The key ingredient of personal responsibility is **choice**. Animals respond to a stimulus because of instinct or habit. For humans, however, there is a brief moment of decision available between the stimulus and response. In this moment, we make — consciously or unconsciously — a choice that influences the quality of our lives.

Suppose, for example, as you're climbing into your friend's car, you realize she's had too much to drink (stimulus). What's your response? You could ignore her drunkenness or get out of the car. You could ask to drive, suggest waiting until she sobers up, or scream at her. What do you choose?

Or, suppose you have an important test tomorrow and a friend calls with free tickets to a great concert (stimulus). What are your possible responses? Which do you choose?

Hundreds (maybe thousands) of times each day, you have an opportunity to make a choice. Some are tiny in their impact (Shall I get my hair cut today or tomorrow?). Some are huge (Shall I stay in college or drop out?). The accumulation of the many choices you make will create the outcome of your life.

The moment of choice looks like this:

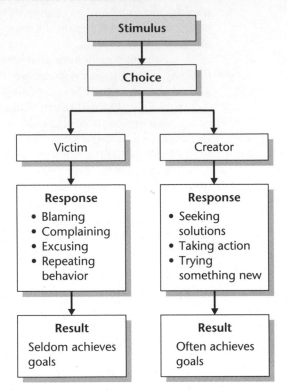

[*T*]*here is a gap or a space between stimulus and response, and . . . the key to both our growth and happiness is how we use that space.*

Stephen R. Covey

Once we accept responsibility for choosing our lives, everything is different. We have power. We decide. We are in control.

Will Schutz

*Properly credentialed institutions with legitimate faculty offer the **possibility** of an education, the **opportunity** to study, the occasion to work with accomplished thinkers. It is the student who must avail himself or herself of these resources. The college educates no one.*

Christopher Monte

In that brief moment between stimulus and response, we can choose as a Victim or as a Creator. We each have it within us to respond either way. When we respond as a Victim, we complain, blame, make excuses, and repeat ineffective behaviors. When we respond as a Creator, we pause at each decision point and ask, "What are my options, and which option will propel me toward my greatest dreams, towards becoming my best, happiest self?"

Successful people are masters of their own choices. In difficult times, a Creator believes, *There's always a better choice, and I am responsible for finding it.*

In truth, sometimes a better alternative does *not* exist. But believing that a better choice exists motivates you to look for it. By looking, you often find choices you otherwise would never have discovered. People with the richest lives seek and find positive choices. They are always creating a better life.

Choosing to accept personal responsibility is the first step towards being an exceptional student — and an exceptional human being.

Irresponsible students (Victims) believe their role is to soak up information poured on them by teachers, then squeeze it back out on tests. If they don't understand the subject, they blame the teacher (or someone or something else). They make excuses. They wait. They grumble. They repeat ineffective actions.

Often they quit. They do little to improve their educations or their lives, all the while believing they have no other choice.

Personally responsible students (Creators) realize that college merely offers them an *opportunity* to learn. They pause at each decision point and consider their alternatives. They seek solutions. They act purposefully. They try something new. They create an education worth having and a life worth living.

The best teacher in the world cannot teach a Victim. The worst teacher in the world cannot stop a Creator.

No matter what is going on outside of you, you have control over what you are learning, and that means you can create your experience in college and in life *as you want it*.

THE FAR SIDE   By GARY LARSON

© 1986 FarWorks, Inc./Dist. by Universal Press Syndicate

8·28   Larson

"Stimulus, response! Stimulus, response!
Don't you ever *think?*"

Journal #2

In this journal entry, you will have an opportunity to adopt the Creator role. When you do, you immediately gain a greater sense of control and an increased ability to create your life as you want it.

1. In your journal, write each of the eight sentence stems below two or more times, completing the sentence differently each time. Each time you complete the sentence stem, your mind will dig deeper into your life experience for greater insights.

For example, for the first sentence stem you might write:

I am a Shawnee. . . .
I am the maker of my own fortune.

Tecumseh

1-1. IF I TAKE FULL RESPONSIBILITY FOR ALL OF MY ACTIONS, *I will have no one to blame if I fail.*

1-2. IF I TAKE FULL RESPONSIBILITY FOR ALL OF MY ACTIONS, *I will get more done.*

1-3. IF I TAKE FULL RESPONSIBILITY FOR ALL OF MY ACTIONS, *I will feel more powerful.*

Remember the five suggestions from the Introduction for creating a meaningful journal: 1) **Be spontaneous.** 2) **Write for yourself.** 3) **Be honest.** 4) **Be creative.** 5) **Dive deep.**

1. IF I TAKE FULL RESPONSIBILITY FOR ALL OF MY ACTIONS . . .
2. IF I TAKE FULL RESPONSIBILITY FOR ALL OF MY THOUGHTS . . .
3. IF I TAKE FULL RESPONSIBILITY FOR ALL OF MY FEELINGS . . .
4. IF I TAKE FULL RESPONSIBILITY FOR MY EDUCATION . . .
5. IF I TAKE FULL RESPONSIBILITY FOR MY CAREER . . .
6. IF I TAKE FULL RESPONSIBILITY FOR ALL THAT HAPPENS TO ME . . .
7. WHEN I AM ACTING RESPONSIBLY . . .
8. IF I WERE TO CREATE MY VERY BEST SELF . . .

2. Write a paragraph (or more) exploring what you have learned in this journal entry about personal responsibility and how you will use this awareness. You might begin, *I have learned that I . . .*

Before beginning, take a few minutes to relax. Remember, it takes time to develop a new habit and experience its benefits.

Relax, think, write.

How could you become more aware of making Creator choices instead of Victim choices?

■ ■ ■ ■ ■ 3. Living Consciously

Unhappiness comes from unawareness.
Will Schutz

Because Creators seem to live richer, fuller lives than Victims do, it's perplexing that so many people choose to live as Victims. One explanation lies in the difficulty of becoming conscious, the state of mind of a Creator.

To make wise choices we must be conscious of our situation, aware of our possible choices, and mindful of our personal responsibility to create our lives as we want them.

Think of the process of maturing as a journey from darkness to light. When we're born, we exist in a kind of mental darkness: we're unconscious (or unaware) of what exists beyond our own immediate needs. As we mature, growing wisdom illuminates our awareness, and we gradually learn what it is to be human and alive. We become more conscious of the impact of others on us and our impact on them. If all goes well, the light of inner consciousness grows brighter, and we see more clearly both what we want and how to achieve it. We see how to stay on course to our dreams while assisting others to pursue their dreams as well. Those individuals who become fully enlightened have mastered the tools for living a personally meaningful and satisfying life. Theirs is a life that is mentally, physically, emotionally, and spiritually exceptional.

And how many of these fully conscious folks have you met in your life? I might have met one or two.

Consciousness, then, is one of our most valuable human qualities. It is an ability unique to mankind among all living creatures. With consciousness, we are able to step outside of ourselves and view ourselves. We can think about what we think about. We can consider what we are doing, then decide what is working and what is not. We can consciously change ourselves. Conscious choice, then, is the extraordinary alternative to instincts and habits. With it, we have one of the greatest tools not only for survival, but also for creating rich, full lives.

Wherever we are in our life, the deepening of the quality of consciousness within us is our most important attainment.
Ira Progoff

Unconsciousness

To live consciously means to seek, to be aware of everything that bears on our actions, purposes, values, and goals, and to behave in accordance with that which we see and know.
Nathaniel Brandon

Despite the ability for consciousness, many human beings — whether eighteen-year-old freshmen or sixty-year-old Ph.D.s — trudge through life in a mental fog that keeps them from seeing the true role they play in creating the outcomes of their lives.

Meet a couple of unconscious people I have known:

Years ago, the president of our college lectured the faculty, administration, and entire staff for thirty minutes about what he called "the most important ingredient of a good college." That ingredient, he said, was respect for others. He assured his audience that he respected each and every one of us, and he asked that everyone at the college treat our students with the same respect, and . . . In mid-sentence he paused . . . and paused . . . glaring off into the audience. Everyone began to get uncomfortable. What the heck was going on? Everyone followed the president's angry gaze to the back row of seats where it settled on a middle-aged man wearing work clothes. Whispers: "Who is he?" "I never saw him before." "I think he's a new custodian." Then silence. All eyes stared at the man, wondering what he might have done.

Finally, the man said nervously, "Is there something wrong?"

The president snapped, "Would you please have the common courtesy to remove your hat while I'm speaking!"

The custodian sank into his chair, wordlessly reached up, tugged a knit cap off his head, and stuffed it between his legs. Then the president resumed his lecture about the importance of "respecting others," unconscious of the pain he had just inflicted.

Here's another example of unconsciousness. A woman in my class asked if she could turn an assignment in late. "I have so much to do, I just couldn't finish it on time."

"It sounds as if your busy schedule could cause you a problem with every assignment. Would you like help organizing your time?" I asked her.

We made a list of her time commitments: college, work, friends, church, sleep, commuting, and so on. We added up all of her weekly time commitments and subtracted them from the 168 hours in a week. It turned out that she had 45 hours left over! That's the equivalent of a full-time job plus overtime . . . yet each week she let this huge part of her life dribble away, wasted. And yet she was sure that she didn't have time to do her college assignments. Unconscious!

Our former college president could never understand why the faculty and staff gave him so little respect; after all, hadn't he made it clear in his speeches how much he respected them? The woman student never turned in one assignment on time the entire semester. Two of them she never turned in at all. She failed the course, but after all, she was so busy!

Now, you may say, "But I'm more conscious than these two people. I would never do such ridiculous things. I'm more aware than that!"

Are you sure? How much do you *really* see, hear, and feel of what's going on around you? Do you see the anger or happiness in other people's eyes? Can you tell who's in love and who's in pain? Can you always tell whether you bring someone joy or hurt his feelings? As you listen to an instructor, are you aware of all the ideas she considers important? When you read a book, are you conscious of the main point of every chapter? How about the main point of this chapter?

Are you conscious of what is directly behind you right now? Are you aware of how you feel right now and why? Do you know what judgements you have made against yourself or others? What excuses you offer or whom you blame for your mistakes? Do you know when you are responding to a stimulus out of habit or out of choice? Are you aware right now whether you are on course or off course? Are you conscious of all you could be doing to live an exceptional life?

*Unless we **think**, clearly and consciously, about each and every choice we make, our choices will **always** be made for us by someone else or by the programs that we carry with us in our subconscious minds.*

Shad Helmstetter

I know of no more elevating fact than the unquestionable ability of man to elevate his life by conscious endeavor.

Henry David Thoreau

Getting conscious

One way to become more conscious is to become familiar with your inner cast of characters. Psychologists call them "sub-personalities," "primary selves," or "aspects." These aspects are constantly chattering in our head about the world, about other people, and about ourselves.

See if you can become aware of an inner voice talking to you right now. Listen. Do you hear it?

Some of you may think, "This is crazy — listening for voices in my head — who ever heard of such a thing?" Thanks for noticing. That doubting voice is one of your aspects talking to you right now. Your inner voices are no small matter. Which inner voice you allow into your consciousness determines the choices you make and the actions you take. Because these actions will determine the outcome of your life, it benefits you to choose your inner voices wisely. And which inner voice you choose will depend on whether you are in Victim consciousness or Creator consciousness.

In Victim consciousness, two of the loudest internal voices are those of your Inner Critic and Inner Defender.

The Inner Critic.   As soon as an uncomfortable situation occurs, our Inner Critic begins to criticize us for the mess we've made. Its voice sounds startlingly like that of our parents (or other authority figures) when they were being judgmental of us or of others when we were children. As soon as we get the slightest bit off course, the Inner Critic immediately points out how it was our fault. Its intention seems to be to protect us from attack by others by criticizing us first, thus shaping up our actions, thoughts, and feelings. This way we will be acceptable to others and win their approval instead of their condemnation.

The Inner Defender.   The flip side of the Inner Critic is our Inner Defender. Our Inner Defender doesn't like to be judged or criticized. As soon as it senses an attack (whether by someone else or by our own Inner Critic), it launches its own assault on others. Our Inner Defender wants to make excuses and blame others for our rotten circumstances. The Inner Defender rationalizes (think of it as "rational lies") our part in creating the situation. It trots out all sorts of excuses that declare, *It's not my fault!* The blame lies with someone else, bad luck, too little money, a troubled childhood, so little time, not enough coffee, too much coffee. The voice of the Inner Defender sounds startlingly like our own voice when we were scared, confused little children trying to figure out how to avoid criticism or punishment.

There's good news and bad news about these inner voices. The good news is they always confirm the Victim's worst beliefs about other people, about the world, about themselves. Victims prove once again that they are "right."

The bad news is that these inner voices distract Victims from taking the very actions that would improve their situation. Victims continue to have conflicts with friends, to mess up college assignments, to be late for life-changing opportunities, to have strained relationships with their children. Their lives are often one disappointment after another. And as long as they point the finger at everyone else, they never change.

Which inner voice occupies your consciousness on a daily basis? Most people have learned to listen to one of these Victim voices more than the other. Do you endure the harsh self-judgments of your Inner Critic? Or do you hear the angry blaming and whiny excusing of your Inner Defender?

Or do you listen to a different voice all together?

The Inner Guide. Creators resist the inner drama of both their Inner Critic and Inner Defender. Instead they listen to the wisdom of their Inner Guide. The Inner Guide objectively observes the events in a Creator's life, asking simply: *Am I on course or off course? If I'm off course, how can I best get back on course?* Our Inner Guide tells us the absolute truth, allowing us to be more fully conscious of the world, other people, and especially ourselves.

We always have a choice about our inner dialogue. We can think and speak as a Victim: blaming, complaining, and excusing. Or we can think and speak as a Creator: telling ourselves the total truth about where we are, deciding where we want to be, and, if necessary, changing our actions and beliefs to get back on course.

Whether we choose to listen to our Inner Critic, our Inner Defender, or our Inner Guide will change the outcome of our life. To illustrate, let's look at what happened to one student. First, we'll view the event as seen through the thoughts of a Victim; then we'll see the same event in the mind of a Creator.

#1 Student's Story as a Victim (heeding his Inner Defender and Inner Critic): *I screwed up again and didn't get my psychology paper done on time. Now the professor is going to take off ten points for lateness. He's so unfair. I wrote the paper in the computer lab, but when I went to print it, nothing happened. I couldn't even find my file. I can't believe what a jerk I am. Maybe I'll just drop the course. I'm probably going to fail anyway.*

#2 Same Student's Story as a Creator (heeding his Inner Guide): *The truth is that I waited until the last minute to write my psychology paper. I went to the computer lab only a few hours before the paper was due. When I tried to save my file, I kept getting an error message that I didn't understand, and the next thing I knew I had erased my whole paper without saving it. I'll rewrite the paper in the computer lab this afternoon, and I'll ask for help with the computer if I need it. I'll turn in the paper tomorrow and accept the ten-point penalty for lateness. In a sense, ten points is a small price to pay for learning to do assignments before they become urgent and to ask for help when I need it. I won't make those same mistakes again.*

Same situation — totally different perspective. The unconscious Victim feels satisfaction knowing he is "right" (in this case he confirms that the teacher is unfair and that he — the student — is a jerk who always screws up); but he remains far off course. By contrast, the conscious Creator listens to the objective facts observed by the Inner Guide, bypasses criticizing the teacher and judging himself and goes right to solving his problem. Within minutes of discovering his mistake, the Creator has learned a valuable lesson and is back on course.

You can see that the Inner Guide thrives on honesty and objectivity. The Inner Guide avoids blaming, complaining, and excusing. The Inner Guide asks:

The essential goal of contemplation is increased awareness of the world outside oneself, the world inside oneself, and the relationship between the two.

Dr. M. Scott Peck

When your conscious awareness watches your own body and mind and all the people and things in the world around you from a deep, calm place inside, you will find that there intuitively wells up within you everything you need to understand.

Ken Keyes

What is *really* happening in my world? What is the absolute truth here? What did I pretend not to know that got me into this situation? How did I create or contribute to what is happening to me? What part did I play in getting off course? What choices can I make to get back on course?

Your Inner Guide is your voice of heightened consciousness. Its total (and sometimes painful) honesty is an essential ingredient in making the wise choices that will lead to success.

Journal #3

In this journal entry, you will have an opportunity to become more conscious. Once you become aware of how you get off course, then you can take actions to get back on course.

In this activity, you'll explore a situation that went badly for you. As in the two students' stories in this section, you'll describe the situation twice: first as a Victim (with the complaining, blaming and excusing of your Inner Defender and Inner Critic), then as a Creator (with the total honesty of your Inner Guide).

1. Write about a time when you felt you were truly a victim. Perhaps you were victimized by a teacher, a parent, an employer, a policeman, a brother or sister, a bad driver, a classmate, a roommate, an adviser, a husband or wife, a coach, a girl friend or boy friend. In this experience, someone "did you wrong."

Write what happened, making it clear how you were victimized. Explain how "they" were responsible for the terrible things that happened to you. Accept no responsibility for what occurred! None! It was all their fault. Let your Inner Defender make great excuses for you and heap the blame on others.

2. Now, rewrite the *same* story taking one hundred percent of the responsibility for what happened. Here is the key: Using the absolute honesty of your Inner Guide, tell how *you* created or contributed to the problem discussed in Step 1. Don't change what happened; just accept responsibility for your part in the problem. Let your Inner Guide tell the truth that your Inner Critic and Inner Defender pretended not to know. These details will let the Creator in you see how to get back on course.

However — and this is very important — as you write your Creator's version of the event, do not blame yourself or others. Do not make excuses, either. What you did is simply an action that got you off course. What others did is simply what they did.

Have fun with this! In your first version of the story, be a great Victim. In your second version, (with the help of your Inner Guide) be a great Creator. You may want to review the examples in this section as models for your Victim and Creator stories.

3. Write a paragraph (or more) discussing what you learned in this journal about living consciously and how you will apply it in your life.

Telling the truth pops the cork. Out flows the person.
Will Shutz

To get maximum value from your efforts, remember to take a few deep breaths and move right into your favorite relaxation method before writing.

Relax, think, write.

How do you make important decisions? How could you improve the quality of your decisions?

■ ■ ■ ■ 4. Managing Your Choices Wisely

Life is a journey with many crossroads, and every crossroad requires a choice. What we're experiencing in our lives today is a result of our past choices. Likewise, what we will experience in five or ten years is the outcome of the choices we'll make from here on.

This is an exciting thought. If we can be conscious of our important choices and manage them wisely, we can more likely create the future that we want.

On the road to your college degree, you will face choices such as these: Shall I . . .

The end result of your life here on earth will always be the sum total of the choices you made while you were here.
Shad Helmstetter

- major in business, science, or creative writing?
- work full-time, part-time, or not at all?
- form a study group or study by myself?
- go to a math tutor or rely on my book?
- ask my teacher a question or stay confused?
- drop a boring course or stick it out?
- study for my exam or go out with friends?

The sum of these choices, plus thousands of others, will determine your degree of success in college and in life. Doesn't it seem wise, then, to develop an effective strategy for choice management?

The Wise-Choice Process

A person defines and redefines who they are by the choices they make, minute to minute.
Joyce Chapman

In the face of any challenge, you can make a responsible decision by answering the six questions of the Wise-Choice Process. This process is a variation of a problem-solving technique developed by Dr. William Glasser.

1. **WHAT'S MY PRESENT SITUATION?** The important information here is, "What exists?" (not "Whose fault is it?"). Keep your Inner Critic — that self-criticizing voice in your head — out of it. Also ignore your Inner Defender — that judgmental voice that blames everyone else for your problems. All you want here are the objective facts of your situation, including how you feel about them. That's a role for your Inner Guide — your wise voice of consciousness that is uncontaminated by blaming, complaining, and excusing.

Man ultimately decides for himself! And in the end, education must be education toward the ability to decide.
Dr. Viktor E. Frankl

I stayed up all night studying for my first history test. When I finished taking the test, I thought I had done well. I hoped for an A. At worst, I expected a B. When I got the test back, my grade was a D. Five students in the class got A's. I feel depressed and angry.

What we really mean by free will, of course, is the visualizing of alternatives and making a choice between them.

Jacob Bronowski

2. **HOW WOULD I LIKE IT TO BE?** You can't change the past, but you can shape your future. If you could create your ideal outcome for this situation, what would it look like?

I would like to get A's on all of my future tests.

3. **DO I HAVE A CHOICE HERE?** The answer is always "YES." No matter how trapped you may feel, if you believe that you <u>do</u> have choices, you will probably find some. Victims seldom move beyond this point in the decision-making process because they assume they have no choice. If you find yourself thinking you have no choice, ask yourself, "What would I do if the survival of someone I love depended on my discovering another option?" Sometimes we don't see another choice simply because we haven't made finding it important enough.

Yes, I always have a choice!

4. **WHAT ARE MY POSSIBLE CHOICES?** Make a list of possible choices. You can create the list by yourself or with the help of a friend, teacher, counselor, or support group. Compile the list without evaluating the suggestions. Don't say, "Oh, that would never work." Don't even say, "That's a great idea." Judgment during brainstorming stops the creative flow of ideas. Move out of judgment into possibility and encourage the most outrageous suggestions possible. One of them may open a door to a choice that might otherwise have remained hidden. Create a list of options that you *could* do, knowing that you are not obligated to do any of them. So make your list long — and be daring!

- *I could continue feeling sorry for myself.*
- *I could complain to my classmates and anyone else who will listen.*
- *I could drop the class and take it next semester with another teacher.*
- *I could complain to the history department head that the teacher grades unfairly.*
- *I could talk to my successful classmates and see how they studied.*
- *I could ask the teacher for suggestions about improving my grades.*
- *I could request an opportunity to retake the test for a higher grade.*
- *I could get a tutor for the next test.*

Let us think of life as a process of choices, one after another. At each point there is a progression choice and a regression choice. There may be a movement toward defense, toward safety, toward being afraid, but over on the other side there is the growth choice. To make the growth choice instead of the fear choice a dozen times a day . . . is a movement toward self-actualization. . . .

Abraham Maslow

5. **WHAT'S THE LIKELY OUTCOME OF EACH POSSIBLE CHOICE?** If you can't predict the outcome of one of your possible choices, stop. You probably need more information. One student stopped her Wise-Choice Process right here when she didn't know the impact that dropping a course would have on her financial aid. She got information from the financial aid office before going on to the next step.

- *Continue feeling sorry for myself: I'd feel lousy, and I'd still have my grade problem.*
- *Complain to classmates: I'd have the immediate pleasure of blasting the teacher and maybe get others' sympathy.*

- *Drop the class: I'd lose three credits this semester and possibly have to make them up in summer school.*
- *Complain to the department head: Probably he'd ask if I've seen my teacher first, so I wouldn't get much satisfaction.*
- *Talk to my successful classmates: I might learn how to improve my study habits and improve my next test score; I might also make new friends.*
- *Ask the teacher for suggestions: I might learn what I need to do next time to improve my grade; at least the teacher would know that I want to do well in the course.*
- *Request an opportunity to retake the test: My request might get approved and give me an opportunity to learn while I raise my grade. At the very least, I'd demonstrate that I'm willing to go the extra mile to do well.*
- *Get a tutor for the next test: It wouldn't help my grade on this test, but it would probably improve my next test score.*

6. **WHICH CHOICE(S) WILL YOU COMMIT TO?** In this final step, decide which choice(s) will likely create the most favorable outcomes and commit to doing it (or them). If no positive choice exists, then consider which option leaves you no worse off than you were before. If no such option exists, then ask which choice creates the least unfavorable outcome(s).

> *I'll talk to my successful classmates, make an appointment with my teacher and have him explain what I could do to improve, and I'll request an opportunity to retake the test. If these choices don't raise my next test score to at least a B, I'll get a tutor.*

Notice that if the situation were different, the options selected would probably be different as well. In the example above, if the student had failed four tests (instead of getting a D on the first test of the semester), a wise choice might be to drop the class. Or, if everyone in the class were receiving D's and F's on the tests, and if the student had already met with the teacher, a responsible option at this point might be to see the department head about the teacher's grading policies.

No matter what your final decision may be, the mere fact that you are making a choice is wonderfully empowering. When you reject the indecision of a Victim and adopt the decision-making of a Creator, you energize yourself. By participating in the Wise-Choice Process, you demonstrate that you believe you *can* change the outcome of your life. You *can* create your future as you wish it to be. You *are* in control of your destiny.

The Road Not Taken

Two roads diverged in a yellow wood,
And sorry I could not travel both
And be one traveler, long I stood
And looked down one as far as I could
To where it bent in the undergrowth;

Then took the other, as just as fair,
And having perhaps the better claim,
Because it was grassy and wanted wear;
Though as for that the passing there
Had worn them really about the same,

And both that morning equally lay
In leaves no step had trodden black.
Oh, I kept the first for another day!
Yet knowing how way leads on to way,
I doubted if I should ever come back.

I shall be telling this with a sigh
Somewhere ages and ages hence:
Two roads diverged in a wood, and I —
I took the one less traveled by,
And that has made all the difference.

—*Robert Frost*

Journal #4

In this journal entry you will have an opportunity to apply the Wise-Choice Process to improve a difficult situation in your life. As you learn to make better decisions, you will dramatically improve the quality of your life!

Think about a current problem, one that you're comfortable sharing with your classmates and teacher. As a result of this problem, you may be angry, sad, frustrated, depressed, or afraid.

Perhaps this upsetting situation has to do with a college course, a grade you received, a teacher's comment, a classmate's action, an unfair requirement. Or maybe the problem relates to a relationship, money, job, or health. Find some situation in your life which isn't the way you want it to be. Now you have an opportunity to be a Creator and change this situation for the better.

When I see all the choices I really have, it makes the world a whole lot brighter.
Debbie Scott, Student

1. Write the six questions of the Wise-Choice Process, and answer each one as it relates to your situation. When you complete the process, see if you don't feel more energized, more powerful, more in control of your life!

The Wise-Choice Process

1. WHAT'S MY PRESENT SITUATION? (Describe the problem objectively and completely.)
2. HOW WOULD I LIKE IT TO BE? (What is your ideal outcome?)
3. DO I HAVE A CHOICE HERE? (Yes!)
4. WHAT ARE MY POSSIBLE CHOICES? (List lots of them.)
5. WHAT'S THE LIKELY OUTCOME OF EACH POSSIBLE CHOICE? (If you can't predict the likely outcome of an option, stop and gather more information.)
6. WHICH CHOICE(S) WILL I COMMIT TO? (Pick from your list of choices in Step 4.)

2. Write a paragraph (or more) about what you learned from doing the Wise-Choice Process. You might begin, *By doing the Wise-Choice Process, I learned that I . . . .*

Relax, think, write.

focus questions

Do you know which words propel you to success, which condemn you to struggle? Do you know how to increase your success by changing the words you think and speak?

◢ ◣ ◢ ◣ 5. Mastering Creator Language

Creators and Victims speak different languages. They might as well be from different planets. Listen carefully to a person's choice of words, especially when something in his life isn't going well. You can tell immediately who accepts responsibility for the outcomes in his life . . . and who doesn't.

Victims think and speak with the voice of their Inner Critic or Inner Defender. Remember, your Inner Critic is the internal voice that criticizes you for everything that goes wrong in your life. The Inner Critic says, "Everything is my fault." Your Inner Defender, on the other hand, tries to protect you by turning criticism outward and blaming everyone else for your problems. The Inner Defender says, "Nothing is my responsibility. It's all *their* fault!"

Listen now to the words of a Victim who is taking a challenging college course. Note the voices of the Inner Defender and Inner Critic:

I hate this course. It's a stupid requirement in the first place. I shouldn't have to take it.

The professor is too boring to pay attention to. All he does is read from his notes. How are you supposed to stay awake?

Going to the support lab is no help. It's noisy in there every afternoon. I try to study for the course, but my housemate is no help. Every time I start to open the book, he's got friends over.

Worst of all, the tests in that course are ridiculous. The professor gave me an F on the first one! No one's passing that class. I bet even Albert Einstein couldn't pass it. I'll never do well in that course, and there's nothing I can do about it.

Or listen to the words of a Victim who wants to lose weight:

I hate being overweight. My clothes don't fit right. I get tired and winded just walking up a flight of stairs. It's awful. I have to lose weight.

It's easy to diet until you get depressed. I've tried going to the gym about twenty different times, but it never lasts.

I've tried every diet known to mankind. But you can hear that junk food calling you when you're trying to study. The next thing you know, you've got an empty bag of cheese puffs next to you. Plus, the TV is always bombarding you with food commercials. I try to ignore them, but it's no use.

I have no self-control, and I've always been that way. I guess some people are just born to be overweight.

If these two Victims don't change their language, it's easy to predict where they'll end up five years from now. The first will still be trying to pass that course; the second will still be overweight. But, if they change their language, they could change their behavior, and if they change their behavior they could change the outcomes of their lives. And so can you.

Let's see what a difference it makes when we translate some of their Victim statements into the language of Creators.

If you want to reach your goals, you need to change your vocabulary.

Zig Ziglar

You must change the way you talk to yourself about your life situations so that you no longer imply that anything outside of you is the immediate cause of your unhappiness. Instead of saying "Joe makes me mad," say, "I make myself mad when I'm around Joe."

Ken Keyes

Victims make excuses

He's too boring to pay attention to.

It's easy to diet until you get depressed.

Victims blame

The professor gave me an F on the first test.

The TV is always bombarding you with food commercials.

Victims complain

It's a stupid requirement in the first place.

I hate being overweight. It's awful.

Victims feel helpless and give up

I'll never do well in that course.

I guess some people are just born to be overweight.

Victims repeat ineffective behavior

Going to the support lab is worthless. It's so noisy in there every afternoon.

I've tried going to the gym about twenty different times, but it never lasts.

Victims "have to" do things

I shouldn't even have to take the course.

I have to lose weight.

Victims pretend their problems belong to others (They say "you" when they mean "I.")

How are <u>you</u> supposed to stay awake?

The next thing <u>you</u> know, <u>you've</u> got an empty bag of cheese puffs next to <u>you</u>.

Creators seek solutions

I find his classes boring. I'm going to tape record his lectures so I can listen to them a little bit at a time.
The next time I feel depressed, I'll go out for a walk instead of snacking.

Creators accept responsibility

I got an F on the first test because I didn't read the assignments thoroughly.
I'm going to record my favorite television programs on my VCR so I can fast forward through the commercials.

Creators take action

I'm going to find out if there's a test I can take to be exempted from this requirement.
I'm going to enroll in a weight reduction class.

Creators profit from past mistakes

Studying alone didn't work for me. I'm going to find others who passed the first test and study with them.
I'm going to stock my refrigerator with low-calorie munchies so I have an alternative to junk food.

Creators try something new

I'm going to visit the support lab when it first opens in the morning; I'll bet there's no crowd that early.
I'm going to jog along the lake this week; maybe I'll enjoy it enough to stick with it.

Creators "choose to" do things

I choose to take this course because it's required for my degree, and my degree will qualify me for the kind of work I've always wanted to do.
I choose to lose weight so I'll look as good on the outside as I feel on the inside.

Creators own their problems (They say "I" when referring to their own problems.)

I find myself falling asleep when I listen to his lectures.
Sometimes I go unconscious and I eat a whole bag of junk food.

Victims distort reality

No one's passing that class. I bet even Albert Einstein couldn't pass it.

I have no self-control.

Victims "try"

I try to study for the course, but my roommate is no help.

I've tried every diet known to mankind.

Most of all, Victims are powerless

There's nothing I can do.
I've always been that way.
I can't . . .
I have to . . .
I should . . .
I quit . . .

Creators tell themselves the truth

A few students are doing well in the class. I guess I haven't done what's necessary to pass the tests in that course.

I have great self-control when it comes to practicing my guitar. Now I just need to transfer that discipline to my eating.

Creators commit and follow through

I'll study for the course for two hours tonight; I'll tell my roommate not to bother me until I'm through studying.

I'm going to make an appointment with a nutritionist and get some expert advice.

Most of all, Creators take control of their choices and their lives

There's something I can do.
I can choose to be different.
I can . . .
I choose to . . .
I will . . .
I'll keep going . . .

Creators accept responsibility for creating the outcomes of their lives, and their words reflect that attitude. Creators resist all excuses, blame, have-to's, lies, and tries. Creators look forward and create their best future!

Whenever you feel yourself slipping into the language of a Victim, ask yourself: *What do I want in my life: excuses or results? What could I think and say that would get me the* **results** *that I want?*

Journal #5

In this journal entry you will have an opportunity to practice Creator language. This is the language of personal responsibility, not excuses, complaints, or blame. When you learn to translate your Victim statements into Creator statements, you will have mastered the language of truly successful people.

1. Draw a line down the middle of one or two journal pages. On the left side of your journal pages, copy the twenty Victim statements below.

2. On the right side of your journal pages, translate the Victim statements into the words of a Creator, just as was done earlier in the journal article.

3. Write a paragraph or more explaining what you just learned about how you use language: Is it your habit to speak as a Victim or as a Creator? Be sure to give examples. What is your goal for your language usage from now on? How will you accomplish your goal? What specific actions will you take? Your paragraph might begin, *While reading about and practicing Creator language, I learned that I . . .*

Relax, think, write.

What you're supposed to do when you don't like a thing is change it. If you can't change it, change the way you think about it. Don't complain.

Advice to Maya Angelou
from her Grandmother

I used to want the words "She tried" on my tombstone. Now I want, "She did it."

Katherine Dunham, African-American Choreographer

VICTIM LANGUAGE	**CREATOR LANGUAGE**
1. *I can never find a parking place.*	
2. *I failed because he's a lousy teacher.*	
3. *It's not my fault that I'm late.*	
4. *I couldn't improve my grade.*	
5. *I've been too upset to get my work done.*	
6. *I should work harder in that class.*	
7. *I have to take English 101.*	
8. *I ought to get a better part-time job.*	
9. *I wish I could write better.*	
10. *That text book is so boring.*	
11. *You can't do homework every night.*	
12. *He's the worst teacher in the school.*	
13. *I had to take a makeup test in math.*	
14. *I'll try to do my best.*	

15. *I couldn't do my homework last night.*
16. *I'll try to pick you up at 8:00.*
17. *I'd die if he/she ever left me.*
18. *My homework didn't get done.*
19. *My parents drive me crazy.*
20. *It's not my fault. I had no choice.*

focus questions Do you think of yourself as a mature adult? Do you know how to tell if, in fact, you are?

■ ■ ■ ■ ■ 6. Making Mature Decisions

[A]n adult is a creation to marvel at; there are so relatively few of them.

Dr. M. Scott Peck

When does adulthood begin? Are you an adult at sixteen, eighteen, twenty-one, twenty-five, or sixty-five? Are you mature when you can drive, drink, vote, join the army, attend college, hold a job, get married, have children, take on a mortgage, retire?

In truth, adulthood has little to do with the passing of years or the roles you play. It has much to do with the maturity of your choices. Adulthood begins when you fully accept personal responsibility for fulfilling your needs and desires without interfering with the rights of others to fulfill their needs.

Children make choices that maximize immediate pleasure. *"I want to feel good **now!**"*

Maturity is approached as the person demonstrates he can and will assume responsibility for his behavior . . . .

Dr. William Passons

Adults enjoy pleasure, too, but they're willing to make choices that reduce immediate pleasure when the future benefits seem worthwhile. *"Even though this would make me feel good now, I'll be better off in the long run if I don't do it."* Adults are also willing to experience discomfort in the present if the payoff in the future makes it worthwhile. *"I don't want to do this now, but I will because I want the future rewards."*

In short, **adults are willing to accept short-term pain to create long-term gain.** The essence of mature decision making is asking, "What will best move me on course to my ideal future?"

Choices . . . always choices!

Joanne was a mass communications major. For as long as she could remember, she had dreamed of being a television newscaster. One of the required courses for mass communications majors was taught by only one teacher. Joanne had taken a course from this professor before and failed. "Any student would hate this guy," she claimed. To her, this professor now stood like a sixty-foot wall between Joanne and her dream. If you had been in Joanne's situation, what choice would *you* have made?

Part of growing up is learning to delay gratification, which helps reduce life's pain and difficulties.

John Bradshaw

Everett told this story: He had once had a high-paying job as a welder. Welding jobs in the area were scarce, and his salary was three times what he could make in any other job he could get. But all was not well. The shift supervisor, Everett said, treated the workers like slaves. If an employee arrived late, the supervisor made him work an hour without pay. Everett, who was in his middle twenties, swore he would never let the supervisor do that to him. In his third month on the job, Everett arrived five minutes late. The shift supervisor started lecturing Everett about promptness and told him to get to work. "And don't expect to be paid for your first hour," he snapped. Everett was furious. What choice would *you* have made?

A man told our class that he had once served prison time for dealing drugs. He swore that he had learned his lesson, and he made an impassioned plea to the other men in the class to stay away from drugs. I learned the rest of the story the following semester from his fiancee. While in college, this man was supporting himself with a minimum-wage job, struggling to make his meager paycheck stretch through the month. Then his fiancee got pregnant. He wanted to marry, and he wanted to be a father, and he wanted a college degree. But he had no money. An acquaintance told him about a quick twenty thousand dollars he could earn. The drug deal was already made. All he had to do was make the delivery. In less than an hour, he could have enough money to get married, to have his child, and to continue college. What choice would *you* have made?

Teresa was studying for her mid-term exam one Saturday afternoon when her sister asked her to go shopping. "C'mon, Teresa, it's the weekend. Are you going to spend your whole life buried in a book? You've got to have some fun, too! Your exams aren't scheduled for another week." Teresa glanced at her books lying before her. Then she looked up at her sister standing at the open door. What choice would *you* have made?

Your choices reveal your maturity

The small child has not the necessary comprehension of time to structure it but simply sets about doing things which feel good, moment to moment. As he gets a little older he learns to postpone gratification for greater rewards.

Thomas Harris

Before we look at the choices these four people made, remember that responsible adults consciously make choices that keep them on course to their dreams . . . without interfering with anyone else's life. Sometimes a mature decision requires postponing pleasure or enduring hardship in the present for a greater reward in the future. A mature person will make sacrifices now for a better life later. An immature person will not.

On the whole, people seem to make more responsible choices as they get older. But I have seen eighteen-year-olds make decisions that demonstrated maturity far beyond their years, and I have seen fifty-year-olds make choices that demonstrated no maturity at all. We can not measure our maturity by how long we've been around; rather, we must base our maturity on the wisdom of our choices to keep us on course to our goals and dreams.

I conceive that pleasures are to be avoided if greater pains be the consequence, and pains are to be coveted that will terminate in greater pleasures.

Michel De Montaigne

So, what choice would you have made if a teacher you disliked stood between you and the career of your dreams? Joanne avoided signing up for the mass communications class taught by the dreaded professor. After one more semester, she dropped out of school and got a job in a department store. Three years later, she has yet to return to college.

What choice would you have made if you were late and your supervisor demanded that you work for fifty-five minutes without pay? Everett quit on the spot. For the next year, he tried with no success to get another welding job. Finally, he enrolled in a job training program, and, after nine months in that program, he got a job as a carpenter's helper, making minimum wage. Shortly thereafter, he decided to enroll in college as a way to get ahead. When I met him in college, he claimed that all of his teachers had unfair rules. He dropped out at mid-semester, and I have never seen him since.

What choice would you have made if offered an opportunity to make a quick twenty thousand dollars in a drug deal? This student accepted the offer and was caught by the police with the drugs in his possession. His fiancee experienced so much stress during the ordeal of his trial that she miscarried, and they lost their baby. As a second-time offender, he received a twenty-year prison sentence (which he is now serving).

Finally, what choice would you have made if someone urged you to leave your studying and go out on a Saturday afternoon for some fun? Teresa decided to finish her studying first, then go shopping if she had time left over. When her sister returned four hours later, Teresa was still studying and still on course to her degree.

Whether you are eighteen or eighty, every choice you make defines you as immature or mature, a child or an adult, a Victim or a Creator, off course or on course.

If you choose as a child does, you will insist on immediate pleasure. You will demand immediate escape from discomfort. You will justify your choices by listening to the blaming and excusing of your Inner Critic and Inner Defender. And you will make these choices even when they take you off course from your dreams.

If you choose as an adult does, you will willingly sacrifice when it means staying on course. You will listen to the objective wisdom of your Inner Guide. This choice may mean giving up immediate pleasure (like forgoing a party to finish a term paper). Or it may mean experiencing discomfort for a while to stay on course (like working at a job you don't enjoy to support yourself through college).

None of this means that you must adopt a bleak, joyless approach to life. In fact, later we'll be exploring how to create greater happiness in our lives as we pursue success in college and in life.

What making mature decisions does mean is this: Sometimes, if we are to stay on course to our goals and dreams, we must exchange short-term pain for long-term gain.

We Real Cool

**The Pool Players.
Seven at the Golden Shovel.**

We real cool. We
Left school. We

Lurk late. We
Strike straight. We

Sing sin. We
Thin gin. We

Jazz June. We
Die soon.

—Gwendolyn Brooks

Sometimes I feel envious when my friends go to parties and I have to go to bed . . . . [W]hatever I've missed, I've made up for. Most kids don't get to go to the Olympics and win three gold medals. It's definitely been worth it. . . .

Janet Evans

Journal #6

In this journal entry you will have an opportunity to evaluate the maturity of your decision making. When you are willing to exchange short-term pain for long-term gain, you will create extraordinary results in your life.

1. With the honesty of your Inner Guide, write and complete the following sentence stem as many times as you can:

In College This Week I Chose To . . .

Let your list contain your major decisions for the past seven days. The more sentences you write, the more you can learn about the maturity of your choices. For example:

1. **IN COLLEGE THIS WEEK I CHOSE TO** *miss my math class on Tuesday*.

2. **IN COLLEGE THIS WEEK I CHOSE TO** *drop my history class*.

3. **IN COLLEGE THIS WEEK I CHOSE TO** *work overtime instead of attending history class*.

4. **IN COLLEGE THIS WEEK I CHOSE TO** *watch television all day on Sunday*.

5. **IN COLLEGE THIS WEEK I CHOSE TO** *major in nursing*.

2. Now, go back and label each decision in your list as ON COURSE or OFF COURSE. Ignore the blaming and excusing voices of your Inner Defender and Inner Critic. Evaluation of your choices is not about making you wrong or bad. It is about evaluating whether or not your choices are keeping you on course to your college degree.

3. Write a paragraph or more about what you learned concerning the maturity of your decisions. Start your paragraph with the main idea (sometimes called the **topic sentence**). For example, you might begin, *I learned that, when it comes to making decisions, I . . .*

In your paragraph, **expand** on your main idea by answering such questions as . . .

• What mature (on-course) decisions did you make this week?
• What benefit will you gain?
• What immature (off-course) decisions did you make this week?
• What price will you pay?
• What are your thoughts about the overall maturity of your choices?
• What changes, if any, will you enact in your decision making?

Relax, think, write.

Chapter 3

■ ■ ■ ■ ■ ■ ■ ■ ■

Once I accept responsibility for creating my own life, I must choose the kind of life I want to create. In other words, I must choose the purpose of my life.

Discovering a Meaningful Purpose ■ ■ ■ ■ ■ ■ ■ ■ ■ ■ ■

I am choosing all the goals for my life.

Successful Students . . .

1. . . . **discover motivating dreams,** providing them with a passionately felt life purpose and consistent motivation.

2. . . . **commit to their dreams,** visualizing the successful creation of their ideal future.

3. . . . **create affirmations** that enhance the personal qualities necessary to achieve their dreams.

4. . . . **choose purposeful short- and long-term goals** that support their dreams.

5. . . . **design a life plan,** giving them a clear picture of the life they wish to create.

Struggling Students . . .

1. . . . have little sense of purpose, passion, or drive in their lives.

2. . . . wander without commitment from one activity to another, holding no positive mental picture of their future.

3. . . . fail to identify and develop the personal qualities necessary to achieve their dreams.

4. . . . have little sense of what they want to accomplish in the coming months and years.

5. . . . tend to invent their life as they live it.

Do you want to feel more motivated? More passionate and alive? Do you know how?

◢ ▬ ◢ ◢ 7. Discovering Your Dreams

Nothing happens unless first a dream.
Carl Sandburg

Do you have dreams that inspire you?

Dreams vault you out of bed in the morning. Dreams motivate you through difficult times. Dreams provide energy when you run headlong into an obstacle. Dreams give your life purpose and meaning.

If you don't have a motivating dream right now, you're not alone. Many people are wandering without a purpose. If you have no motivating purpose for your life, simply make it your intention to find one. Let your dream be to discover your dreams.

Our dreams stand as beacons beckoning us on to greater growth and accomplishments.
Virginia Satir

Many people search for years before they find their purpose in life. Later, they realize that experiences which earlier seemed meaningless or even painful were, in fact, essential preparation for discovering their dreams. Be patient with yourself as you search for your dreams. Trust that you'll discover your dream at exactly the right moment. In the meantime, enjoy the quest for your dreams!

College offers a wonderful opportunity to discover your dreams. In college you'll be exposed to hundreds, even thousands, of new people, ideas, and experiences. With each new encounter, be conscious of your energy. When your voltage rises, pay attention. Something within you is getting inspired.

Think about the roles you have chosen for your life. A life role is any function to which we regularly devote large amounts of time and energy. Right now, for example, one of the major roles you're playing is that of college student.

Man is what his dreams are.
Benjamin Mays, President, Morehouse College

How many of the following roles are you also playing: friend, employee, employer, athlete, brother, sister, church member, cheerleader, son, daughter, roommate, husband, wife, parent, grandmother, grandfather, tutor, choir member, pet owner, musician, neighbor, counselor, business owner, volunteer? Do you play other roles as well?

What dreams do you have for yourself in each of your life roles? If you were to picture your ideal outcome for each of your roles twenty years from now, what would you see? For example, what do you dream of accomplishing in your role as a student? Twenty years from now will you have a two-year associate of arts (A.A.) degree? Will you have a four-year bachelor of arts (B.A.) or bachelor of science (B.S.) degree? Will you go on to graduate school and earn a master of arts (M.A.) or master of science (M.S.) degree? Will you go even further and obtain a doctor of philosophy (Ph.D.) degree, a medical doctor (M.D.) degree, or a doctor of jurisprudence (J.D.) law degree? Any of these futures could be yours.

I swing big, with everything I've got. I hit big or I miss big. I like to live as big as I can.
Babe Ruth

Philosopher Joseph Campbell gave this wise advice for living a meaningful life: "Follow your bliss." Become conscious of when you have found your bliss. When the thought of a future achievement or experience excites you, give it your time and energy.

Whatever you do, don't be limited by puny dreams. Create outrageously bold intentions. Realize that you have special talents to accomplish wonderful things, so dare to dream big! If you want to be a doctor, don't settle for being a nurse. If you want to be a nurse, don't settle for being a hospital clerk. If you want to be a hospital clerk, don't settle for being a doctor. Go for what *you* want!

Don't be limited by doubts about how you will accomplish your dreams. Trust that the perfect method will show up when you have established and committed to a passionate desire.

Don't be limited by concerns that you may have picked the wrong dream. Trust that if a better dream comes along, you will adopt it with even greater enthusiasm.

Don't be limited by what others say you *should* do. Trust your passions. You might wait for years for the motivation to do what others say you should do. Already within you is the boundless energy necessary to create the unique dreams that inspire *you*.

Some say our dreams are already present by the time we are five years old. Imagine the excitement of charging after your dreams each day with the enthusiasm and energy of the five-year-old within you! What are the dreams that live in your heart of hearts? What were your greatest dreams before you stopped dreaming? We human beings are incredibly powerful creators when we are on course to our personally meaningful dreams!

College, choices, and Latin (Latin?)

I had no big dreams as a college freshman. I lacked a vision of what I wanted to accomplish in my role as a student (or any other roles, for that matter), and my choices showed it. I remember the afternoon that my freshman adviser looked over my course selections for my first semester. He crossed out a course that I had picked and signed me up for Latin.

Latin? What the heck was I going to do with an ancient language? I guess my face shouted my doubt. My adviser scraped his desk chair a little closer to me, a fatherly smile spreading across his face. I could smell the coffee on his breath. "Latin, you see, contains the roots of much of the English language," he said kindly. "Studying Latin will improve your vocabulary." He kept nodding in approval of his own advice.

Well, what did I know? I wasn't sure why I was in college anyway. I didn't have any reason *not* to take Latin. I wanted to be agreeable. I wanted him to like me. "Okay," I said. And that's how I happened to take Latin.

A year later, in my sophomore year, I was still drifting. The time had come to declare my major, and I was baffled. I thought I might major in English. My roommate thought that was a bad idea. He counted off on his fingers all the reasons why no one should ever major in English. "Plus," he asked with finality, "what can you *do* with a degree in English?"

I wasn't sure. It didn't occur to me to ask someone who knew. "Well, how about psychology, then?" I wondered aloud.

"Hmmmmm." My roommate was pondering my future. He'd attended a private high school. I was impressed. Finally, he nodded. "Psychology is good," he said.

It makes no difference what your dream is — the important thing is that you declare one and dedicate yourself to it.

Joyce Chapman

Always dream and shoot higher than you know you can do. Don't bother just to be better than your contemporaries or predecessors. Try to be better than yourself.

William Faulkner

And that's how I happened to become an undergraduate psychology major. (Later, by the way, as I got clearer on what I wanted to create in my life, I returned to graduate school for advanced degrees in both English and psychology — so it's never too late to change course.)

Without a dream to guide my energy, I was a Ping-Pong ball, bouncing back and forth between other people's ideas of what I should do. Worse, I didn't even realize I had another choice. I didn't know that I could be living my life in pursuit of a motivating dream. Years later, I wished my freshman adviser (or anyone else) had said, "Hold it, young man. Have you considered what your life is all about? Have you considered discovering the dreams that will catapult you out of bed each morning, shoot you off into your day, keep your energy surging well into the evening, give you peaceful, contented rest at night? Have you got at least one dream, young man? Do you know that you deserve to have a dream?"

I hope by now you're wondering to yourself, "So, what *are* my greatest dreams?" Or, if you believe you've already discovered your dreams, perhaps you're wondering, "Are there even *bigger* dreams for me?"

Discovering your biggest dreams is one of the greatest gifts you can give yourself. A dream that expresses what you truly value guides the choices that you make every day. And, as we already know, the choices you make determine the outcome of your life. If you wish to live a rich, personally fulfilling life, remember that you are responsible for choosing and creating the outcomes that you want.

Through the years, I have had the joy of working with students who discovered incredibly wonderful and motivating dreams: becoming an operating-room nurse, writing and publishing a novel, traveling around the world, operating a refuge for homeless children, building a house on the ocean, marrying and raising a beautiful family, living in perfect health, playing professional baseball, starting a private school, finding a cure for muscular dystrophy, writing songs for Aretha Franklin, becoming a college teacher, healing emotional wounds from childhood, earning a million dollars before the age of thirty-five, swimming in the Olympics, managing a mutual fund, having a one-woman art show, feeling total self-worth and confidence, becoming a fashion model, owning a clothing boutique, being elected a delegate to the state legislature, eliminating hunger on the planet, spending a year as a foreign exchange student in Africa, feeling continually filled with peace and harmony, and more.

But what do *you* want? What will excite and motivate *you*? What is it that *you* want to have, do, or be? The only consistent motivation in life is a personally inspiring dream. What is your dream?

In your journal entry, you will have an opportunity to explore your dreams and develop internal motivation. Let your dreams guide your every choice from now on. You'll achieve more from your actions than ever before.

Perhaps along the way, your dreams will change. Great! That will mean you've defined your life's purpose even more clearly. Whatever dreams you create will be perfect . . . for now.

In short, don't worry. If you look deep within yourself, you will discover the very best dreams for yourself at this moment of your life. Then, "follow your bliss!"

Journal #7

In this journal entry, you will have an opportunity to explore your dreams. People with motivating dreams make better choices. They are better able to know when they are on course. They are more likely to live a positive, energized, exciting, fulfilling life.

Take a deep breath and relax. It is time for some no-limit dreaming. You can begin creating a magnificent life today.

1. Write a list of the major roles that you have chosen in your life. Next to each role, write your biggest dream(s) for that role. Remember that a life role describes anything to which you consistently devote large amounts of your time and energy. After defining your roles, ask yourself: *If I knew that I could not fail, what would I love to accomplish or experience in this role during my life?* Be as specific as possible. Describe what you would like to have, do, and be in each role. For example . . .

I started getting successful in school when I saw how college could help me achieve my dreams.

Bobby Marinelli, Student

ROLE: Student	DREAM: Earn a Ph.D. in psychology.
ROLE: Partner	DREAM: Be happily married to someone I love and who loves me enough to support my personal growth.
ROLE: Worker	DREAM: Have my own counseling practice assisting children to develop high self-esteem.
ROLE: Self-nurturer	DREAM: Be in great shape, physically and emotionally; travel for a month in Europe.

If you uncover a dream that doesn't fit into any of your current roles, create a new role that will allow you to pursue this dream. For example, if you realize that one of your dreams is to write a book, you would create a role of author.

2. Choose two of your dreams and write a separate paragraph (or more) about each one. In each paragraph discuss **what** the dream is and **why** you have chosen it (and anything else you'd like to say about it). Without worrying about how you'll create it, write a complete and honest discussion of a future that inspires you! You may wish to begin, *One of the dreams that I want to accomplish in my lifetime is . . . .* Your second paragraph might begin, *A second dream that inspires me is . . . .*

Relax, think, and write.

focus questions   Do you have a strong commitment to your dreams? Do you know how to make your commitment even stronger?

◼◻◼◼◼ 8. Committing to Your Dreams

Many people doubt that they can achieve what they truly want. When a big, exciting dream creeps into their thoughts, they shake their heads at the idea. "Oh, sure," they mumble to themselves, "how am *I* going to accomplish that dream?" This is merely the voice of your Inner Critic, and you can choose to ignore it.

In truth, you don't need to know how to achieve a dream when you first think of it. What you do need is an unwavering commitment, fueled by a strong desire. Once you promise yourself that you will do whatever it takes to accomplish your dream, you often discover the method for achieving it in the most magical ways.

Certainly the disease of our age is lack of purpose, lack of meaning, lack of commitment on the part of individuals.
Carl Rogers

Commitment creates method

A commitment is an unbending intention, a decision that you are unwilling to change despite setbacks. A commitment is a singlemindedness of purpose that promises to overcome all obstacles regardless of how positive or negative you may feel in any particular moment. During the summer between my sophomore and junior years in college, I made such a commitment.

That summer, I used all of my savings to visit my roommate who lived in Hawaii. While there, I met a beautiful young woman who lived on Oahu, and we spent twelve blissful days together.

When you have a clear intention, methods for producing the desired results will present themselves.
Student Handbook,
University of Santa Monica

Perhaps like you, one of my dreams has always been to have a wonderful love relationship. So, before leaving Hawaii, I promised to return during Christmas break. Back in college, six thousand miles away, my commitment was sorely tested. I had no idea how, in just three months, I could raise the necessary money to return to Hawaii. I had little extra time; I was attending college full-time and playing varsity lightweight football. Committed to my dream, however, I invented and rejected one scheme after another for quickly (and legally) raising a large sum of money.

Then, one day, as if by magic, I discovered a possible solution. I was glancing through *Sports Illustrated* magazine when I noticed an article about crew (rowing). The author was a student at Yale University. Bingo! Until that moment, all I'd had was a commitment. When I saw that article, I had a plan. A long shot, yes, but a plan, nonetheless: Maybe the editors of *Sports Illustrated* would buy an article from me about my sport, lightweight football. Maybe the article would earn me enough money to return to Hawaii. Every evening for weeks, I worked on an article. Finally, I stuck it in an envelope, dropped it in the mail, and crossed my fingers.

A few weeks later, my manuscript came back, rejected. On the printed rejection form, however, a kind editor had handwritten, "Want to try a rewrite? Here's how you might improve your article. . . ."

I spent another week revising the article, mailed it directly to the editor who had encouraged me, and waited anxiously. Days passed. Then weeks. Soon Christmas break was only seven weeks away. By then, I had just about given up hope of returning to Hawaii in December.

Then my phone rang one afternoon, and the caller identified himself as a photographer from *Sports Illustrated*. "I'll be taking photos at your football game this weekend. Where can I meet you?"

And that's how I found out that my article had been accepted. Better yet, *Sports Illustrated* paid me enough money to return to Hawaii. I spent Christmas in Honolulu, on the beach at Waikiki, with my girlfriend on the blanket beside me.

Suppose I hadn't made a commitment to return to Hawaii? Would reading *Sports Illustrated* have sparked such an outrageous plan? Would I, at twenty years of age, have ever thought to raise money by writing a feature article for a national magazine? Doubtful.

How commitment contributes to success

What intrigues me as I recall my experience is this: The solution for my problem was there all the time; I just didn't see it until I made a commitment. Our brains cannot be conscious of everything. There's just too much going on both outside and inside of us for us to be aware of it all. When we make a commitment, we are in effect choosing what our brain will focus on. Commitment causes us to think of and do the most amazing deeds, actions we would otherwise not even have imagined.

A part of our brain, called the **reticular activating system,** seems to be the gatekeeper that allows only selected stimuli and thoughts into consciousness. Have you ever noticed that if you decide to buy a certain car, all of a sudden those cars are everywhere? They were there all the time, of course, but now that we've told our brain what we want to see, it complies.

By committing to our dreams, we program our brains to look for solutions to our problems and to keep us going when the path gets rough.

Victims seldom commit to any personally meaningful outcome, so they wait for motivation and solutions to come from outside them. In college they wait for the perfect teacher to stimulate them, the perfect textbook to inspire them, the perfect course to inflame them. Creators know that long-term motivation lies within, not without.

Whenever you're tempted to look for motivation outside yourself, remember

Until one is committed there is hesitancy, the chance to draw back, always ineffectiveness. Concerning all acts of initiative (and creation), there is one elementary truth, the ignorance of which kills countless ideas and splendid plans: that the moment one definitely commits oneself, then Providence moves too. All sorts of things occur to help one that would never otherwise have occurred. A whole stream of events issues from the decision, raising in one's favour all manner of unforeseen incidents and meetings and material assistance which no man could have dreamt would have come his way.
William Hutchison Murray,
Scottish mountaineer

Always bear in mind that your own resolution to succeed is more important than any one thing.
Abraham Lincoln

this: Motivation surges up from a *commitment* to a passionately held purpose.

The key to making and keeping your commitment is visualizing the pleasure you'll derive when you achieve your dream.

Visualize your ideal future

We human beings pursue what gives us pleasure. And we do our best to avoid what causes us pain. Use this psychological truth to your benefit.

To make or strengthen a commitment, visualize yourself accomplishing your dream and imagine the pleasures you'll experience when you do. Consider also the pleasures you'll experience on the journey to creating your dream. Let these positive outcomes and positive feelings draw you like a magnet toward your dream. You see, all of our accomplishments are created twice. Before we can create them in the world, we must create them in our minds.

BOOTH

"I'll run through it again. First, the exhilaration of a work completed, followed by the excitement of approaching pub date. Reviews pouring in from everywhere while the bidding for the paperback rights soars to insane figures. An appearance on Merv Griffin or Dick Cavett, sandwiched in between like Engelbert Humperdinck and Juliet Prowse. Finally, a flood of letters from people to whom your name, yesterday unknown, now has the shimmer of national renown. Hit those keys!"

Some years ago, I happened to glance at a three-ring notebook carried by one of my students. Taped to the cover was a photo showing her in our college's graduation cap and gown. In the picture, her face was aglow with success.

"Tell me about that photo," I asked. "Have you already graduated?"

"Not yet. But that's what I'll look like when I do."

"How did you get the photo, then?"

"My sister graduated from this college a few years ago," she explained. "After the ceremony, I put on her cap and gown and had my mother take this picture of me. Whenever I get discouraged in school, I look at this photo. I imagine myself walking across the stage, receiving my diploma from the college president. I hear my family in the audience cheering for me, just like we did for my sister, and then I stop feeling sorry for myself and get back to my school work. This picture reminds me what all my efforts are for."

A few years later, at her graduation, I remember thinking, "She looks just as happy as she did in the photo. Maybe even happier."

Life will test our commitment to our dream. To keep our commitment strong in times of challenge, we need a clear picture of our desired results. We need a mental image that, like a magnet, will draw us steadily into our ideal future.

In Journal #7, you defined what you want to *have, do,* and *be* in your future. Now imagine having already achieved these dreams. Once you can picture this desired future in your mind, you are well on your way to creating it in the world.

The power of visualizing makes sense when you remember that it's difficult to get anywhere if you don't know where you're going. A mental movie of your dreams as already accomplished allows you to begin with your desired end in mind and to know what you must do to get there.

Effective visualizing

Here are four keys to an effective visualization.

1. **RELAX.** Visualizing seems to have the most positve impact when it is experienced during the *alpha* waves produced by deep relaxation.
2. **USE PRESENT TENSE.** Visualizing works best when you imagine yourself experiencing your success **now**. Thus, in writing or speaking about your ideal outcome, use the present tense for all verbs. *I am walking across the stage to receive my diploma.* (Not past tense, *I was walking across the stage,* and not future tense, *I will be walking across the stage.*)
3. **BE SPECIFIC**. It is essential to imagine the scene as concretely and as specifically as possible. Use all of your senses as you would in a real experience. What do you see, hear, smell, taste, touch?
4. **FEEL THE FEELINGS.** Events gain power to influence us when accompanied by strong emotion. Imagine your accomplishment to be just as grand and magnificent as you wish it to be. Then feel the excitement of your success.

Visualizations are a powerful way to influence the positive outcome of one's future. Psychologist Charles Garfield notes that athletes have used visualizations to win sports events; psychologist Brian Tracy reports salespeople's use of visualizations to succeed in the business world; Dr. Bernie Siegel, a cancer specialist, has chronicled patients who improved their health using visualization; and psychologist Denis Waitley has documented cases of prisoners of war who maintained their sanity and will to survive by visualizing positive outcomes during their ordeals. As a student, you, too, can use the power of visualization to achieve your ideal outcomes in college — and in life.

Make a commitment to your dreams. Create a singlemindedness of purpose that promises to overcome all obstacles in your way. Visualize the pleasures of achieving your dream.

Finally, consider this: Keeping your commitment may be even more important than actually achieving your dream. It has been said that life is a journey, not a destination. When you are on course to a personally meaningful dream, you will learn and grow in ways that you cannot imagine today. Regardless of the outcome, the journey toward a personally motivating dream is rich and rewarding.

So, create lofty dreams. And, from deep within you, commit to their achievement.

Visualization takes advantage of what almost might be called a "weakness" of the body: it cannot distinguish between a vivid mental experience and an actual physical experience.
Dr. Bernie Siegel

Journal #8

In this journal entry you will have an opportunity to visualize the accomplishment of two of your most important dreams. Once you can picture these ideal outcomes, you will have strengthened your commitment to and increased the likelihood of creating the future you desire.

First, get comfortable. Take a deep breath and let it out with a sigh. You may wish to take a few more deep breaths and fully relax so that you can experience the *alpha* brain waves that make visualizations most effective.

1. Write a visualization of the moment in your future when you are actually realizing the accomplishment of your biggest dream in your role as a student. Describe the scene of your success as if it is happening to you *now*. For example, if your dream is to graduate from a four-year college with a 4.0 average, you might write, *I am now dressed in a long, blue graduation robe. I feel the tassel from my graduation cap tickling my face. I look out over the thousands of people in the audience, and I see my mother, a beaming smile spreading across her face. I hear the announcer call my name. I feel a rush of adrenalin, and chills tingle on my back as I take my first step out on the stage. I see the college president smiling, reaching his hand out to me in congratulations. I hear the announcer repeat my name, adding that I am graduating with highest honors having obtained a 4.0 average. I see my classmates standing to applaud me. Their cheers flow over me, filling me with pride and happiness. I walk . . .*

2. Repeat Step 1 for a dream that you have in another of your life roles.

Whatever the mind of man can conceive and believe it can achieve.
Napoleon Hill

Remember the four keys to an effective visualization:

1. Relax and create *alpha* brain waves.
2. Write your victory scene using **present tense verbs** . . . it is happening now!
3. Write your victory scene **concretely, specifically**. What do you see, hear, and feel?
4. Write your victory scene with **emotion**. Imagine it to be just as grand and magnificent as you wish it to be. You deserve it!

Read your visualizations often. Ideal times are right before you go to sleep and when you first awake in the morning. You may even wish to record your visualizations on a cassette tape and listen to them often.

Relax, think, write . . . your ideal future.

What personal qualities will you need to achieve your dreams? How can you strengthen these qualities within yourself?

9. Creating a Personal Affirmation

> *I was saying "I'm the greatest" long before I believed it.*
>
> Muhammad Ali

To adopt new beliefs, we can now systematically choose affirming statements, then consciously live in them.
Joyce Chapman

You'll need special personal qualities to achieve your dreams. For example, if your dream is a happy family life, you'll need to be loving, supportive, and communicative. If your dream is to play professional tennis, you'll need to be confident, athletic, and determined. If your dream is to discover the cure for cancer, you'll need to be creative, optimistic, and strong-willed. In each case, you may need other personal qualities in addition to these, but these few will certainly be essential.

Now think of the dream you have for your education. What are the personal qualities that you'll need to accomplish it? Will you need to be intelligent, persistent, articulate, responsible, goal-oriented, emotionally stable, focused, motivated, organized, playful, forgiving, curious, confident, honest, enthusiastic, organized, self-nurturing?

The potential for developing all of these personal qualities, and more, exists in each healthy human being. Whether each person fulfills that potential is another matter. During childhood, a person's judgment of his or her personal qualities seems to be based mostly on what others say. For example, if your friends, family, or teachers told you as a child that you're smart, you probably internalized this quality and labeled yourself "smart." But if no one said you're smart, perhaps you never realized your own natural intelligence. Worse, someone important may have told you that you're dumb, and thus began the negative mind chatter of your Inner Critic.

How we become the labels that others give us is illustrated by a mistake made at a school in England. A group of students at the school were labeled "slow" by their scores on an achievement test. Because of a computer error, however, their teachers were told that these children were "bright." As a result, their teachers treated them as bright. By the time the error had been discovered, the academic scores of these "slow" students had risen significantly. Why? Having been told and treated as if they were bright, the kids started to act bright. Perhaps, like these children, you have positive qualities waiting to be labeled, nurtured, and strengthened.

As children we tend to depend on others to tell us our personal strengths and weaknesses, but as adults **we can choose what we believe about ourselves.** As one of my psychology teachers used to say, "In your world, your word is law." If you say something is true, that thought becomes your truth. Your self-talk defines your reality. Suppose, for example, you want to be more organized. If you tell yourself over and over, "I am organized, I am organized, I am organized," you increase the chances that you will, indeed, take actions to get organized. Your words are the parent to both your new beliefs and your new actions.

Claiming your desired personal qualities

An effective way to strengthen desired qualities is to create a personal affirmation. A personal affirmation is a statement about ourselves in which we claim our desired qualities as if we already had them in abundance.

Here are some examples of personal affirmations:

- *I am a bold, happy, loving man.*
- *I am a confident, creative, selective woman.*
- *I am a spiritual, wise, and curious man, finding happiness in all that I do.*
- *I am a powerful, conscious, and drug-free woman, creating an abundance of love in my life.*
- *I am a successful, perceptive, and light-hearted man, and I love life.*
- *I am a supportive, organized, and secure woman, and I am creating harmony in my family.*

Affirmations assist us to breathe life into personal qualities that were smothered by what important adults told us when we were children. One of my colleagues, for example, said that whenever she made a mistake as a child, her father would say, "I guess that proves you're NTB." "NTB" was his shorthand for "Not Too Bright." Imagine the challenge of feeling intelligent when you keep getting a message from your father that you're NTB! After a while, she didn't even need her father around, because her Inner Critic was happy to remind her that she's NTB. She could benefit from an affirmation that says, "I am VB (Very Bright)." An affirmation, then, is a method for weakening the negative influence of your Inner Critic.

Recently I observed a well-dressed mother lifting her toddler so he could drink from a water fountain. "Don't get yourself all wet," she warned. "*You always make a mess of everything!*" What a negative thought to inflict upon this impressionable little person! With luck, one day he'll learn to tell himself that he can choose to be messy sometimes and he can choose to be neat sometimes, and regardless of which one he chooses, he's a really great person.

Thoughtless words by adults have stunted the development of many kids' positive qualities. What limiting messages did you receive as a child? Can you recall the sting of negative criticisms told to you over and over by an important adult in your life? Perhaps you were constantly reminded that you were "homely" or "stupid" or "clumsy" or "always screwing up." If so, today you can create an affirmation that supports the rediscovery and growth of your shriveled positive qualities. For example, you could say, "I am a beautiful, intelligent, graceful woman, turning any mistake into a powerful lesson."

Many people report that their positive affirmations seem like lies. The negative messages from their childhood (chanted by their Inner Critics) feel more like the truth. If so, try thinking of your affirmation as prematurely telling the truth. You may not feel beautiful, intelligent, or graceful when you first begin to claim these qualities, but, just as the "slow" children responded to being called bright, with each passing day you will grow into the truth of your chosen qualities. Using affirmations is like becoming your own parent by acknowledging the positive qualities that no one has thought to tell you about . . . until now.

Living your affirmation

Of course, simply creating an affirmation is insufficient to offset years of negative programming. Affirmations need reinforcement to gain strength and influence in your life. Here are six ways to empower your affirmation.

First, realize that you already possess the qualities you desire. You already *are* creative, persistent, loving, intelligent . . . whatever. These are your natural human qualities waiting to be rediscovered and nurtured. To confirm this reality, simply recall a specific event in your past when you displayed your desired quality. This desired quality may be hidden, but it is available within you. You simply have to remember who you are.

Second, give power to your affirmation by repeating it over and over until it becomes as familiar to you as your name. One student said her affirmation while working out on a rowing machine. The steady pace of the exercise provided the rhythm to which she repeated her affirmation. What would be a good time for you to repeat your affirmation?

Third, say your affirmation while looking at yourself in the mirror. This approach can assist you to attribute the positive qualities to the person in the mirror (YOU!).

Fourth, be vigilant about all the other words you use to describe yourself. Your description of yourself defines who you think you are; thus, your words define your future. If you want to be intelligent, keep your Inner Critic from saying things like, "Boy, am I stupid. I never do anything right." Keep your Inner Defender from claiming, "It's not my fault. She's the worst teacher in the whole college." Instead, *consciously choose* to say, "I got a 50 on the math test. I'm intelligent, so I can learn from my mistakes." In other words, rather than pinning a negative label on yourself or someone else, let your Inner Guide describe what you did, what your positive quality is, and what you'll do differently in the future.

Fifth, use your affirmation when life tests you.   In the midst of life's many challenges, let your affirmation remind you of the personal qualities that will assist you to stay on course to your dreams. You can then take an action that not only keeps you on course, but also strengthens the very qualities you want to develop in yourself.

Sixth, you can record your affirmation on a three-minute loop tape.   These ever-repeating tapes are made for telephone answering machines and are sold at many electronics stores. You can listen to your affirmation tape as you commute to work, eat lunch alone, wait for a friend, or during any other free time. Another great time to listen to (or say) your affirmation is right before doing any school assignment or taking a test. To make listening even more enjoyable, you can record your favorite slow instrumental music in the background to induce *alpha* brain waves.

Some years ago when I began planning the student success courses at my college, I had difficulty expressing my enthusiasm for this new program. Looking back, I believe my reluctance was a way of protecting myself from disappointment if others didn't get excited, too. Finally, I realized that if I didn't express my enthusiasm for the program, I couldn't expect others to support it.

That's when I created an affirmation to help me call forth and fully express my enthusiasm. I would say my affirmation at times of anxiety, such as right before making a presentation to a faculty or student group. Before long, I was fully expressing to others the enthusiasm I felt inside. Others caught this enthusiasm, and the program began with wonderful support.

So, decide what personal qualities will assist you to stay on course to your dreams. Your personal affirmation will help to bring them forth!

Journal #9

In this journal entry you will have an opportunity to create a personal affirmation. Your affirmation will help you develop the personal qualities you need in order to achieve your dreams.

First, take a moment to breathe deeply and relax.

1. Write a one-sentence statement of your greatest dream for your role as a student.

2. Write a list of personal qualities that would assist you to achieve this educational dream. Write these qualities as adjectives. *For example:*

*persistent, intelligent, hard-working, fun, enthusiastic, loving, articulate, or-
ganized, friendly, confident, relaxed, and so on. Write as many qualities as
possible.*

3. Circle the three qualities on your list that seem the *most essential* **if
you are to achieve your dream as a student.**

4. Write three versions of your personal affirmation. Do this by filling
in the blanks in sentence formats A, B, and C below. Fill the blanks with the
three personal qualities you circled in Step 3 above. NOTE: Use the same three
personal qualities in each of the three formats below.

Format A: I am a _____, _____, _____ man/woman.
Example: *I am a strong, intelligent, persistent woman.*

Format B: I am a _____, _____, _____ man/woman, _____ing
_____.
Example: *I am a strong, intelligent, persistent woman, creating my
        dreams.*

Format C: I am a _____, _____, _____ man/woman, and I
_____.
Example: *I am a strong, intelligent, persistent woman, and I love life.*

**5. Choose the one sentence from Step 4 that you like best and write
that sentence five or more times.** This repetition will allow you to begin taking ownership of your affirmation and these desired qualities.

**6. Write one paragraph each about the three qualities from your af-
firmation. In each of these three paragraphs, tell about a specific event
in your life when you demonstrated this quality.** For example, if one of
your desired qualities is persistence, tell a story about a time in your life when
you were persistent (even a little bit!). Write the story like a scene from a book,
with enough specific details that readers will feel as though they are seeing
what you experienced. Your paragraph might begin, *The first quality of my affirmation is . . . A time when I demonstrated that quality was. . . .*

Relax, think, write.

Do you know why it is important to have goals? Do you know the essential qualities of an effective goal?

■ ■ ■ ▲ 10. Choosing Purposeful Short- and Long-term Goals

When a man does not know what harbor he is making for, no wind is the right wind.

Seneca

By committing to personally meaningful dreams, we create energy and motivation in our lives. The next step toward success is choosing meaningful short- and long-term goals.

Short-term goals define the specific destinations we plan to reach within the next few months. Long-term goals define the specific destinations we plan to reach in a year or more. Each short-term goal realized is a stepping stone toward the achievement of one of our long-term goals, and each long-term goal realized is a stepping stone toward the achievement of one of our dreams.

Possessing written goals — both short-term and long-term — keeps us on course to our dreams. Yet many students resist setting academic, personal, and professional goals for themselves. According to psychologist Brian Tracy, people don't set goals because 1) they don't realize the importance of goals and 2) they don't know how to set goals. Let's eliminate these two reasons so you can experience the power of having goals in your life.

*People who have unclear goals, unclear pictures of themselves, and make unclear choices, end up with an unclear future — and never a **chance** at reaching what they thought they had wanted.*

Shad Helmstetter

Why goals are important

People who don't realize the importance of goals haven't heard about a study done at Yale University. The researchers first asked members of the Yale graduating class of 1953 if they had specific, written, long-term goals. Only 3 percent did. The other 97 percent did not. Twenty years later, the researchers contacted these same Yale graduates to see what had happened in their lives. They found that the 3 percent with goals were living lives that were measurably better than those of the 97 percent without goals. In one area in particular, the results were quite remarkable: The 3 percent of Yale graduates who had set specific goals for their lives had accumulated more personal wealth than that accumulated by the *entire* other 97 percent.

One student I know who completely changed her life by setting goals is Joan. While growing up, Joan dreamed of becoming a famous singer. After high school, she started singing in night clubs. She married her manager, and the two of them lived in a trailer, moving from town to town as Joan's singing jobs demanded. Life on the road was exhausting. She recorded a song, but it didn't sell. Her dreams began to unravel. Marital problems complicated her career. Career problems complicated her marriage. She grew tired of the uncertainty in her life, living from day to day without feeling emotionally or financially secure. Fi-

I wanted to be the greatest hitter who ever lived. A man has to have goals — for a day, for a lifetime — and that was mine, to have people say, "There goes Ted Williams, the greatest hitter who ever lived."

Ted Williams

nally, in frustration, she divorced her husband and gave up her dream of singing professionally.

Although disappointed, Joan didn't stop setting goals. She needed to earn a living, so she set a short-term goal to become a hairdresser. Shortly after Joan graduated from cosmetology school her mother died, leaving Joan enough money to settle some debts, buy her first new car, and pay for a new long-term goal. She decided to go to a community college (where I met her) and major in dental hygiene, a career that would provide her with a greater income than cosmetology.

Two years later, Joan graduated with honors and went to work in a dentist's office. Still lacking a dream that excited her, Joan chose another long-term goal: her bachelor's degree. Joan worked days in the dentist's office while at night she pursued her B.S. degree. A few years later, she again graduated with honors.

Then, she set another long-term goal: to earn her master's degree. Earlier in her life, Joan had doubted that she was "college material." With each academic success, her confidence grew. "One day I realized that, once I set a goal, it's a done deed," Joan said.

That awareness inspired Joan to begin dreaming again. As a child, Joan had always imagined herself as a teacher. Master's degree now in hand, she returned to our college to teach dental hygiene. A year later, she was appointed department chairperson. In only six years, Joan had gone from a self-doubting freshman to head of the college's dental hygiene department. Thanks to her many successes, Joan was brimming with new self-confidence. She decided to go for her biggest dream of all: She wanted to earn a great deal of money and experience financial security for the first time in her life.

And that's when Joan decided that she would leave teaching, open her own business, and become wealthy. After researching career choices, she chose the role of insurance agent as the career most likely to accommodate her new dream quickly. Perhaps by now you can guess what happened. Joan set and accomplished hundreds of short-term goals and dozens of long-term goals in the course of building her own successful insurance agency. Today, Joan is one of the top insurance agents with a national company; she has her own office, a custom-built home, and a six-figure income.

How to set a goal

To be effective, a goal needs five qualities. You can remember these essential qualities by applying the DAPPS rule to your goals. "DAPPS" is an acronym, a memory device in which each letter of the word stands for one of five qualities:

Dated. Effective goals have specific deadlines. A long-term goal generally has a deadline of a year or more away, maybe even five or ten years away. A short-term goal usually has a deadline within a few months. As the deadline approaches, your motivation typically increases. This energy helps you finish strong. If you don't meet your deadline, you have an opportunity to examine what went wrong and create a new plan. Without a deadline, you might stretch the pursuit of a goal over your whole life, never reaching it!

We . . . believe that one reason so many high-school and college students have so much trouble focusing on their studies is because they don't have a goal, don't know what all this studying is leading to.
Muriel James and
Dorothy Jongeward

Goals are dreams with a deadline.
Anthony Robbins

Achievable.   Effective goals are both ambitious and realistic. It's unrealistic to say you'll complete a marathon next week if your idea of a monster workout has been flicking the button on your television remote. You're just setting yourself up for failure. Still, if you're going to err, err on the side of optimism. When you set goals that are at the outer reaches of your present ability, stretching to reach them causes you to grow. Listen to other people's advice, but trust yourself to know what is achievable for you.

Personal.   Effective goals are *your* goals, not goals thrust on you by someone else. Goals are stepping stones to a higher purpose that you have chosen (or are seeking) for your life. Ask yourself if each of your current goals contributes to *your* personal dreams. If not, trade them in for goals of your own. You don't want to be lying on your death bed and realize that you have lived someone else's life. Trust that you know better than anyone else which goals and dreams are right for you.

Positive.   Effective goals focus your energy on what you *do* want rather than on what you *don't* want. Translate negative goals into positive goals. For example, a negative goal to quit smoking becomes a positive goal to be "smoke free." A negative goal to stop being late to classes becomes a positive goal to arrive on time to every class. A negative goal to not fail English becomes a positive goal to pass English with a B or better. I recall a race car driver who explained how he miraculously kept his spinning car from smashing into the retaining wall: "I kept my eye on the track, not the wall." Focus your thoughts and actions on where you *do* want to go rather than on where you *don't* want to go, and you, too, will stay on course.

Specific.   Effective goals state what you want in specific, measurable terms. It's not enough to say, "My goal is to do better this semester." Or "My goal is to work harder at my job." How will you know if you've achieved these goals? What concrete evidence will you have? How will you measure your success or failure? Effective goals are stated with specific, observable outcomes so that when your deadline arrives, anyone (especially you) can see whether you did or did not achieve your goals. "I will achieve a 3.5 or better grade average this semester. On my job, I will volunteer for all offerings of overtime." Being specific helps keep you from fooling yourself that you achieved a goal when, in fact, you did not.

Now let's apply the DAPPS rule to some possible long- and short-term goals for college. Suppose your dream is to earn a master's degree in biology. An effective stepping stone to that dream might be the following long-term goal:

Earn my bachelor of science degree in biology from the University of Maryland by June, 2001.

As stepping stones to this long-term goal, you would set a number of short-term goals. Here are short-term goals that you might set this semester to stay on course to your bachelor's degree:

1. *Earn an A in Bio 101 by 12/15.*
2. *Earn an A in Eng 101 by 12/15.*
3. *Earn an A in Math 107 by 12/15.*
4. *Apply for a scholarship for next semester by 11/15.*
5. *Apply for a job in the college science learning center by 10/25.*

If you remember to apply the DAPPS rule, all of your goals will be Dated, Achievable, Personal, Positive, and Specific. These five qualities make for very effective goals. Of course, you will later want to identify and carry out the necessary actions to achieve these goals. We will explore in Chapter 4 how you can do that. For now, we want to clearly define the outcomes we seek.

Goals will lift you up!

Choosing heartfelt goals will fan the fire started in your soul by your dreams. You'll stop waiting for someone or something "out there" to give you motivation.

A truly motivated person is someone pursuing a purposeful goal, a goal that is a logical stepping stone to a greater dream . . . even if you can't see the dream! Your teachers, your jobs, your relationships, and your college may come and go, but as long as you have inspiring goals and lofty dreams, you'll seldom lack for motivation.

Journal #10

In this journal entry you will have an opportunity to choose long- and short-term goals for your role as a student. These goals will be the stepping stones to your dreams

First, take a deep breath, and allow your body and mind to relax.

1. To focus your mind, write a one-sentence statement of your greatest dream as a student. This will probably be the same dream you have worked on in previous journals.

2. Write a list of your *long-term goals* leading to this dream. Remember, long-term goals usually take a year or more (and as long as five, ten or even twenty years) to accomplish. Here are some examples of well-defined long-term goals that follow the DAPPS rule:

MY LONG-TERM GOALS:

1. *Complete my A.A. degree in arts and science from Baltimore City Community College by 5/99.*
2. *Complete my B.A. degree in education from Morgan State U. by 5/01.*
3. *Attend my junior year abroad, preferably in Germany or Spain.*
4. *Be elected president of the student government in my senior year.*

3. Write a list of your *short-term goals* leading to this dream. Remember, short-term goals usually take at least a few months to accomplish. In college, it is convenient to think of short-term goals as anything you want to accomplish during one semester. Again, be sure to use the DAPPS rule in writing your short-term goals. For example:

MY SHORT-TERM GOALS:

1. Earn an A in Soc 101 by 12/20.
2. Earn an A in Eng 101 by 12/20.
3. Earn a B or better in PE 110 by 12/20.
4. Join the school choir by 10/29.
5. Take at least one page of notes in every class period this semester through 12/20.
6. Attend every class this semester through 12/20.

4. Write two paragraphs. In the first paragraph discuss what you have learned about yourself and your *long-term goals*. In the second paragraph discuss what you have learned about yourself and your *short-term goals*. Your first paragraph might begin, *I have learned that I . . .*

Relax, think, write.

focus questions Do you have a clear and compelling vision for your future? Do you know how to create one or improve the one you have?

■ ■ ◢ ■ II. Designing Your Life Plan

A life plan defines your desired destination in life, and it charts your best route for getting there. A life plan makes it easier to stay conscious of whether you are on course or off course. It gives your Inner Guide something positive to focus on when your Inner Critic or Inner Defender are distracting you from your dream.

The starting point of any life plan is to define one's personal mission. A mission states your chosen life purpose. Psychologist Charles Garfield defines a mission as "an image of a desired state of affairs that inspires action — determines behavior and fuels motivation."

Peak performance begins with a commitment to a mission.
Charles Garfield

To begin defining your mission, recall the life roles that you have picked, the dreams you have committed to, the long- and short-term goals you have chosen.

With your dreams and goals in mind, ask yourself, "What is at the center of all of these choices? What holds them together? What do I want my life to mean?" At the center of all of your dreams and goals lies your personal mission.

Don't be limited by a small vision. Invent a magnificent purpose. Create an outrageously bold intention. Dare to think big! And don't worry about being wrong. You can expect to revise your mission statement dozens of times during your life. Consider this version only as a work in progress. Have fun creating it!

Writing your mission statement

I know what it means to operate without a mission and a life plan. For years I drifted on the winds of chance. Only since the late 1980s have I truly had a sense of purpose. I feel like a slow learner, but today I am guided by my chosen purpose. I am open to changing, but until I do, I'll make my decisions to support this mission:

> MY MISSION IS to learn, adopt, and teach strategies that will empower me and others to live rich, personally fulfilling lives.

Each time I read my mission statement I am renewed. My energy level rises. I experience a positive urgency that vitalizes my life. With my purpose clearly in mind, I drift off course less often and get back on course more quickly.

A mission statement is a very personal document, one that can guide your choices for a lifetime. It is your personal constitution, and you can write it to fit your values and your personal style. There are as many ways to write a mission statement as there are people writing them. My suggestion is to start with a one-sentence statement. Later you may wish to expand it. Remember, this statement defines what is at the center of your life.

To find your purpose in life is one of the greatest gifts that you can give yourself. Purpose (or lack of it) determines the choices we make. And the choices we make determine the outcomes of our lives.

If you believe that you already know your life purpose, why not pretend that there may be an even greater purpose available to you and that you might discover it today.

In your journal entry, you will be writing the first draft of your mission statement and your life plan. Likely they will both change in the future. In the meantime, you will have a guide for making purposeful choices. You will accomplish more from your actions than ever before. Later, if your mission changes, it will mean only that you have even more clearly defined what your life's purpose is.

Your life plan

Once you have written your mission statement, you will be ready to put together your life plan. You will have all the pieces:

YOUR MISSION

YOUR LIFE ROLES

YOUR DREAMS IN EACH ROLE

YOUR LONG-TERM GOALS FOR EACH DREAM

YOUR SHORT-TERM GOALS FOR EACH LONG-TERM GOAL

A quality personal mission statement is a significant investment of time, but the benefits of this activity over a lifetime are incredible.
A. Roger Merrill

Outstanding people have one thing in common: an absolute sense of mission.
Zig Ziglar

Start from the bottom and you'll see how each of these is a stepping stone to the one above it. Your short-term goals are stepping stones to your long-term goals. Your long-term goals are stepping stones to your dreams. Your dreams are stepping stones to fulfilling your life roles. Your life roles are stepping stones to achieving your mission. Taken together, these elements form the design of a conscious life plan. By choosing our destinations in life and by staying on the course we have chosen, we create a richer, fuller experience of life.

Take a look at the first page of a life plan that one student, Maria, designed for herself. See if you don't agree that she is on course to experiencing a life worth living. Maria wrote . . .

MY MISSION IS to grow in love for myself and others, especially my husband and children, and to offer counseling and support groups for troubled teenagers, assisting them to live happy, productive lives.

MY AFFIRMATION: I am a loving, wise, and supportive woman, using my talents to improve the lives of others.

MY ROLE: college student

MY DREAM IN THIS ROLE: master's degree in social work.

MY LONG-TERM GOALS IN THIS ROLE:

1. Associate of Arts degree from BCCC by June, 1999.
2. Bachelor of Arts degree from Morgan State U. by June, 2001.

MY SHORT-TERM GOALS IN THIS ROLE:

1. Earn an A in English 101 by 5/20.
2. Write an essay of five hundred or more words with fewer than three grammar errors by 5/20.
3. Earn an A in PSY 101 by 5/20.
4. Learn and apply five or more psychological strategies that will help my family be happier and more loving by 5/1.
5. Earn an A in CSS 110 by 5/20.
6. Consciously adopt five or more new success behaviors and teach these strategies to my children by 4/15.
7. Learn to use a word processor well enough to prepare all of my written assignments by 3/1.
8. Take at least one page of notes in every class period this semester.
9. Turn in every assignment on time this semester.

This is the first page of Maria's six-page **life plan**. She created one page for each of her chosen **life roles**. Each page began with her **mission** and **affirmation** (the same each time). Then, she went on to define her **dream(s)**, **long-term goals**, and **short-term goals** for each of her other five life roles: parent, wife, employee, group leader for troubled teenagers, and friend.

By consciously designing her life, Maria is well on her way to creating a rich, personally fulfilling life. Get ready. You're about to design a great life for yourself, too!

Journal #11

In this journal entry, you will have an opportunity to design your life plan. People with a life plan generally experience high levels of motivation and a clear sense of direction in their lives.

Except for your mission statement, you have already written in previous journal entries almost everything you need for your life plan. Simply go back to those journal entries and copy the information onto your life plan. Feel free, of course, to revise any of the choices you made earlier.

As you write your goals in your life plan, both long-term and short-term, remember to apply the DAPPS rule. Make sure that each goal is <u>D</u>ated, <u>A</u>chievable, <u>P</u>ersonal, <u>P</u>ositive, and <u>S</u>pecific.

First, relax and prepare to design the outcome of your life. To focus your mind, glance back at Maria's life plan on page 59. Use it as a model for your own life plan.

1. Title a clean page in your journal: MY LIFE PLAN. Below that complete the following just as Maria did.

My Mission: (Write a one-sentence mission statement for your life.)
My Affirmation: (Refer to Journal #9)
My Life Role: (Write one of your major roles in your life, for example, student.)
My Dream(s) in this Role: (Refer to Journal #7)
My Long-Term Goals in this Role: (Refer to Journal #10)
My Short-Term Goals in this Role: (Refer to Journal #10)

2. Turn to a clean page in your journal, and repeat Step #1 for a second life role. Then repeat this process for as many life roles as you wish. The more roles that you consider, the more complete will be your vision of your life. You will wind up with one page for each of your life roles. Taken together, these pages are your plan for a great life!

3. Write a paragraph about what you have learned by designing your life plan. Remember, at this time you don't need to know *how* to achieve your goals, dreams, and mission. All you need to know is *what* you want to create in your life. In the next chapter, you will begin learning strategies for accomplishing your life plan.

For now, relax, think, and write your life plan!!

I have a dream that one day on the red hills of Georgia, the sons of former slaves and the sons of former slave owners will be able to sit together at the table of brotherhood . . . that my four little children will one day live in a nation where they will not be judged by the color of their skin but by the content of their character.

—Martin Luther King, Jr.

Chapter 4

■ ■ ■ ■ ■ ■ ■

Once I accept responsibility for creating my life and discovering my purpose, the next step is to take purposeful actions that will turn my dreams into reality.

Taking Purposeful Actions ■ ■ ■ ■ ■ ■ ■

I am taking all of the actions necessary to achieve my goals.

Successful Students . . .

1. . . . **act on purpose**, performing deeds that move them on course to their goals and dreams.

2. . . . **write their own rules**, consciously adopting a personal code of conduct that governs their choice of actions.

3. . . . **develop self-discipline**, demonstrating focus and persistence in pursuing their goals and dreams.

4. . . . **master effective self-management**, regularly planning their purposeful actions.

5. . . . **set high standards**, expecting excellence of themselves in the completion of their purposeful actions.

6. . . . **visualize successfully doing purposeful actions**, mentally rehearsing behaviors necessary for their success.

Struggling Students . . .

1. . . . wait passively or wander from one unpurposeful activity to another.

2. . . . submit to or rebel against the rules made by others.

3. . . . give up or change course when their actions do not immediately lead to success.

4. . . . live disorganized, unplanned lives with uncertain futures.

5. . . . are satisfied with mediocrity and incompleteness in the work they do.

6. . . . seldom mentally rehearse the specific actions necessary to achieve their goals, more often picturing their own failure.

▌▐ ▪ ■ 12. Acting on Purpose

Do not confuse a creator with a dreamer. Dreamers only dream, but creators bring their dreams into reality.

Robert Fritz

Creators do more than dream. Creators take purposeful actions that move them steadily toward their goals and dreams.

Thomas Edison did more than dream of inventing the light bulb; he performed over ten thousand experiments before achieving his goal. Martin Luther King did more than dream of the day when people of all races would be equal; he spoke and organized and marched and wrote. Roger Banister did more than dream of breaking the four-minute mile; he trained day in and day out for years. College graduates did more than dream of their diploma; they attended classes, read books, wrote papers, conferred with teachers, applied for scholarships, joined clubs, rewrote papers, formed study groups, did library research, asked questions, went to support labs, sought out tutors, and more!

It is not enough to be busy . . . the question is: what are we busy about?

Henry David Thoreau

When we consider the accomplishments of successful people, we may forget that these people weren't born successful. Most created their success through the persistent repetition of purposeful actions: They did what was necessary over and over and over.

By contrast, Victims procrastinate, seldom taking purposeful actions until a pressing deadline finally forces them to act. Their Inner Defender may even convince them that they work better under the threat of a deadline. But Creators know a powerful secret for turning dreams into reality:

Do important actions *before* they become urgent.

Try Quadrant II

The significance of **importance** and **urgency** in choosing our actions is illustrated in the chart of the Quadrant II Time Management System® on the next page (from Stephen Covey's book *The 7 Habits of Highly Effective People*). This chart shows that our actions fall into one of four quadrants, depending on how purposeful and how urgent they are. How we spend our time and energy significantly influences the degree of our success, so as you read about the four quadrants, ask yourself, "In which quadrant am I living my life?"

Words show a man's wit, but action shows his meaning.

Ben Franklin

QUADRANT I ACTIONS (Important & Urgent) are important activities done under the pressure of deadlines and last-minute crises. One of my college roommates began his junior paper (the equivalent of two courses) just three days before it was due. His writing was important and *very* urgent. He worked on the paper for seventy-two hours straight and, exhausted, turned it in without

	Urgent	Not Urgent
Important	**Quadrant I** *Example:* Staying up all night cramming for an 8:00 A.M. test.	**Quadrant II** *Example:* Creating a study group in the first week of the semester.
Not Important	**Quadrant III** *Example:* Attending a hastily-called meeting that has nothing to do with your goals.	**Quadrant IV** *Example:* Mindlessly watching television until 4:00 A.M.

I am personally persuaded that the essence of the best thinking in the area of time management can be captured in a single phrase: organize and execute around priorities.
Stephen Covey

even proofreading it, fifteen minutes before the deadline. He fell deeper and deeper into his pattern of procrastination, and in our senior year it caught up to him. He failed out of college. People who spend their lives in Quadrant I are constantly dashing about putting out brush fires in their lives. They frantically create modest successes in the present while sacrificing extraordinary success in the future. Worse, Quadrant I is the quadrant in which people experience stress, develop ulcers, and flirt with nervous breakdowns.

QUADRANT II ACTIONS (Important & Not Urgent) are important activities done *without* the pressure of a looming deadline. When you engage in an important activity with time enough to do it well, you can create your greatest dreams. Because they lack urgency, Quadrant II actions are easily postponed, even forever. Almost all of the suggestions in this book belong in Quadrant II. You could postpone forever taking actions such as keeping a journal, relaxing, listening to your Inner Guide, using the Wise-Choice Process, using the language of Creators, identifying your mission, discovering and committing to your dreams, visualizing your dreams, creating a personal affirmation, picking your life roles, choosing your long- and short-term goals, and designing a life plan. Billions of people are born, exist, and die without doing even one of these activities. However, when you take purposeful actions such as these, you do more than merely exist. You create a rich, full life. Quadrant II is where you will find Creators!

Act before there is a problem; bring order before there is disorder.
Lao Tzu

QUADRANT III ACTIONS (Not Important & Urgent) are unimportant activities done with a sense of urgency. How often have you responded to the demand of your phone ringing, then gotten trapped into long conversations that kept you from taking more important actions? You were caught in Quadrant III. Do I detect an Inner Defender excusing, "But I don't have any choice. It might be an important call"? What if you let an answering machine pick up your calls? If it's someone you want to talk to right then, pick up the phone. Otherwise, return the call when you've completed your purposeful tasks. That way, you'll never waste time (as Victims do) talking to people who are unimportant to your life. Anytime we allow someone else's urgency to talk us into an activity that is unimportant to our own goals and dreams, we have allowed ourselves to be drawn into Quadrant III.

QUADRANT IV ACTIONS (Not Important & Not Urgent) are simply wasted time. Everyone wastes some time, so it's not something to judge yourself for (though your Inner Critic will probably try). Instead, listen to your Inner Guide, become more conscious of your time . . . and minimize your wasteful choices of behavior. A college teacher I know recently surveyed his class and found that many of his students watch television more than forty hours per week. That's like having a full-time job for which you receive no pay and no benefits! Another example of Quadrant IV behavior is listening to someone complain about how terrible life is. You can choose to stand there and listen for ten or twenty minutes, or you can excuse yourself by simply saying, "I'm sorry, I have an important appointment." The appointment is with yourself. As in Quadrant III, actions in Quadrant IV are wasteful because they don't move us closer to our goals and dreams. They may even move us further away. Wiser choices always exist in Quadrants I and II. It is important to note that true recreation (re-creation) should not be confused with a Quadrant IV activity. Recreation like sports, travel, exercise, movies, and games can be true Quadrant II behaviors.

Creators spend as much time as possible in Quadrant II, where they undertake purposeful actions with time to do them well. In college, for example, Creators make appointments with their teachers early in the semester to discuss problems they are having with the course. They start and lead study groups in all of their classes. They tape record summaries of their class notes and listen to them at every opportunity. They predict questions on upcoming tests and carry the answers on 3 x 5 study cards. And they do all of these actions even though they could go the whole semester without taking any of them. They don't need external urgency to motivate their taking purposeful actions. They have created their own urgency by the commitment they have made to their dreams.

By contrast, Victims spend much of their time in Quadrants III and IV where unimportant actions like complaining, excusing, and blaming are repeated over and over, knocking them farther and farther off course.

Creators say "No" to Quadrant III and Quadrant IV activities. Sometimes this means saying "No" to other people: *No, I'm not going to be on your committee this semester. Thank you anyway.* Sometimes Creators say "No" to themselves: *No, I'm not going to sleep late this Saturday morning. I'm going to get up early and study for the math test. Then tonight I can go to the movies with my friends without getting off course.*

When we say "No" to Quadrants III and IV, we are freeing up time to say "Yes" to Quadrants I and II. Imagine spending just thirty additional minutes each day taking purposeful actions. Think how dramatically that one small choice could change the outcome of your life!

While it is true that without a vision the people perish, it is doubly true that without action the people and their vision perish as well.
Johnetta B. Cole,
President, Spelman College

The great aim of education is not knowledge but action.
Herbert Spencer

Journal #12

In this journal entry, you will have an opportunity to see the degree to which you are acting on purpose. As you begin to spend more time in Quadrants I and II, you will see a dramatic improvement in the results you are creating.

1. Make four columns in your journal. At the top of each column write one of the four quadrants. Remember, they are the following:

Quadrant I: Important & Urgent

Quadrant II: Important & Not Urgent

Quadrant III: Not Important & Urgent

Quadrant IV: Not Important & Not Urgent

2. Below each column heading, list any actions that you have taken in the past few days which belong in that quadrant. Include the day of the week and approximate amount of time spent in the activity. You may wish to start with today and work backward. For example, Quadrant IV might look like this:

Quadrant IV: Not Important & Not Urgent

1. Tuesday: Watched TV for two hours.
2. Tuesday: Wasted time on phone for one hour.
3. Monday: Watched TV for three hours.
4. Monday: Cleaned my apartment for two hours. (It didn't need it.)
5. Sunday: Watched TV for three hours.

3. Write a paragraph (or more) about what you have learned about your use of time.

Effective writing anticipates questions that a reader may have about your topic, and it answers these questions clearly. Your reader may wonder, for example, what exactly you discovered after looking at how you used your time? Did you use your time purposefully or unpurposefully? What specific evidence did you use to draw this conclusion? If you keep using your time this way, are you likely to reach your goals and dreams? Why or why not? What most often keeps you from taking purposeful actions? How do you feel about your discovery? What different choices, if any, do you intend to make about how you use time?

Choose to relax before undertaking this journal activity. Relaxation, by the way, is a Quadrant II activity; it is important but not urgent. You could postpone it forever. But then you'd miss out on its benefits.

Relax, think, write.

Whatever you can do, or dream you can, begin it. Boldness has genius, power, and magic in it. Begin it now.

Goethe

Remember to reread the visualization of your dream (Journal #8) often to help you stay motivated. Also, remember to say your affirmation (Journal #9) each day to enhance the personal qualities that will keep you on course to your dreams!

Do you have your own personal rules to keep you on course?
Do you know which personal rules will propel you to success in college . . . and in life?

■ ■ ◢ ◩ 13. **Writing Your Own Rules**

That man is free who is conscious of being the author of the laws he obeys.

Ancient folk saying

Successful people love rules.

Does that idea seem strange? Do you wonder how anyone could possibly love rules? Do you, instead, resent and resist rules?

If so, try this: Don't love other people's rules. Create and love your own.

Victims don't do that. Instead, they angrily rebel against other people's rules, believing all rules are bad. Or they begrudgingly submit to them, believing all rules are required.

The most important thing is to have a code of life, to know how to live.

Dr. Hans Selye

In part, Creators are successful because they consciously live by their own personal rules. Creators' rules are designed to help them choose actions that will keep them on course. A teacher who grew up during the Depression has this rule for himself: *Always pay cash.* This rule works well for him. A man I know who is wealthy has this rule for himself: *Never pay cash.* This rule works well for him. Different dreams and different circumstances call for different rules.

Each of us needs our own code of conduct, our own commandments for success. That's why **Creators consciously choose action rules that keep them on course to achieving their goals and dreams.**

Your success in college and in life depends on the quality of your personal rules, those you are aware of and those you aren't. Rules are merely the thoughts we use to create patterns of behavior: *I will always . . . I will usually . . . I will seldom . . . I will never . . . .*

Most people are unaware of the rules they live by. As a result, their actions are habits (patterns of behaviors) that they perform unconsciously. In college, Victims miss classes they could have attended because, according to their rules, absence is okay. Victims do mediocre work on assignments because their rules give them permission to do less than their best. Victims come to class unprepared because, by their personal rules, homework is optional. Of course when Victims flunk out of school, they blame their failure on others or use it to judge themselves harshly.

I think you're going to be very surprised to discover that you may be living by rules of which you're not even aware. Rules have to do with the concept of should and should not.

Virginia Satir

You'll want to uncover and change any self-defeating action rules you now have. These rules are holding you back.

You'll want to become conscious of and preserve any empowering action rules you now have. These rules are keeping you on course.

Finally, you'll want to write new action rules that will support even greater accomplishments. Think of the most successful students you know. Observe them carefully and note what actions they take consistently. You'll quickly see what their personal action rules are. Maybe you will want to adopt them as your own.

For your consideration: Three success rules

Consider three action rules as the foundation of your personal code of conduct. I have polled thousands of college instructors at faculty development workshops I have conducted, and these are the three actions they consistently identify as belonging to their most successful students.

RULE 1: SHOW UP. Commit to attending every class from beginning to end. Someone once said that 90 percent of success is simply showing up. Makes sense, doesn't it? How can you be successful at something if you're not there? Studies have shown a direct correlation between attendance and grades (as one measure of success). Claude Olney, a business law professor at Arizona State University, once figured out that his students dropped about one-half letter grade for each class they missed. That means a student who missed eight classes or more probably failed. At Baltimore City Community College, a study found that, on average, the more classes students missed, the lower their grades were, especially in introductory courses. If you can't get motivated to show up, maybe you need a new dream.

RULE 2: DO YOUR BEST WORK. Commit to doing your best work on all assignments, including turning them in on time. You'd be amazed at how many sloppy assignments teachers see. But it isn't just students who are guilty. A friend in business has shown me hundreds of job applications that screamed to be thrown in the trash. One book publisher includes this "special note" in its guideline for prospective authors: "It is in your own best interest that the material you submit be of professional quality. Many otherwise viable publishing proposals have gone unreviewed or have reviewed poorly due to improper preparation of initial materials. This includes poor quality originals for duplicating, grammar, punctuation and spelling errors, inadequate typing/word processing. . . . You owe it to yourself to put forth your very best effort." And this advice, you will recall, is for professionals! Doing your best work on assignments is a rule that will propel you to success in all that you do.

> *Play the revolutionary and challenge the rules — especially the ones you use to govern your day-to-day activities.*
> Roger von Oech

RULE 3: PARTICIPATE ACTIVELY. Your education, like your life, is not a spectator sport. Commit to getting involved. Come to class prepared. Sit forward in your chair. Listen attentively. Think deeply about what is being said. Ask yourself how you can apply the information you're learning toward the achievement of your goals and dreams. Take notes. Ask questions. Answer questions. Request a conference with your teacher. Read ahead. Start a study group. If you participate at this active level of involvement, you couldn't keep yourself from learning even if you wanted to.

> *[E]veryone has the choice, even at a young age, to take charge of their lives and make their own rules.*
> Gay and Kathlyn Hendricks

Some students resist adopting these three basic rules of success. They say, "But what if I get sick, or what if my car breaks down on the way to class, or what if my child has to go to the hospital, or what if I don't have time, or what if I don't like talking in class?" I trust that by now you recognize the voice of the Inner Defender, the internal excuse-maker.

And, yes, something may happen that will keep you from following your rules. So realize that each rule is simply your **intention**. You **intend** to attend every class from beginning to end. You **intend** to do your very best work and to turn assignments in on time. You **intend** to participate actively. You are making a commitment *to yourself* to live by these rules because they will help *you* to be successful . . . and you may need to break your own rules if something of a higher value (like your health) demands it. If, for example, you do miss a class for unexpected and important reasons, you needn't let your Inner Critic judge you. Simply ignore its harsh judgments and attend your next class with a renewed commitment to live up to your personal rules.

Exceptional students follow not only these three basic rules of success, they add their own. They promise themselves to take actions that will move them step by step toward achieving their goals and missions. As a result, successful students often create personal rules that are much more demanding than any teacher, employer, parent, or anyone else would ever impose on them. They know what they **must** do to be a success.

He noblest lives and noblest dies who makes and keeps his self-made laws.
Sir Richard Francis Burton

Your commitment to your dream demonstrates your intention on the level of thought. Your commitment to your action rules demonstrates your intention on the level of behavior. Once we follow our own rules long enough, they are no longer simply rules. They become habits. And once our positive actions become habits, few obstacles can block the path to our success.

Today is the day to start loving action rules — your own!

Journal #13

In this journal entry, you will have an opportunity to write your own action rules for success in college. By following your own code of conduct, you will stay on-course toward your greatest dreams.

To focus your mind, ask yourself, "What do successful students do? What actions do they consistently take?" Now write the action rules for your success, rules with which you can cooperate.

1. At the top of a journal page write: MY PERSONAL ACTION RULES FOR SUCCESS IN COLLEGE. Below that, write a list of your own rules for success. List only those actions to which you are willing to commit.
Consider adopting the following as your first three personal rules. Remember, they were identified by thousands of college teachers as the three most important actions for students' success in college:

1. Attend every class from beginning to end.
2. Do my very best work on all assignments and turn them in on time.
3. Participate actively.

NOTE: In this journal entry, we are exploring the actions of successful students. So, as you list your rules, don't include attitudes such as: *Think positively.* We'll look at attitudes later. Instead, choose rules that lead to **observable actions** such as: *Ask questions when confused. Form a study group. Read difficult assignments until I understand them. Say my affirmation daily. Review notes before every class.* It's an action only if someone else can see or hear you do it.

2. On your list of action rules, label each one as follows:

MUST   (*I must follow this rule to be successful.*)

or

SHOULD (*I should follow this rule to be successful.*)

3. Write a paragraph or more about what you have learned about your own action rules. Remember to answer any questions your ideas may raise in the minds of your readers. If possible, give experiences, yours or others', that demonstrate the practical value of each rule.

Relax, think, write.

On the next page is a list of action rules that my students have come up with over the years. This list may give you ideas for your own personal action rules for success. If you consistently performed every one of these actions, you would be an exceptional student, indeed!

focus questions How strong is your self-discipline? Do you know the essential ingredients of self-discipline?

■ ■ ■ ■ ■ 14. Developing Self-Discipline

> *Self-discipline is self-caring.*
> Dr. M. Scott Peck

Most goals and dreams are achieved by taking purposeful actions persistently over time.

The problem is, our culture loves instant pleasures. Many of us never learned the rewards of persistence, of taking small steps daily toward a distant and personally meaningful goal.

Few of us learned the value of self-discipline. Victims think of self-discipline the same way they think of responsibility. Both, they believe, are *difficult*. Both require *major sacrifices*. Both are done with *gritted teeth*. (Chain-gang music would go great here, too.)

In truth, self-discipline is the visible evidence of both maturity and self-love. Self-discipline is the willingness to do whatever has to be done, whether you want to or not, until you achieve your goals and dreams. Case in point: Every January first, America's athletic clubs are wall-to-wall with people who have made New Year's resolutions to get in shape. A month later, the crowds are gone, reminded that getting (and staying) in shape takes commitment, focus,

Perhaps the most valuable result of all education is the ability to make yourself do the thing you have to do, when it ought to be done, whether you like it or not.

Thomas Henry Huxley

MY PERSONAL ACTION RULES
FOR SUCCESS IN COLLEGE

1. Attend every class from beginning to end.
2. Do my very best work on all assignments and turn them in on time.
3. Participate actively.
4. Speak as a Creator.
5. Make a list of my life roles and dreams.
6. Write visualizations of my dreams; read them often.
7. Create a personal affirmation; say it often.
8. Write down my long- and short-term goals and review them often.
9. Use a weekly written schedule.
10. Keep lists of purposeful actions for each of my life roles.
11. Revise assignments based on feedback from my teacher and classmates.
12. Take good care of my health: Get proper rest, eat well, exercise regularly.
13. Associate with winners and positive people.
14. Follow directions carefully.
15. Use the library and appropriate labs (science, reading, writing, math, computer).
16. Avoid drugs, including excessive use of alcohol.
17. Bring course tools (books, notebooks, pens, and such) to every class.
18. Do assignments early.
19. Find a good study place and study there often.
20. Sit up front in every class.
21. Laugh and have fun.
22. Make appointments with my teachers about anything that confuses me.
23. Bring at least three questions to every class.
24. Listen carefully.
25. Take good notes in every class; review them often.
26. Work with a tutor.
27. Compete with myself to do better than last time.
28. Give myself frequent small rewards for daily successes.
29. Talk positively to myself.
30. Create possible test questions from which to study.
31. Talk in class when appropriate; otherwise focus on the person speaking.
32. Request assistance from family and friends when needed.
33. Join or create a study group.
34. Take frequent breaks while studying.
35. Read difficult assignments twice or even three times.
36. Look at myself in the mirror every day and say, "You're an A student."
37. Remind myself daily that I am capable, lovable, and worthy of a great life.

and persistence. In other words, it takes self-discipline. Here's the question that gets answered by our actions: Do I love myself enough to do what it takes to have a healthy, well-conditioned body?

And so it goes with every important goal I set! My actions reveal whether I have the self-discipline to stay on course even when I don't feel like it. If I am mature and love myself enough to achieve my goals and dreams, my self-discipline will be stronger than my laziness.

Self-discipline is commitment made visible through purposeful actions.

Most students want to be successful. But *wanting* and *doing* are worlds apart. It's easier to go out with friends than it is to go to class . . . day after day. It's easier to spend hours on the phone than it is to read a challenging textbook . . . hour after hour. It's easier to watch television than it is to do research at the - library . . . night after night. It's even easier to vacuum the living room than it is to sit in front of a blank sheet of paper and write and revise . . . again and again.

Many people choose immediate pleasure. Few choose the far-off rewards of persistent and purposeful actions. Many begin the journey to their dreams; sadly, few finish. Yet all we need to do is put one foot in front of the other . . . again and again and again until the prize is ours. Self-discipline is what a Creator has and a Victim lacks.

Developing self-discipline is like building a muscle. Almost all the benefits of exercise come at the end of a workout when the strain seems the greatest. Within days, however, the muscles are stronger. When you push through your resistance to do purposeful actions over and over, the world rewards you with results . . . and your self-discipline muscles grow even stronger.

I can't guess how many perfectly capable students I've seen quit while on the path to their academic goals because they hadn't learned to flex their self-discipline. You can't get in shape with a one-hour workout and you can't master a college course with a one-night burst of studying.

This is great news, I hope you realize. If you *are* one of those rare individuals who's committed to taking consistent actions toward your goals and dreams no

matter what, you have a great advantage over many of the students at your college. In fact, you have a great advantage over many of the people on this planet.

Self-discipline has three essential ingredients: **commitment, focus,** and **persistence.** We have already discussed how to create commitment in Section 8. Now let's look at how to develop focus and persistence.

Focus

Staying focused is a challenge. Distractions constantly tug at our minds, and, like a child, the unfocused mind dashes from one distraction to another. We must be willing to be responsible for our attention.

Baseball Hall-of-Famer Henry Aaron hit more home runs than any other baseball player in history. When a particular pitcher was giving him trouble, Aaron would focus his entire attention on everything the pitcher did. But a baseball game, like life, presents many distractions: the crowd, teammates, opposing players, nagging injuries, even one's own wandering thoughts. As "Hammering Hank" drew closer to breaking Babe Ruth's home-run record, he had to deal with still other distractions: hate mail and death threats. But Aaron had developed a strategy to help him focus his attention. He would hold his baseball cap in front of his face to block out all distractions; then, peeking through one of the cap's little air holes, he would focus solely on the pitcher. In this ingenious way, Aaron concentrated on what he had to do in that moment to get a hit. Like Henry Aaron, you'll hit more home runs in life if you're able to focus. When you study, a strong focus can keep you from being pulled off course by distractions.

I have developed a focusing strategy for those times when I find myself reading in a noisy place. I put my book on a table in front of me. I put my elbows on the table, place my thumbs in my ears, and hold my hands beside my eyes. This way I can neither hear nor see distractions; all I can see is the book in front of me.

Everyone has experienced losing focus for minutes, for an hour, even for a day. But struggling students often lose focus for days and weeks at a time. They start coming late, skipping classes, doing sloppy work, ignoring assignments. They forget why they're in college.

For many students, the time to beware losing focus is about halfway into the semester. This is when your Inner Defender starts giving you all of those excuses to justify your not taking purposeful actions: *I've got all the lousy teachers, my schedule stinks, I'm still getting over the flu, I don't need this kind of hassle, next semester I could start all over.* And your Inner Critic chimes in with practiced self-criticism: *I never could do math, I'm not as smart as my classmates, I don't know how to manage my time, I've been out of school too long, I'm too old, I'm too young, I'm not really college material, anyway.*

Your Inner Guide can help you regain focus with the asking of one question: "What are my goals and dreams?" This question reminds you of your motive — your reason — for taking actions. If your goals and dreams don't motivate you to take purposeful actions, then perhaps you need to rethink where you want to go in life.

. . . I'm not bragging, but I think I focus on things very well.
Henry Aaron

The quickest tool for refocusing is always the single question: What is your dream?
Joyce Chapman

Persistence

Focus is self-discipline in thought. Persistence is self-discipline in action. Here's the question your Inner Guide can ask when you aren't persistently taking the actions you know will gain you your goals and dreams: "Do I love myself enough to keep going?" This question reminds you that you're taking these actions out of caring for yourself. You are the one who will benefit most from the accomplishment of your goals and dreams . . . and you are the one who will pay the price of disappointment if you fail.

When Luanne enrolled in my English 101 class, it was her sixth time taking the course. She needed to master standard English to pass the course. Although there was nothing wrong with Luanne's intelligence, I wasn't so sure about her self-discipline.

Early in the semester, we had a conference, and I asked Luanne about her dreams. She told me she dreamed of working in television, and her eyes sparkled. I asked her if learning to write and speak well — including mastering standard English grammar — would be a stepping stone to her success. She hesitated. It was as if a part of her knew that agreeing would commit her to many hours of work.

Finally she said, "Yes."

"Great! So, what's one action that you're not doing now that if you did it every day for a month or more, you would improve your grammar?" I wanted to help her discover a Quadrant II activity (Important but Not Urgent) and assist her to make it a new habit.

"Probably studying my grammar."

"Do you care enough about yourself to do that?"

"What do you mean?"

"I mean do you love yourself enough to do whatever it takes to create your dream of working in television? That includes studying standard grammar every day until you master it."

She paused. "I think so. . . ."

"Well, here's a chance to find out." I handed her a Thirty-Two-Day Commitment form (see page 76). "I'm inviting you to make a commitment to study grammar for thirty-two days in a row. You can check off on this form each day that you keep your promise to yourself. This is how you can develop self-discipline. Will you do it?"

"I'll try."

"C'mon, Luanne. You've been *trying* for five semesters. My question is, 'Will you commit to studying grammar for, say, thirty minutes every day for the next thirty-two days?' That's long enough to create a powerful new habit."

She thought again. She was standing at another of life's important crossroads. Her choice would make all the difference in the outcome of her life.

"Okay, I'll do it," Luanne answered.

And, bless her soul, she really meant it. Each time I passed the writing lab, there was Luanne. The tutors joked that they were going to start charging her rent.

Great works are performed not by strength, but perseverance.

Samuel Johnson

[I]n studying the source of people's success, I've found that persistence overshadows even talent as the most valued and effective resource in creating and shaping the quality of life.

Anthony Robbins

But that's not all Luanne did. She attended every English class. She did every writing assignment. Each week she came to see me to go over her essays. She made flash cards, writing her problem sentences on one side and the corrections on the other. She carried her flash cards with her everywhere. In short, Luanne was taking the actions of an exceptional student. Luanne was finally demonstrating the persistence of true self-discipline.

As mentioned earlier, English 101 students at our college must pass one of two essays that are graded by other teachers. In her five previous semesters, Luanne had passed none of the ten exam essays that she had written. And the first exam this semester brought her more bad news.

Both of her exam readers said her grammar errors still tipped the scale against her. But, there was some good news. She had gotten her highest score ever.

I watched Luanne as we reviewed the graders' comments, wondering how she would respond. It was another important moment of choice for her. Would she respond as a Victim or a Creator? Would she quit or persist?

"Okay," she said finally, "show me how to correct what I did wrong." We went over her essay sentence by sentence. The next day she went to the writing lab earlier; she left later. She rewrote the exam essay for practice. With the application of self-discipline, Luanne's new rules were turning into positive habits.

That semester, the second exam was given on the Friday before Christmas. In order to finalize grades, all of the English 101 instructors met that evening to grade the essays. I promised to call Luanne with her results.

The room was quiet except for rustling papers as two dozen English teachers read one essay after another. At about ten o'clock that night, I received the graded essays from my class. I looked quickly through the pile and found the essay with Luanne's social security number. She had passed!

I went to the telephone to call her. Another teacher asked who I was calling at such a late hour. "I'm calling my student, Luanne, to tell her she passed."

"Luanne passed!" the other teacher exclaimed. "That's terrific! I had Luanne last semester."

"Good for her," another teacher chimed in. "I taught Luanne, too."

"Me, too," said another. "I knew she could do it if she ever got serious."

As I dialed the phone, teachers who had taught Luanne told others about her success. There is nothing quite so inspiring as the victory of someone who will not quit on her dream.

"Merry Christmas, Luanne," I said into the phone, "you passed!"

I heard her delight on the other end of the phone line, and at that moment, two dozen teachers in the room began to applaud.

Journal #14

In this journal entry you will have an opportunity to apply self-discipline by planning and carrying out a thirty-two-day commitment. A thirty-two-day commitment is a strategy for developing self-discipline by persistently performing a purposeful action until it becomes a habit. Thirty-two days is the length of time behavioral psychologists suggest is long enough to break an old habit or start a new one.

1. To focus your mind, write one of your most important short-term goals for this semester. You can simply copy one from your life plan in Journal #11.

2. Write and complete the following sentence stem, five or more times:

I WOULD MOVE STEADILY TOWARD THIS GOAL IF EVERY DAY I . . .

Remember, choose actions that others can see you do. Also, choose actions that you can do even on weekends. For example, you wouldn't pick "attend class" because you can't attend class every day for thirty-two days straight. If your short-term goal is to earn an "A" in English, you might complete the sentence with specific actions such as these:

1. **I WOULD MOVE STEADILY TOWARD THIS GOAL IF EVERY DAY I** *spent at least fifteen minutes doing exercises in my grammar book.*
2. **I WOULD MOVE STEADILY TOWARD THIS GOAL IF EVERY DAY I** *wrote at least two hundred words in my journal.*
3. **I WOULD MOVE STEADILY TOWARD THIS GOAL IF EVERY DAY I** *rewrote one of my previous essays, correcting the grammar errors that my teacher marked.*

Chances are, all of these actions will fall in Quadrant II (Important but Not Urgent).

3. On the Thirty-Two-Day Commitment chart (page 76), write ONE action from your list in Step 2. Do that by completing the sentence stem at the top of the form (Because I know . . .). For the next thirty-two days, put a check beside each day that you keep your commitment. See if you aren't amazed by what you accomplish after the next thirty-two days of taking this purposeful action!

4. In your journal, write a paragraph (or more) about your thoughts and feelings as you begin your thirty-two-day commitment. Answer questions such as: *What is your goal? What were some possible actions you considered? What action did you choose? How will this action, when performed consistently, assist you to reach your goal? What challenges might you experience in keeping your commitment? How will you overcome these challenges? How do you feel about undertaking this commitment?* What other questions might someone possibly ask you about your thirty-two-day commitment?

IMPORTANT: If you miss a day on your thirty-two-day commitment, don't judge yourself. Simply ask your Inner Guide what got you off course, renew your commitment to yourself, and start over at Day 1. Don't turn this success strategy into an opportunity for self-judgment!

Relax, think, write.

By making and keeping promises to ourselves and others, little by little, our honor becomes greater than our moods.

Stephen Covey

Success is . . . the long-term consequence of making and keeping promises — promises to others . . . and promises to yourself . . . the more you exercise your self discipline, the stronger it gets.

Harvey Cook

32-Day Commitment

Because I know that this commitment will keep me on course to my goals, I promise myself that every day for the next 32 days I will take the following action: _____

_____

_____

Day 1		Day 17	
Day 2		Day 18	
Day 3		Day 19	
Day 4		Day 20	
Day 5		Day 21	
Day 6		Day 22	
Day 7		Day 23	
Day 8		Day 24	
Day 9		Day 25	
Day 10		Day 26	
Day 11		Day 27	
Day 12		Day 28	
Day 13		Day 29	
Day 14		Day 30	
Day 15		Day 31	
Day 16		Day 32	

Does it seem as though there's just not enough time to do all that you need to do? Do you know the secret to better time management?

■ ■ ■ ■ ■ 15. Mastering Effective Self-Management

Like as the waves make towards the pebbled shore,
So do our minutes hasten to their end.

William Shakespeare

At the end of class one day, I asked my students to pass in their assignments. A look of panic came over one man's face. "What assignment?" he moaned. "You mean we had an *assignment* due today?"

On another day, a woman walked into class, stopped short, and smacked herself on the forehead with the palm of her hand. "Oh, no," she wailed. "I told my boss I'd come to work today!"

At lunch, I heard one student ask another: "Did you study for the test today?" "No," the other replied, "I didn't have time."

Time is the coin of your life. It is the only coin you have, and only you can determine how it will be spent.

Carl Sandburg

Do these situations sound familiar? Do the 168 hours in your week seem to slip away? Do you wonder how some people always seem to be more efficient, effective, and organized than you are? Do you wonder how to manage your time?

If so, here's the secret: Stop trying to manage time. No matter what we mortals do, time just keeps on ticking. You can't manage minutes or Mondays or months. **All you can manage is yourself.**

You have already taken most of the steps of effective self-management in previous journal entries. You identified your life roles and dreams. You chose your long- and short-term goals. You picked purposeful actions that you could take toward your short-term goals. With these steps, you have laid a foundation for effective self-management.

Effective self-management means creating a plan to spend most of your time each week in Quadrants I and II doing purposeful activities. By planning and organizing your actions around your goals and dreams, you minimize wasted time. Three helpful tools for effective self-management are a monthly calendar, a daily actions list, and a weekly planner. You may want to use one, two, or all three of these tools. The important thing is to try each of them and see which of them supports you to persistently take actions important to your success.

The first tool, a **monthly calendar**, like the one on page 82, provides you with an overview of upcoming appointments, commitments, and assignments. Record on your monthly calendar your class hours, work schedule, lab hours, doctor's appointments, parties, committee meetings, times you care for your children, job interviews, sports practices and games, and the due dates of all class assignments, including tests, research papers, final exams, lab reports, and quizzes. A monthly planner is the easiest self-management tool to use, and it can be used all by itself.

The second self-management tool, a **daily actions list,** like the one on page 83, is a record of every action you want to accomplish that day. By listing your actions under each of your roles and its corresponding goals, you can keep moving ahead toward all of your dreams. Whenever you have free time during the day, instead of slipping unintentionally into Quadrants III or IV, check your list for purposeful actions to do. As you complete an action, you can cross it off your list. As you think of important new actions, you can add them to your list. In this way, each daily actions list will usually last you a week or more. At that time, copy any remaining actions to a clean list. If you keep transferring the same action from week to week, you'll quickly become aware of your procrastination. At that time you can decide what to do about it. You could choose to take the action immediately. You might break it into smaller steps and add those to your list. Or you might realize that the action isn't purposeful and you'll cross it off your list altogether. I wouldn't have survived college without my daily actions list.

The third tool, a **weekly planner**, like the one on page 84, allows for even more detailed organizing of your life than the monthly calendar. Sunday night is a great time to make a written plan for the upcoming week. You can start by transferring time commitments from your monthly planner to your weekly schedule. Then you can see where you have free time to schedule Quadrant II activities from your daily actions list. A weekly planner gives you an overview of your week in one quick glance.

Using your self-management tools

Experiment with all three tools to see which one (or combination) works best for you. Many Creators use all three of the tools mentioned here. Once you get a sense of what system works best for you, you'll probably want to buy a planner. There are dozens of different types available at stationery and office supply stores.

I know few successful people who don't use some sort of written self-management plan. Watch people who currently have the jobs you want. See if they aren't carrying a little book with them everywhere they go. That's their planner.

Regardless of what written planning system you decide to use, there are four basic steps to effective self-management.

> **FOUR STEPS TO EFFECTIVE SELF-MANAGEMENT**
>
> 1. Review your roles, goals, and dreams.
>
> 2. List purposeful actions.
>
> 3. Schedule purposeful actions.
>
> 4. Do what you plan!

1. Review your roles, goals, and dreams. Begin each planning session by reviewing your roles, goals, and dreams. You can do this by reviewing your life plan. The purpose here is to keep your destination clearly in mind, which helps you keep motivated and focused. If you're using a weekly actions list, write your roles and goals in the shaded boxes.

2. List purposeful actions. On your monthly calendar, look for purposeful actions that you have scheduled for today, such as attending a class. Transfer these scheduled activities to your daily actions list, recording them under the appropriate role and goal. Then add any additional purposeful actions as they occur to you. This way, you begin turning your goals and dreams into reality by breaking them into little action steps that you can do today, tomorrow, or later this week. For example, suppose that your short-term goal for Math 107 is to earn an A. Your daily actions list will contain Quadrant I actions (Important and Urgent) like these:

ROLE/GOAL: Math 107 Student/Grade of A
1. Attend classes on time (MWF).
2. Read pages 29–41 & do problems 1–10 on page 40.
3. Study 2 hours or more for Friday's test on Ch's 1–3.

When the seniors in the College Board study were asked what contributed to a successful and satisfying career in college, 73 percent said the "ability to organize tasks and time effectively."

Tim Walter and Al Siebert

Each of these three actions is **important**, and each is relatively **urgent** because it is due this week. Notice that each action is written to heed the DAPPS rule, just as your goals are. Each action is **D**ated, **A**chievable, **P**ersonal, **P**ositive, and **S**pecific. Especially be specific. Vague items such as *Do homework* are little help when the time comes to perform your action steps. Much more helpful is something specific: *Read pages 29–41 & do problems 1–10 on page 40.* Being specific assists your Inner Guide to compare what you *planned* to complete with what you *actually* completed. Creators use this comparison for designing course corrections, not blaming or excusing.

Listing Quadrant I actions is a great start toward effective self-management. Exceptional students, however, go an important step further. They also list Quadrant II actions, actions that are **important** and *not* **urgent**. Your action list for Math 107 might continue with Quadrant II actions like these:

4. Make appointment with Prof. Finucci and ask her advice on preparing for the math test on Friday.
5. Attend weekly appointment with math lab tutor.
6. Meet with study group and compare answers on practice problems.

In college I learned how to manage more tasks than anyone could possibly finish. Literally. We learned how to keep a lot of balls in the air at the same time. You couldn't study for every class every day, so you had to decide what could be put off till later. The experience taught us to set priorities.

Dennis Hayes
Founder, Hayes Modems

These Quadrant II behaviors are the sorts of activities that struggling students postpone or ignore altogether. You could go through the entire semester without doing any of these purposeful actions, because none of them is urgent. But when you do choose Quadrant II actions, oh, what a different outcome you will create!

Remember, as you accomplish the tasks on your weekly actions list, check them as complete. As you think of additional actions, add them to your list. In time, you will find that once they are written down, most of your actions get completed.

3. Schedule purposeful actions.
If you are using a weekly planner, it is time to schedule your purposeful actions on that form. Take these three steps:

1. Schedule actions that occur regularly each week, such as classes, team practices, or work hours (from your monthly planner).
2. Schedule Quadrant I actions (from your daily actions list).
3. Schedule Quadrant II actions (from your daily actions list).

By scheduling purposeful actions each week, Creators leave little time for un-purposeful actions. Remember, though, that true recreation is a Quadrant II activity and is just as important to your success as homework. Don't forget to schedule some fun and recreation.

4. Do what you plan!   It is one thing to schedule your purposeful actions. It is quite another to do them. Once you have scheduled your priorities, let nothing keep you from carrying out your plan — except for a rare emergency or one-time opportunity. Make a habit to say, "No" to low-priority alternatives.

Researchers at the University of Georgia found that self-management activities such as these had a positive impact on grades. In fact, they found that self-management attitudes and skills are even better predictors of grades than the Scholastic Aptitude Test (SAT). Your written self-management system will keep you on course to your dream if you use it regularly.

The rewards of effective self-management

You will rarely meet a truly successful person who doesn't use some sort of written self-management plan. That's because it has so many benefits. You stay conscious of your goals and dreams. You keep your life in balance by working on all of your priorities instead of just one or two. You see clearly how you use (and abuse) your time. You're more likely to keep purposeful commitments. You're less likely to be tempted by frivolous distractions. You schedule and carry out purposeful actions before they become urgent. And most important, you effectively chart your persistent steps towards achieving your goals and dreams.

Some people resist using a written self-management system. They don't feel comfortable with the self-imposed structure. If this is true of you, I urge you to experiment with the three tools: the monthly calendar, the daily actions list, and the weekly planner. You may find that you'll discover a unique system of written self-management that works just right for you.

Consistently using a written self-management system is a habit that takes time to establish. You may begin with great energy, then find that a week has gone by without using your planner. Your Inner Critic may want to blame you. Your Inner Defender may want to excuse you. As always, ignore these destructive voices.

Instead, ask your Inner Guide where you went astray and simply begin your planning anew. In time, your skills in using a written self-management system will improve. You'll learn how to adapt the various tools to your own needs and work style. You'll discover that sometimes you'll just have to abandon the best-laid plan because something of a higher priority demands attention. The truth about planning is that sometimes it doesn't work. But, when you *do* make a plan, your chances of achieving your goals and dreams improve dramatically.

Journal #15

In this journal entry, you will have an opportunity to experiment with the three tools of a written self-management system. Mastering effective self-management will assist you greatly in turning your dreams into reality. Keep in mind that you can adapt the tools of self-management to suit your own style.

Take a few moments to breathe deeply and relax.

1. On the Monthly Calendar (page 82), fill in the days of the month; then write in all of your upcoming time commitments and college assignments.

2. On the Daily Actions List (page 83), do the following two steps:

A. In the shaded boxes, write your Roles/Goals. You may wish to consider each course you are taking as a role. Add other life roles as well. For example:

Role: Employee
Goal: Get a new job paying $10+ per hour

B. In the spaces below each Role/Goal, write a list of purposeful actions that you will take this week. For example:

Role: Sociology 101 Student
Goal: Earn an A
1. Read textbook, pages 13–28. (Quad I)
2. Study for Friday's quiz. (Quad I)
3. Have conference with teacher about my research paper. (Quad II)
4. Meet with study group. (Quad II)
5. Attend all classes on time. (Quad I)

Remember, you can check off each action as you complete it. Also, you can add new actions to your list as they occur to you.

3. On the Weekly Calendar (page 84), schedule the actions from Step 2 by writing them in the appropriate time slots. Each morning, refer to your weekly calendar to see what time commitments and actions steps you have scheduled for that day.

4. In your journal, write a paragraph (or more) about your thoughts and feelings about using a written self-management system. Remember that good writing answers questions that an interested reader would ask about your topic. For example, *which planner or combination of planners (if any) seems best for you? Why? Will keeping a written self-management system be a challenge for you? What might get in your way of using a written self-management system? What experience (if any) have you had with written planners? How do you feel about putting your action steps in writing each week? What successes could it create?*

Relax, think, write.

Monthly Calendar

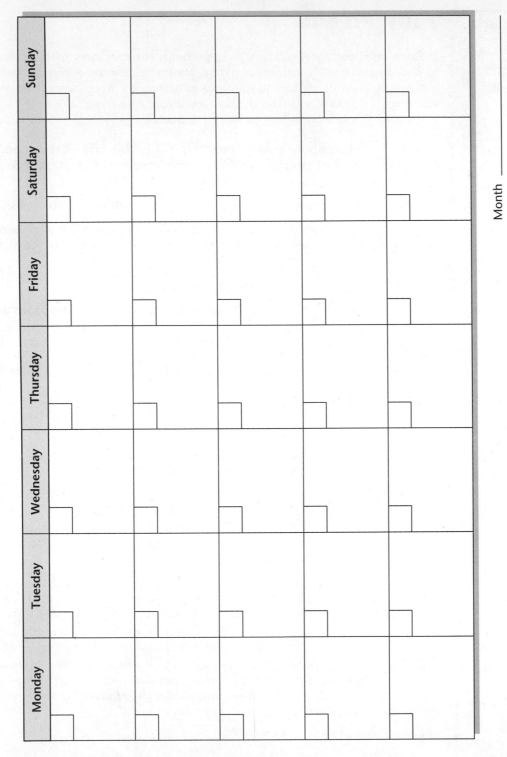

Month _____

Daily Actions List

Role:	
Goal:	

Role:	
Goal:	

Role:	
Goal:	

Role:	
Goal:	

Role:	
Goal:	

Telephone Calls	

Miscellaneous Actions	

Role:	
Goal:	

Role:	
Goal:	

Role:	
Goal:	

Weekly Calendar

Monday	Tuesday	Wednesday	Thursday	Friday	Saturday	Sunday
7:00	7:00	7:00	7:00	7:00	7:00	7:00
8:00	8:00	8:00	8:00	8:00	8:00	8:00
9:00	9:00	9:00	9:00	9:00	9:00	9:00
10:00	10:00	10:00	10:00	10:00	10:00	10:00
11:00	11:00	11:00	11:00	11:00	11:00	11:00
12:00	12:00	12:00	12:00	12:00	12:00	12:00
1:00	1:00	1:00	1:00	1:00	1:00	1:00
2:00	2:00	2:00	2:00	2:00	2:00	2:00
3:00	3:00	3:00	3:00	3:00	3:00	3:00
4:00	4:00	4:00	4:00	4:00	4:00	4:00
5:00	5:00	5:00	5:00	5:00	5:00	5:00
6:00	6:00	6:00	6:00	6:00	6:00	6:00
7:00	7:00	7:00	7:00	7:00	7:00	7:00
8:00	8:00	8:00	8:00	8:00	8:00	8:00
9:00	9:00	9:00	9:00	9:00	9:00	9:00

Do you perform all of your purposeful actions with excellence? How would it change your life if you did?

■ ■ ▲ ■ ■ 16. Setting High Standards

Years ago, I came across a story (I don't remember where) that had a profound impact on me. Here's my version of it:

One September morning, on their first day of college, two dozen freshmen made their way into the biology laboratory. They pulled chairs around the laboratory tables, sat down, and glanced about for the teacher.

Because this was their first college class, most of the students were a bit nervous. A few introduced themselves to tablemates. Others kept checking their watches.

At exactly nine o'clock, the professor, wearing a crisply pressed white lab coat, entered the room. "Good morning," he said. He set a white plate in the middle of each laboratory table. On each plate lay a small fish.

"Please observe the fish," the professor said. "Then write down your observations." He turned and left the room.

The students looked at each other, puzzled. This was *strange*! Oh, well. They took out scrap paper and wrote such remarks as *I see a small fish*. One student added, *It's on a white plate*.

Satisfied, they set their pens down and waited. And waited. For the entire class, they waited. A couple of students whispered that it was a trick. They said the professor was probably testing them to see if they'd do something wrong. Time crawled by. Still they waited, trying to do nothing wrong. Finally, one student mumbled that she was going to be late for her next class. She picked up her books and stood. She paused. Others rose as well and began filing out of the room. Some looked cautiously over their shoulders as they left.

When the students entered the lab for their second class, they found the same white plates with the same small fish already waiting on their laboratory tables. At exactly nine o'clock, the professor entered the room. "Good morning. Please take out your observations of the fish," he said.

Students dug into their notebooks or bookbags. Many could not find their notes. Those few who could, held them up for the professor to see as he walked from table to table.

After visiting each student, the professor said, "Please observe the fish. Write down all of your observations." Then he left, closing the door behind him.

The students looked at one another, puzzled. They peered at the fish. Those

I just tried to make a habit to do the best I could. . . . I did that in school, I did it in the practice of law, and I did it in every job I've ever had.

Sandra Day O'Connor
Supreme Court Justice

You are really never playing an opponent. You are playing yourself, your own highest standards, and when you reach your limits, that is real joy.

Arthur Ashe

few who had found their notes glanced from the fish to their notes and back again. Was the professor crazy? What else were they supposed to notice? It was only a fish. About then, one student spied a book on the teacher's desk. It was a book for identifying fish, and she snatched it up. Using the book, she quickly discovered what kind of fish was lying on her plate. She read eagerly, recording in her notes all the facts she found about her fish. Others saw her and asked to use the book, too. She passed the book to other tables, and her classmates soon found what was written about their fish. After about fifteen minutes the students sat back, very pleased with themselves. Chatter died down. They waited. But the professor didn't return. As the period ended, all the students carefully put their notes away.

The same fish on the same white plate greeted each student in the third class. The professor entered at nine o'clock. "Good morning," he said. "Please hold up your observations." All of the students held up their notes immediately. They looked at each other, smiling, as the professor walked from table to table, looking at their work. Once again, he walked toward the door. "Please . . . *observe* the fish. Write down *all* of your observations," he said. And then he left.

The students couldn't believe it. They grumbled and complained. *This guy is nuts. When is he going to teach us something? What are we paying tuition for, anyway?* Students at one table laughed heartily at a name someone had thought up for the teacher. Students at another table, however, began observing their fish more closely. Other tables followed their example.

The first thing all the students noticed was the biting odor of aging fish. A few students recorded details about the fish's color that they had failed to observe in the previous two classes. They wondered if the colors had been there originally or if the colors had appeared as the fish was aging. Each group measured its fish. They poked it and described its texture. One student looked in its mouth and found that he could see light through its gills. Another student found a small scale and each group weighed its fish. They passed around someone's pocket knife. With it, they sliced open the fish and examined its insides. In the stomach of one fish they found a smaller fish. They wrote quickly, and their notes soon overflowed onto three and four sheets of paper. Finally someone shouted, "Hey, class was over ten minutes ago." They carefully placed their notes in three-ring binders. They said goodbye to their fish, wondering if their finny friends would be there on Monday.

They were, and a vile smell filled the laboratory. The professor strode into the room at exactly nine o'clock. The students immediately thrust their notes in the air. "Good morning," the professor said cheerfully, making his way from student to student. He took longer than ever to examine their notes. The students shifted anxiously in their chairs as the professor edged ever closer to the door. How could they endure the smell for another class period? At the door, the professor turned to the students.

"All right," he said. "Perhaps now we can begin."

The students had wondered when their professor was going to teach them something, yet all along he was helping them discover one of life's essential lessons — when you're doing a purposeful task, only your best work will do.

Excellence: The not-so-secret ingredient of success

What would your life be like today if you had always given your very best effort on all of your important work?

What if right now you decided to give your very best effort every day for one week? For one month? For one year? For twenty years? What wondrous future could you create for yourself if every purposeful action you performed from this moment on you did with excellence?

Quality is a choice. "Made in Japan" used to mean "junk." Today "Made in Japan" means "excellence." Sometime in the latter half of the twentieth century, Japanese manufacturers made a choice to do their best. That choice has changed the world . . . theirs and ours.

You can choose the quality of your education and the quality of your life. You can consciously choose to live with excellence as your standard. If you don't choose excellence, mediocrity wins by forfeit. Every day the quality of your actions announces your decision to the world.

Employers complain about their employees' careless work. Teachers complain about their students' shoddy efforts. It's no mystery why they complain. Many people seem guided by mediocrity instead of excellence. This is good news for you . . . just as it was good news for the Japanese. If you do your best, you will lift yourself above the masses. You will become invaluable to those whose rewards you seek.

What is your level of excellence in college right now? Forget for a moment what your grades are and what your teachers or classmates may have said about your work. Listen, instead, to your Inner Guide for a more personal truth. How does the quality of your present effort stack up against the quality of work of which you're capable? What could you create if you were willing to hold yourself to a higher standard of excellence . . . starting right now?

To achieve excellence, you don't have to seek perfection. Every word you write doesn't have to rival Shakespeare. Every doodle you draw doesn't have to top Rembrandt. But when performing an action purposeful to your dreams, how can you possibly tolerate less than your best effort? Don't your dreams deserve your best? Don't *you* deserve your best?

I once did an experiment with the help of an English teacher whose students had just turned in a set of compositions. I glanced at each essay for about ten seconds and predicted whether the teacher would pass it or fail it. Mind you, I did not *read* the essays. I simply looked at them. Were words crossed out? Were the margins even? Were the pages neat or crumpled? Was the paper white or stained? Was the essay typed or handwritten, easy or impossible to read? Was the essay short or long? With these few observations as my only data, I wrote my predictions on whether each essay would pass or fail. Without revealing my predictions, I returned the papers to the teacher. The following day, we compared my guesses with her actual grades. I had correctly predicted her passing or failing grades on eighteen of the twenty-two essays.

Granted, this experiment was hardly a scientific study. Still, it's revealing. I'll bet you could have done as well in predicting the outcomes yourself. Your Inner Guide knows excellence when he or she sees it.

I always remember an epitaph which is in the cemetary at Tombstone, Arizona. It says: "Here lies Jack Williams. He done his damndest." I think that is the greatest epitaph a man can have — when he gives everything that is in him to do the job he has before him. That is all you can ask of him, and that is what I have tried to do.

Harry S. Truman

Excellence survives the scrutiny of comparison. Like it or not, your assignments are compared to those of your classmates; your job application is compared to those of your competitors; your job performance is compared to that of your fellow workers. Even your lover or spouse compares your behaviors to those of others. Excellence crushes mediocrity every time.

But even more important than living up to other people's standards of excellence is living up to your own potential. Setting high standards stretches you to the greatest use of your unique talents.

Ask yourself this question: Is there a higher standard of excellence in the pursuit of my dreams and goals to which I would like to commit?

If so, wouldn't this be a great day to do it? Wouldn't this be the perfect day to start giving your very best to the creation of your life!

Journal #16

In this journal entry you will have an opportunity to set high standards for the quality of your work in college and in life. When you choose excellence as your standard, you catapult yourself to the top of your class or profession.

1. Through the eyes of your Inner Guide, look back at your previous journal entries and observe their quality. As you glance at each entry, listen (don't write yet) as your Inner Guide observes:

- Did I write spontaneously?
- Did I write for myself?
- Have I been honest?
- Have I added creative touches, such as pictures, symbols, or photos?
- Do my thoughts demonstrate my best thinking? In other words, have I dived deep?
- Have I revised or added to journals that I knew were incomplete?
- Am I seeking the most value from each journal entry or merely trying to get them done?
- Is this the best journal work I can do?
- Will I be proud to find my journal in a drawer twenty years from today?

2. Write a letter of four paragraphs from your Inner Guide to you. The subject of the letter is the quality of your journal. Let your Inner Guide write one paragraph each about the following:

1. The quality of your journal compared to what you are capable of: Rate the journal on a scale of one to ten (ten being best). Explain the rating. Be specific. Give examples.
2. What gets in your way of doing your very best work?
3. Ideas for improving the level of excellence of your journal. Be specific.
4. Ideas for improving the level of excellence of your life. Be specific.

This letter from your Inner Guide to you might begin: *Dear (YOUR NAME), I have been looking over your journal, and I'd like to tell you the honest truth about its quality* . . . Have your Inner Guide use answers to the questions in Step 1, as well as your own questions, to support its evaluation of the quality of your journal.

Remember to ignore any blaming, complaining, or excusing by your Inner Critic or Inner Defender. This activity is not about being right or wrong, good or bad. It's about objectively observing the quality of your present standards. It's about assessing if you are capable of doing better. It's about consciously choosing your best effort.

Why not decide to hold yourself to a higher standard of excellence even as you do this journal entry?

Do your BEST relaxation, your BEST thinking, your BEST writing.

> *All morning I worked on the proof of one of my poems, and I took out a comma; in the afternoon I put it back.*
>
> Oscar Wilde

Do the pictures you create in your mind support your success? Do you know how to use mental images to achieve greater success?

▪ ▪ ▪ ▪ ▪ 17. Visualizing Successfully Doing Purposeful Actions

We choose what we believe will happen in our future. Then we often mentally rehearse it happening.

Few of us realize that we are creating these movies in our minds. Even fewer realize their power. Actions that we graphically and repeatedly imagine are recorded by our brains as memories. When we picture these events over and over, they affect our future actions as if they had actually happened.

In the past few decades many athletes have begun using mental imaging to great advantage. First, they relax their minds with slow (sixty beats per minute) classical music. This relaxation technique assists them to achieve *alpha* brain waves just as you have been doing with your relaxation techniques. Once relaxed, these athletes picture themselves successfully performing their event over and over in their minds. They know that if they repeatedly perform their sport flawlessly in their imagination, they will move closer to perfection in their physical performance.

Musicians also benefit from mental rehearsal. A friend of mine is a professional clarinetist. One day I saw her sitting quietly by herself, eyes closed, hands resting in her lap, her fingers twitching strangely. "Are you all right?" I asked.

She opened her eyes as if returning from a trance. "Sure," she said. "Why do you ask?" I mentioned the strange twitching of her fingers. "Oh that," she said, laughing. "I was mentally practicing a Beethoven symphony that we're performing in concert this Friday."

> *Peak performers develop powerful mental images of the behavior that will lead to the desired results. They see in their mind's eye the result they want, and the actions leading to it.*
>
> Charles Garfield

Health is another area in which visualization may be beneficial. Cancer specialist Dr. Bernie Siegel tells the amazing story of Glen, a child who had developed a brain tumor that his doctors said was untreatable. Glen was sent home to die. His parents, however, took Glen to the Mayo Clinic where Glen learned to use mental movies. Glen pictured rocket ships flying around in his head, shooting at the tumor. After months of such visualizing, Glen got a CAT scan of his brain, and the tumor was gone. Unfortunately, healing doesn't always result from such visualizations, and many medical experts remain unconvinced that recoveries such as Glen's are caused by the power of thought. Still, enough stories like Glen's exist to convince Dr. Siegel and others of the healing power of visualizations. In fact, the National Institutes of Health has created the Office of Alternative Medicine to study the effectiveness of alternative medical treatments, including visualizations.

Nothing is more important yet less understood than the power of the mind. Many people believe that exploring inner (not outer) space is the next great frontier.

Although many questions about the power of visualization remain unanswered, enough is already known that you can use it to improve your success in college and in life. Psychologist Charles Garfield once performed an experiment to determine the impact of visualization on a group of people who were afraid of public speaking. These nervous speakers were divided into three sub-groups:

If we picture ourselves functioning in specific situations, it is nearly the same as the actual performance. Mental practice helps one to perform better in real life.

Dr. Maxwell Maltz

Group 1 read and studied how to give public speeches, but they delivered no actual speeches.

Group 2 read about speech making and also gave two talks each week to small audiences of classmates and friends.

Group 3 read about effective speaking and gave one talk each week to small groups. In addition, this group watched videotapes of effective speakers and, twice a day, **mentally rehearsed** giving speeches of their own.

Experts on public speaking evaluated the effectiveness of these speakers both before and after their preparation. The experts were unaware of the three sub-groups and the different ways that each group had prepared for its speeches. Here are the results of the experts' evaluations:

I generally meditate for a thirty-minute period before speaking [to groups], and I visualize everything going smoothly and my audience and myself enjoying and appreciating the entire experience.

Wayne Dyer

Group 1 did not improve. Merely reading about effective speaking did not make the participants more effective in giving speeches.

Group 2 improved significantly. Practicing speaking to an audience greatly improved the participants' skills.

Group 3 improved the most. These participants had not only seen what excellent speakers do, they had played a **mental movie** over and over of themselves doing exactly what excellent speakers do.

Many students — whether in a speech class or somewhere else — achieve less than their potential. One reason is that they seldom picture themselves taking the actions of excellent students. They fail to create a mental movie of themselves starring as a successful student, doing what successful students do.

Worse, they may create an image of their own failure. Has your Inner Critic ever filled your head with thoughts like these: *I know I'm going to fail my final exams. It doesn't matter how hard I study. As soon as I walk into the exam room, I freeze up. I read the first question, and my mind goes blank. I start to feel hot and sweaty. I always feel so stupid. I hate exams.*

A student who thinks this way has a powerful ability to visualize. Unfortunately, he is using this skill to defeat himself.

What if he were willing to envision a more positive future? What if he erased from his mind long-running movies of failure? What if he replaced that film with a positive rehearsal of actions that would lead to his success? His new mental movie might look like this:

I walk into my exam fully prepared. All semester I have been taking the purposeful actions of a successful student. I have attended all of my classes on time. I have done my very best work on all of my assignments and turned them in on schedule. I have participated actively! I have studied effectively, and I am fully prepared for this test. Walking into this exam room, I feel totally confident. I find a comfortable seat and take a few moments to breathe deeply, relax, and focus myself. I concentrate on the subject matter of this test. I let go of all my other cares and worry. I feel excited about the opportunity to show how much I have learned about this subject. The teacher walks into the room and begins handing out the exams. My confidence is supreme. I know that anything the teacher asks will be easy for me to answer. The teacher smiles at me supportively as she hands me the exam. As I glance at the questions on the test, I see that they ask exactly what my study group and I have prepared for all semester. Alert and aware, I begin to write. Every answer I write flows easily from the storehouse of knowledge I have in my mind. I work steadily and efficiently for the entire exam period. After finishing, I check my answers. I hand in the exam with a comfortable amount of time remaining. As I leave the room, I feel a pleasant weariness. I am supremely confident that I have done my very best.

As you experience this mental movie, notice how it uses the four keys to successful visualizing that we discussed in Section 8:

1) **Relax.** Create *alpha* brain waves to focus your attention.
2) **Use the present tense** as if you are experiencing the actions now.
3) **Be specific.** Use as many senses (sight, sound, smell, taste and touch) as possible to make the scene as real as possible.

> *I was sitting there with my eyes closed, watching plays in my head. I was in my own private basketball laboratory, making mental blueprints for myself.*
>
> Bill Russell
> Hall of Fame Basketball Player

> *We live on two levels — the public level, which is our **doing**, which is observable, verifiable; and the private stage, the thinking stage, the rehearsing stage, on which we prepare for the future roles we want to play.*
>
> Fritz Perls

4) **Feel the feelings.** Let yourself experience the emotional pleasure of successfully doing purposeful actions.

When you follow these four guidelines, you will create an experience that your mind will record as if it had really happened. After enough repetition, the actions in your mind will improve the actions in your life.

You get to choose the movies you play in your mind. You can watch yourself failing. Or you watch yourself succeeding.

Which will you choose?

Journal #17

In this journal entry you will have an opportunity to visualize yourself successfully doing a purposeful action, one that will move you toward the achievement of one of your academic goals for this semester. Once you learn to visualize success, you can use this technique to improve the results you create in all of your life roles.

Take a deep breath and relax.

1. Write one of your most important academic goals for this semester from your life plan (Journal #11). Continue using the DAPPS rule.
For example:

My short-term academic goal for English this semester is to write an essay of five hundred words or more that is free of grammar, spelling, and punctuation errors.

2. Write a list of specific actions that would be effective stepping stones to achieving this academic goal. The more actions you list, the more choices you will be creating for yourself. Your list will probably contain mostly Quadrant II actions. For example:

The following actions will help me achieve my goal in English:
1. Meet with my professor weekly to discuss any errors in my essays.
2. Read and study ten pages per night in my grammar book.
3. Write on 3 x 5 cards my sentences that contain errors. Put the corrections on the back of the card. Carry the cards with me and study them at least five times per day.

3. Circle ONE action from your list in Step 2; then write a visualization of yourself carrying out that action.

Use the four keys to effective visualizing:
1. **RELAX.**
2. **USE THE PRESENT TENSE.** Imagine doing the actions now. (*I knock* on the professor's office door, not "*I knocked . . .*" or "*I will knock . . .*")

3. **BE SPECIFIC**. Use your senses. Let yourself see, hear, and feel (even smell and taste, if appropriate) all that you experience as you take this action.

4. **FEEL THE FEELINGS**. Include the good feelings that you have as you perfectly perform the actions that will create your goals and dreams.

As a model for your writing, reread the visualization on page 91.

4. Write a paragraph or more summing up your thoughts and feelings about visualizing successfully doing purposeful actions.

The quality of your actions begins with the quality of your thoughts. Choose your thoughts wisely.

Relax, think, write.

Chapter 5

■ ▪ ▪ ▪ ▪ ▪ ▪ ▪

Once I accept responsibility for taking purposeful actions to achieve my chosen goals and dreams, the next step is to develop mutually supportive relationships that make the journey easier and more enjoyable.

Developing Mutually Supportive Relationships ▪ ▪ ▪ ▪ ▪ ▪ ▪ ▪

I am developing mutually supportive relationships
that will assist me to more easily reach my goals and dreams.

Successful Students . . .

1. . . . **develop interdependence**, recognizing that life is richer when giving to and receiving from others.

2. . . . **request assistance**, benefiting from the skills and knowledge of others.

3. . . . **create a support network**, utilizing an interactive team approach to success.

4. . . . **listen actively**, demonstrating a desire to truly hear another person's thoughts and feelings.

5. . . . **communicate effectively**, leveling with others about what they are thinking and feeling.

Struggling Students . . .

1. . . . remain exclusively dependent, co-dependent, or independent in relation to others.

2. . . . seldom if ever request help from legitimate resources.

3. . . . work alone, seldom cooperating with others for the common good of all.

4. . . . talk constantly and interrupt often, demonstrating little desire to hear another person's perspective.

5. . . . communicate ineffectively by placating and blaming.

How would you like to make accomplishing your success a little easier and a whole lot more fun? Do you know how?

■ ■ ■ ■ ■ **18. Developing Interdependence**

No man is an island, entire of itself; every man is a piece of the continent, a part of the main.

John Donne

One semester, in the eleventh week, Martha made an announcement. "This is the last time I'll be in class. I'm withdrawing from college. I just wanted to say how much I'll miss you all."

A concerned silence followed Martha's announcement. Her quiet, solid presence had made her a favorite with classmates.

"My babysitter just moved," Martha explained, "and I've been trying to find someone I trust to look after my one-year-old . . . with no luck. My husband took his vacation this week to take care of her, but he has to go back to work. I have to drop out of school to be with my baby. Don't worry," she added weakly, "I'll be back next semester. Really, I will."

Nobody but nobody can make it out here alone.

Maya Angelou

"But there's only a few more weeks in the semester. You can't drop out now!" someone said. Martha merely shrugged her shoulders.

Finally one of the other women in the class said, "My kids are grown and out of the house, and this is the only class I'm taking this semester. I'd be willing to watch your child for the next few weeks if that would help you get through the semester. The only thing is, you'll need to bring your baby to my house because I don't have a car."

"Thanks, but I don't have a car either," Martha said. "I guess I just wasn't meant to go to school this semester."

"Wait a minute," a man in the class said. "Not so fast. Aren't we learning that we're all in this together? I have a car. I'll drive you and your child back and forth until the semester's over."

Martha sat for a moment, stunned. "Really? You'd do that for me?" In three minutes Martha's fate had changed from dropping out of school to finishing her courses with the help of two classmates.

Each of us decides whether we'll go for our dreams alone . . . or if we'll seek and accept assistance from others along the way. What's your choice?

In western culture we often glorify the solitary hero, the strong individual who stands alone against all odds. This script makes good cinema, but does it help us stay on course to our dreams? In fact, can anyone today really be independent?

After all, who of us actually goes unaided by others? We eat food grown *by others*. We wear clothes sewn *by others*. We live in houses built *by others*. We work at businesses owned *by others*. We watch televisions manufactured *by others*, many living clear on the other side of the world. When you really think about it, loners are fooled by the illusion of independence.

Our lives are intertwined with the lives of many other people. Some of them support us to pursue our goals. A few stand in our way. Most are neutral. Creators consciously increase the number of people who help them and decrease the number who hinder them. Creators give assistance; they also ask for and accept assistance. Creators know that life can be easier and more enjoyable when people cooperate for their mutual benefit.

As a student, you can realize great benefits by developing mutually supportive relationships with other self-motivated students. College is a great place to meet people who can play an important role in the quality of your life. You help them and they help you . . . and everyone wins.

Even the Lone Ranger had help

When it comes to relating to others, there are four kinds of people:

Dependent people believe: *I can't achieve my goals by myself. I need other people to do the work for me.*

Co-dependent people believe: *I'll work on my goals as soon as I've helped everyone else get their goals.*

Independent people believe: *By working hard, I can get some of what I want all by myself. I'll just do without the rest.*

Interdependent people believe: *I know I can get some of what I want by working alone, but I'll accomplish more and have more fun if I give and receive help.*

Which belief do you hold? Which belief will best assist you to stay on course to your dreams?

Support groups and twelve-step programs have shown the value of interdependence, people coming together to accomplish what might be impossible for one person alone. Overweight people gather at Overeaters Anonymous to lose weight *with the support of others*. Alcoholics attend Alcoholics Anonymous meetings to stay sober *with the support of others*. Computer hackers join others at computer clubs to learn new ideas. Budding authors join writers' groups to seek advice and encouragement from like-minded souls. Look through your telephone book for support groups; the list is impressive.

Moving from dependence to independence is a major step toward maturity. But moving from independence to *inter*dependence demonstrates the greatest maturity of all in human development.

Truly mature people gladly give and seek assistance.

Developing interdependence will not only keep you on course in college, it will also support your success in ways that you can't even imagine now. A friend of mine who buys old houses, remodels them, and resells them for a tidy profit, ran into difficult times. His completed houses weren't selling, he was short of money to begin any new projects, and bankers were unwilling to lend

I decided to go for what I wanted . . . and if I couldn't get it by myself, like a good American should, well, I wasn't proud — not any more — I was going to get some help.
Barbara Sher

Dependent people need others to get what they want. Independent people can get what they want through their own effort. Interdependent people combine their own efforts with the efforts of others to achieve their greatest success.
Stephen Covey

him additional money. Creditors began to get ugly, and for a few weeks he considered declaring bankruptcy. Then, he came up with an ingenious plan to raise capital: He asked friends to contribute money to his "investment fund," agreeing to pay them higher interest rates than banks were paying at the time. Within two weeks, he had accumulated enough money not only to sustain himself until his properties sold, but to buy two new houses to remodel. He was back in business. And he couldn't have done it alone.

Perhaps the most destructive relationships are those based on co-dependence. Co-dependent people are fulfilled, not by their own successes, but by someone else's approval or dependence upon them. *I am worthwhile*, the co-dependent sadly believes, *only if someone else can't get along without me*. Co-dependent people abandon their own dreams and even endure abuse to keep the approval of others.

One of my students had been in college for seven years without graduating. John was a bright fellow who was creating results far below his potential. During a class discussion about co-dependence, he shared a recent experience that had happened to him. He had been studying for a mid-term test in history when a friend called and asked for help with a test in biology (a course that John had already passed). John set his own studies aside and spent the evening tutoring his friend. The next day John failed his history exam. In his journal, he wrote, "I've learned that in order to be successful, I need to make my dreams more important than other people's approval. I have to learn to say 'No.'" Because they have difficulty saying "NO," co-dependents like John often spend time in Quadrant III, engaged in activities that are urgent to someone else but not really important to their own goals and dreams.

The problem with co-dependence, dependence, and independence is that giving and receiving are out of balance. The co-dependent person *gives* too much. The dependent person *takes* too much. The independent person prefers neither to give nor take anything.

By contrast, the interdependent person finds a healthy balance of giving and receiving, and everyone benefits. That's why building mutually supportive relationships is one of the most important Quadrant II behaviors you'll ever undertake. The support you receive from interdependent relationships will very likely determine whether you stay on course to your dreams. It may also determine how fast you get there and how much you enjoy the journey.

Journal #18

In this journal entry, you will have an opportunity to identify whether you are primarily a dependent, co-dependent, independent, or interdependent person. Remember, **dependent** people *need* others to achieve even their simplest goals. **Co-dependent** people give continuously to others at the expense of achieving their own goals. **Independent** people insist on pursuing their goals alone. **Interdependent** people realize they can create more in their lives if they give and receive assistance in mutually supportive relationships.

1. Write and complete the following ten sentence stems two or more times each.

1. A specific situation when someone assisted me was . . .
2. A specific situation when I assisted someone was . . .
3. A specific situation when I made assisting someone more important than my success and happiness was . . .
4. When someone asks me for assistance I usually feel . . .
5. When I think of asking someone else for assistance I usually feel . . .
6. What most often gets in the way of my asking for help is . . .
7. If I often asked other people for assistance . . .
8. If I joyfully gave assistance to others . . .
9. If I gratefully accepted assistance from others . . .
10. One goal that I could use assistance with today is . . .

2. Write about what you discovered in Step 1: How would you describe your typical relationship to others: 1) dependent, 2) co-dependent, 3) independent, or 4) interdependent? Why do you think so? How do you feel about yourself in this regard? Are there any changes you wish to make? Fully describe how you would prefer to relate with others. Give specific examples and evidence from your own experience. Write as many fully developed paragraphs as necessary to explore this topic.

Relax, think, write.

You need a village to raise a child.
   African Proverb

focus questions   Do you ask for help when you need it? Do you know how to make an effective request?

■ ■ ■ ■ 19. Requesting Assistance

Ask, and it shall be given you; seek, and ye shall find; knock, and it shall be opened unto you.
For everyone that asketh, receiveth; and he that seeketh, findeth; and to him that knocketh it shall be opened.
   The Bible, Matthew 7:7,8

Donald hated where he was living: he had to walk sixteen blocks to catch a bus to the college, his neighborhood was run-down, the local supermarket was outrageously expensive, his wife disliked their neighbors, his daughter hated her elementary school, and their tiny apartment was barely big enough for the three of them. He felt trapped.

"Sure I'd move if I could," Donald said. "But where am I going to find a better place that I can afford while I'm going to college?"

"Request assistance," I suggested. "Let people know how they can help you. No one will know that they could help you unless you ask."

"I don't even know who to ask."

"Then ask everyone. What have you got to lose?"

Later in the semester, Donald came to class with a huge grin. Over the weekend, he and his family had moved into a new apartment. It was bigger, closer to the college, in a better neighborhood, his daughter loved her new school, and, their rent had gone down twenty-five dollars per month.

"I decided to ask everyone I met if they knew about a nice, affordable apartment in a better part of town," Donald said. "A man at my church gave me the name of an elderly woman who wanted to rent a basement apartment in her huge house. She lives alone and was willing to keep the rent low if we'd check on her a couple of times a day. I never thought I could afford such a great place."

Request assistance from college resources

When you have a problem, you have a choice: You can tackle the problem alone . . . or you can request assistance. College is a great place to perfect the supportive habit of asking for help.

Nearly every college spends a chunk of your tuition on support services. These services are designed to help you succeed in college, but they go to waste unless you use them. Do you know what support services your college offers, where they are, and how to use them?

Academic problems? Request assistance from one of your college's tutoring labs. Many colleges have a writing lab, a reading lab, and a math lab. Other sources of help might include a science learning center or a computer lab. Your college may also have a diagnostician whose job it is to test students for learning disabilities and to suggest ways for overcoming them. Academic help exists at your college. Ask for it.

Money problems? Request assistance from your college's financial aid office. Money for college is available in the form of grants and scholarships (which you don't pay back), loans (which you do pay back, usually at low interest rates), and student work programs, which offer money-making jobs on campus. Your college may also have a service that can find you an off-campus job, perhaps one in the very field you wish to enter after graduation.

Personal problems? Request assistance from your college's counseling office. Trained counselors are available at many colleges to help students through times of emotional upset. It is not unusual for students to experience some sort of personal difficulty during college; the interdependent ones ask for help.

Health problems? Request assistance from your college's health services office. Many colleges have doctors whom students can consult inexpensively or even for free. Health-related products may be purchased far less expensively through some colleges' health service office. Your college may even offer health insurance for students.

At fifty I am still completing the process of learning how to ask for help, how not to be afraid to appear weak when I am weak, how to allow myself to be dependent and unself-reliant when appropriate.

Dr. M. Scott Peck

That man is great who can use the brains of others to carry out his work.

Donn Piatt

Problems deciding on a career?   Request assistance from your college's career office. There you can take tests to discover your aptitudes, discover where job opportunities are, learn how to write or improve your resume, and practice effective interviewing skills.

Problems getting involved socially at your college?   Request assistance from your college's student activities office. Here you'll find out about sports, student-sponsored activities, service projects, student professional organizations, and clubs just waiting for you to join them.

Request assistance from your instructors

College instructors hold weekly office hours to meet with students outside of class. Yet, it is the rare student who takes advantage of this valuable resource for assistance.

This is good news for you. If you're interdependent and willing to ask your instructors for help, you'll probably experience little competition for their time. Find out when they have office hours. Make an appointment. Beforehand, jot down a couple of questions. Students who request conferences, keep their appointments, and come prepared with questions and requests send an impressive message to their teachers: *I'm committed to my success . . . and I want your help!*

Meeting with your teachers is a Quadrant II (Important and Not Urgent) action that can pay off handsomely. Your teachers have years of specialized training. Some of them sell their knowledge and skills outside of the college as consultants, but you've already paid for their help with your tuition. All you have to do is ask. Most teachers went into their profession because they like their subject and they enjoy helping people. When you make a request of them, you tap their desire to be of service. As a bonus, if you get to know your teachers, one of them may turn out to be an important mentor or trusted guide in your life.

Make effective requests

Making an effective request is a skill. The key is to apply the DAPPS rule to your requests. Whenever possible, make your requests **D**ated, **A**chievable, **P**ersonal, **P**ositive, and (most of all!) **S**pecific. Here are some translations of vague, spongy Victim requests to specific, clear Creator requests:

1. I'm going to be absent next Friday. It sure would be nice if someone would call and tell me what I miss.

1. *John, I'm going to be absent next Friday. Would you be willing to call me Friday night and tell me what assignments I missed?*

2. I don't suppose you'd consider giving me a few more days to complete this research paper?

2. *I'd like to request an extension on my research paper. I could have it to you by noon on Friday. Would that be acceptable?*

3. Do you think you could help me with my math sometime?

3. Would you meet with me for about an hour to help me with my math homework? Great! Saturday morning at ten o'clock is good for me. Would that work for you?

When you make specific requests, the other person can respond with a clear "yes" or "no." If the person says "No," all is not lost. Discover if he will negotiate:

1. *If you can't call me Friday night, could I call you on Saturday morning to get the assignments that I miss?*
2. *Well, if Friday isn't acceptable to you, could I turn my paper in on Thursday by 5:00?*
3. *If an hour is too long, would you be willing to help me with my math for just thirty minutes?*

A Creator seeks definite yes or no answers. Victims often accept "maybe" or "I'll try" for fear of getting a "no," but it's better to hear a specific "no" and be free to move on to someone who will say yes.

Once, during the meeting of a college faculty committee, the members present changed the date of the next meeting. The committee chairperson made a request of the corresponding secretary, and the following conversation resulted:

Chairperson: Would you send out a notice today about the new date for our next meeting?
Secretary: I'm really busy, but I'll see what I can do.
Chairperson: I understand that you're busy, but the people who weren't here today need to know about the schedule change as soon as possible so they can rearrange their plans. Will you be able to get the memo out today?
Secretary: I'll do my best.
Chairperson: I know you'll do your best. But I want to be sure that the memo will go out today. If you can't do it, just say so, and I'll get it taken care of some other way.
Secretary: No, that's all right. I'll get it out today.
Chairperson: Thanks, I really appreciate your help.

Notice how the chairperson moved her colleague from maybe to yes by assertively and effectively making her request. Even a Creator is sometimes reluctant to make a commitment because he needs more information or more time. In that case, you can always make another request. The chairperson could have said, *Would you be willing to tell me by three o'clock if you'll get the memo out today?* or *Would you be able to get it out by ten o'clock tomorrow morning, then?*

One of my mentors gave me a valuable piece of advice: "If you go through a whole day without getting at least a couple of no's, you aren't asking for enough help in your life."

Would you be willing to make two requests today?

As an interdependent person, I have the opportunity to share myself deeply, meaningfully with others, and I have access to the vast resources and potential of other human beings.
Stephen Covey

Requesting is the act of asking for something from someone else. A complete request requires: (1) a speaker, (2) a listener, (3) terms of fulfillment (exactly what is being asked for), (4) a time agreement, and (5) a response (accept, decline, counteroffer).
John Hanley

Know how to ask. There is nothing more difficult for some people, nor for others, easier.
Baltasar Gracian

Journal #19

In this journal entry you will have an opportunity to practice requesting assistance. When you become skillful at making effective requests, you will find that achieving your goals becomes both easier and more enjoyable.

First, take a moment right now to relax. Breathe deeply and let yourself get comfortable. To focus your mind, think about one of your most challenging academic goals.

1. Write and complete each of the following seven sentence stems (once each):

1. One of my most challenging academic goals this semester is . . .
2. My biggest obstacle to achieving this goal is . . .
3. Someone (besides me) who could assist me to overcome this obstacle is . . .
4. My biggest fear about asking this person for assistance is . . .
5. The worst thing that could happen if I asked is . . .
6. The best thing that could happen if I asked is . . .
7. The most likely thing to happen if I ask is . . .

2. Write a letter to this person and request assistance. You can decide later if you actually want to send the letter.

Here are some possibilities to include in your letter:

- Tell the person what your most challenging academic goal is for this semester.
- Explain how this goal is a stepping stone to your dream.
- Describe your dream and explain why it is so important to you.
- Identify your obstacle, explaining it fully.
- Discuss why you believe this person is ideally qualified to assist you to overcome your obstacle.
- Admit any reluctance or fear you have about asking for assistance.
- Request *exactly* what you would like this person to do for you.

Remember, for effective requests, use the DAPPS rule. Make your request **D**ated, **A**chievable, **P**ersonal, **P**ositive and **S**pecific.

Relax, think, write your request.

Have you said your affirmation today? Did you do your thirty-two-day commitment today? Are you using your daily action list today? What inner voices are you listening to today?

Do you have a support network that will help you to achieve your greatest dreams in college and in life? Do you know how to build one?

▪ ▪ ▪ ▪ ▪ 20. Creating a Support Network

To reach your goals you need to become a team player.

Zig Ziglar

One underused ingredient of success is called **OPB.** OPB stands for two things, really:

Other People's Brains and **Other People's Brawn.**

Are you pursuing your goals alone? Or, are you benefiting from a supportive network of people whom you've consciously chosen to assist you? For solving most problems, ten brains are better than one. For accomplishing most tasks, twenty hands are better than two.

Create a project team

[D]evelop an inner circle of close associations in which the mutual attraction is not sharing problems or needs. The mutual attraction should be values and goals.

Denis Waitley

If you're tackling a big project, why not create a team to help you? The purpose of a project team is to accomplish one particular task. In business, when a project needs attention, an ***ad hoc* committee** is formed to complete the project. *Ad hoc* in Latin means "toward this." In other words, an *ad hoc* committee comes together for the sole purpose of solving one problem. Once the task is complete, the committee disbands.

One of my students created a project team to help her move. More than a dozen classmates showed up, including a fellow who provided a small truck. In one Saturday morning, the team packed and delivered all of her possessions to her new apartment.

What big project do you have that would benefit from the assistance of a group of people? The only thing standing between you and a project team is your willingness to ask for help.

Create a study group

One of the best strategies for success in college is to form a study group. A study group differs from a project team in two ways. First, a study group is formed to help everyone on the team excel in a particular course. Second, a study group meets many times throughout a semester.

Love thy neighbor as thyself, but choose your neighborhood.

Louise Beal

In fact, some study groups become so successful that members stay together semester after semester. In his sophomore year, my son teamed with two other students in the business curriculum at his university, and they took courses together for the next three years. By helping and challenging each other, all three graduated with 4.0 averages in their majors.

Here are three suggestions for assembling an effective study group:

1. Choose only Creators.   As the semester begins, make a list of potential study group members by observing which classmates consistently attend class, which ones come prepared, and which ones participate actively. In other words, look for students who follow the three essential action rules for success that we discussed in Section 13 (page 67). Keep an eye out also for that quiet student who doesn't say much, but whose occasional comment reveals a special understanding of the subject. After the first test or essay, find out how the students on your list did. Now invite three or four of the most successful students to form a study group with you. You have created a team with great potential.

2. Choose group goals.   Unfortunately, great potential doesn't guarantee an effective study group. In fact, many students have had bad experiences with study groups and now insist on studying alone. Realize that a study group is only as effective as you make it. The entire team must agree upon common goals. You might say to prospective study-group members, *My goal in our math class is to master the subject and to earn an A. Is that what you want, too?* There's no point teaming with students whose goals don't match your own.

> *My driving belief is that great teamwork is the only way to reach our ultimate moments, to create breakthroughs that define our careers, to fulfill our lives with a sense of lasting significance.*
>
> Pat Riley

3. Choose group rules.   Once the group has agreed upon common goals, the third step is to agree upon effective team rules. Pat Riley, one of the most successful professional basketball coaches ever, has his players create a "team covenant." Before the season, they all agree on the rules they will follow to stay on course to their goal of a championship. Your team should do the same. Decide where you will meet, how often, what time, and what will take place during the meetings. Many study groups fail because they turn into social gatherings. You might consider rules like these:

> **Rule 1:** *We will meet in the library every Thursday afternoon from one o'clock to three o'clock.*
> **Rule 2:** *Each member will bring twenty new questions to every meeting. Questions will be written on one side of a 3 × 5 card; the answers will be written on the back, including the source (textbook page or lecture date).*
> **Rule 3:** *All written questions must be asked, answered, and understood before any socializing.*

When you organize a study group of Creators who agree on common goals and action rules, what could possibly stop you from achieving your desired outcomes?

Create a success team

> *[S]tudents have always known the advantages of teaming up with a study buddy for homework or exam cramming.*
>
> Barbara Sher

Project teams are great for completing a single important task, and study groups maximize learning in a particular course. We can make even greater use of effective networking in our lives by creating our own success team.

A success team is a group that meets regularly over an extended period of time — maybe even years — with but one purpose: to apply OPB (other peoples' brains and brawn) to assist everyone on the team to achieve their greatest goals and dreams.

Business leaders know the importance of a board of directors to the success of their business. Why not create a board of directors for our own personal and professional success?

Creating a success team is an old idea. Andrew Carnegie became wealthy in the steel industry more than one hundred years ago. He gave away millions of dollars for the construction of libraries and performance halls, including Carnegie Music Hall in New York City. Carnegie attributed his achievements in part to his success team. Calling themselves the Master Mind Group, Carnegie and five other men met every Tuesday morning for breakfast. Their purpose was to offer each other suggestions about how each could reach his goal.

I belong to a weekly success team that benefits me in many ways. By discussing my goals and dreams, I stay conscious of what I want to create in my life. By telling the team about my recent actions, I remind myself that it takes deeds not wishes to create my goals. By identifying my obstacles, I see them more clearly. By sharing my victories, I strengthen my confidence and ability to overcome obstacles. By exploring my feelings, I stay conscious of my encouraging as well as my discouraging emotions. By examining what I have learned, I continue to grow. By getting suggestions, I consider effective actions I might otherwise have overlooked. By accepting assistance, I use other people's brains and other people's brawn to move me toward my goals. By listening to the dreams, actions, challenges, frustrations and victories of others, I am inspired to persevere. By offering information, suggestions and assistance to my team, I have the privilege of contributing to others' success and happiness. In sum, by being in a group, I am offered the wonderful opportunity to give and receive help.

Taking time to create a support network in college is one of the most important Quadrant II activities you can undertake. Creators develop relationships in college that continue to support them for years — even for a lifetime. Don't get so caught up with the daily grind of college that you fail to create a support network of fellow travelers. Give to them and they will give back to you . . . and all of you can reach your dreams.

Many of us are in the habit of collaborating only with people who are like us. One of the greatest benefits of your college experience is meeting people of diverse backgrounds. These people can often be of great assistance to us, and we to them, simply because we bring different ideas, skills, experiences, abilities and resources to the relationship. Be sure to network with people who are older or younger than you, who are from different states or countries, who are of different races or cultures, who have different religions or political preferences.

Start a telephone list of the people you meet in college. You might want to even write a few notes about them: their major or career field, their families, hobbies, interests, and especially their strengths. Keep in touch with these peo-

Nobody in business works in a vacuum. We work in teams, divisions, committees, work groups.

Dan Gutman

ple during college. Keep in touch with them after college. It has been said that success is not only **what** you know but **who** you know.

Friends helping friends is a key to success

When I joined the bank, I started keeping a record of the people I met, and put them on little cards, and I would indicate on the cards when I met them, and under what circumstances, and with whom, and sometimes I put on the cards a little notation which would help me remember a conversation or something of that sort. And then I extended that, and did it in addition to alphabetically — geographically, and by company, so that if I know I'm going to call on a company, I will take out the cards of that company and look at the names of the people that I've met there before, which will help me remember if I see them again.
David Rockefeller
Chairman of the board, Chase
Manhattan Bank

A story is told of a man who prayed to know the difference between heaven and hell. An angel visited and took the man to see for himself. First, the angel escorted him to hell. There, the man saw a banquet table that stretched from one horizon to the other. The table overflowed with beautifully prepared meats, vegetables, drinks, and desserts. Along the banquet table sat the prisoners of hell, but despite the bounty of food, all had sunken, withered looks. Then the man saw why. The poor souls in hell could scoop up anything they wanted from the bountiful table, but their elbows would not bend, and they could not place the food into their mouths. Living amidst all that abundance, the citizens of hell were starving.

Then the angel whisked the man to heaven where he saw the same endless banquet table that he had seen in hell. Once again, the table was heaped with a bounty of splendid food. Then the man saw the most amazing similarity of all: As in hell, the citizens of heaven could not bend their elbows to feed themselves.

"I don't understand," the man said. "Is heaven the same as hell?"

The angel said nothing, only pointed. The residents of heaven were healthy, smiling, laughing, and obviously contented as they sat at the banquet tables. Then the man saw.

The citizens of heaven were feeding each other.

Journal #20

In this journal entry you will have an opportunity to experience an imaginary success team meeting.

Afterwards, you may decide to start networking, using OPB to assist you to achieve your greatest goals and dreams.

To focus your mind, think about any three people with whom you would like to form a success team. These people can be living or dead, real or imagined, people you know or people you don't know (but would like to). Your success team can include Albert Einstein, your mother, Superman, your fifth-grade teacher, Mother Teresa, a friend, Michael Jordan, or anyone you choose!

1. To choose your success team, write and complete the following three sentence stems:

1. As the first person on my success team I choose _____ because . . .
2. As the second person on my success team I choose _____ because . . .
3. As the third person on my success team I choose _____ because . . .

2. Complete each of the following sentence stems as you might say them at your success team meeting:

1. A challenging GOAL I have in college/life right now is . . .
2. Recent *specific* ACTION STEPS I've taken toward this goal are . . .
3. Today my major OBSTACLE to this goal is . . .
4. The EMOTION that I feel most as I journey toward this goal is . . .
5. On the journey to this goal, an important LESSON I have recently learned is . . .
6. My next three *specific* ACTION STEPS toward this goal will be to . . .
7. To achieve this goal, I could use ASSISTANCE with . . .

3. Complete the following sentence stems as you believe Person One on your support team (from Step 1) would complete them.

PERSON SPEAKING: _____

1. One suggestion I have to help you reach this academic goal is . . .
2. One outside resource that you could make use of to reach this academic goal is . . .
3. I would be willing to assist you to reach this goal by . . .

4. Repeat Step 3 in the voice of Person Two on your support team.

5. Repeat Step 3 in the voice of Person Three on your support team.

6. Write a paragraph or more discussing the most important thing(s) you learned in this imaginary success team meeting.

Relax, think, write.

focus questions

Do you know how to strenthen a relationship with active listening? Do you know the essential skills of being a good listener?

Take a major step toward your success in college — choose to start a study group. Don't just think about it — do it. DO IT TODAY!!

◼ ◼ ◼ ◼ ◼ 21. Listening Actively

When people talk, listen completely. Most people never listen.
Ernest Hemingway

I was strolling along a sidewalk recently when I saw a friend walking toward me. I smiled and said, "Hi."

He smiled back and said, "Fine."

This tiny incident illustrates the major obstacle to listening. My friend didn't hear what I *had* said ("Hi."). He heard and responded to what he *thought* I had said ("How are you?"). Poor listeners let their own thoughts and expectations distort what the other person is actually saying. Good listeners, by contrast, clear their minds and listen for the entire message conveyed by the other person's words, tone of voice, gestures, and facial expressions.

No matter how well one person communicates, unless someone else listens actively, the communication will go astray. In my brief greeting on the sidewalk, of course, no harm was done. In other situations, however, poor listening skills can cause great damage. Imagine the potential problems created if good listening skills are absent when . . .

A doctor says to a nurse: *Decrease the patient's dosage of medicine . . .* but the nurse is expecting the doctor to increase the dosage.

An employer says to an employee: *Include last year's sales figures in the report for comparison . . .* but the employee is preoccupied with how to get the report done on time.

A teacher says to a class: *I must have your assignments on time so I can get the semester grades turned in . . .* but the students know the teacher has accepted late papers in the past.

In some cases, the immediate problem caused by poor listening can be fixed (the employee can rewrite the sales report, for example). But the relationship may be injured beyond repair (the employer may never again trust the employee, even passing him over for future promotions).

Listening effectively means that you accept 100 percent responsibility for receiving the same message that the speaker sent, uncontaminated by your own thoughts or feelings.

Effective listening means active listening, and active listening begins with empathy. Empathy is the ability to understand another person's words *as she means them,* and to feel the other person's emotions *as she feels them.* To empathize is to experience life as if, for that moment, you are the other person. To empathize with someone does not mean that you necessarily agree with him. It means that you understand what he is thinking and feeling. And you actively let him know that.

With empathetic listening, you send this message: *I am doing my very best to see the world through your eyes.*

How to listen actively

Active listening is a learned skill. To achieve understanding of another person's whole communication, follow these four steps:

Step 1: Listen to understand.   Change your purpose for listening. Most people listen for the purpose of responding. In fact, they are not really listening; they are busy thinking about what they will say next, waiting for the smallest opening to insert their own opinion. Effective listening, founded on empathy, begins with the intention to understand. Make it your first purpose to discover what the other person thinks and feels about his or her experience.

Step 2: Clear your mind and remain silent.   You are not the other person. You have not had his exact experiences, nor his unique thoughts and feelings about his experiences. Turn off your Inner Critic and Inner Defender. Clear your mind and be quiet. Enjoy just *being* with your companion. You have nothing to prove. For now, be a receiver, not a sender. Let your mind listen for thoughts. Let your heart listen for emotions. Let your intuition listen for a deeper message hidden beneath the words. Let your companion know that you are actively listening. Sit forward. Nod your head when appropriate. Offer verbal feedback that you are actively listening: *"Mmmmm . . . . I see . . . . . Uh huh . . . ."*

Step 3: Reflect the other person's thoughts and feelings.   Like a mirror, reflect your understanding of the speaker's thoughts and feelings. In your own words, restate the totality of what you heard, both the ideas and the emotion (if present). Then verify the accuracy of your understanding. For example . . .

- *You're really angry about the comments your teacher wrote on your research paper. His comments seem sarcastic rather than helpful. Is that it?*
- *I want to be clear about this essay that you're assigning. The outline for the essay is due October third and the final draft is due November first. Have I got it right?*

The quieter you become, the more you can hear.
Baba Ram Dass

Notice that while reflecting, you add nothing new to the conversation. Don't offer advice or tell your own experience.

And, when the other person asks you a question, be sure you understand what the person is actually asking. Family therapist Virginia Satir told a story about a six-year-old child who asked his mother, "Mommy, how did I get here?" His mother launched into a long and thorough explanation about how babies are created. An hour later, the puzzled little boy said, "I meant, when we moved here, did we come in a train or in an airplane?"

What you hear when you listen isn't necessarily what they are saying. What you hear is your own interpreted version of what they are saying.
John Hanley

Step 4: Ask the person to expand or clarify.   Invite the speaker to share additional information and feelings. The more actively you listen, the better your chances are of truly empathizing with the person.

- *I want to be sure I understand you. Would you say a bit more about that?*
- *Could you give me an example of what you mean?*
- *How did you feel when that happened?*
- *That's amazing. What happened next?*
- *I'm not sure I know what you mean by that. Can you say it a different way?*
- *That's a point of view I hadn't thought of. Tell me more.*

While listening actively, be especially alert for a speaker's vague use of pronouns such as *this, that,* and *it.* If you aren't positive what these words refer to, you may misunderstand the message. If a speaker says, "I always have a problem with *this,*" or "I get so angry whenever someone does *that,*" or "I don't know if *it* matters any more," ask the speaker to clarify what *this, that,* and *it* mean to him.

I want to be sure I understand. When you said that you always have a problem with this, *what did you mean by* this?

Use active listening in your college classes

At the end of a class, I often ask students to write and complete this sentence stem: *Today I learned/relearned . . .* I am always impressed with how much learning most students create during a class experience.

Occasionally, however, a student will write, *Today I learned NOTHING.* How can this be? Two students sit in the same class for an hour, one learns valuable lessons while the other learns nothing! I submit that it may be as simple as this: One student listened actively . . . one student didn't. (Why one student didn't listen actively we will explore later.)

Successful students are active listeners. In class, they clear their minds and take the alert posture of one about to hear something of great value. They reflect the teacher's ideas to confirm that they are hearing accurately. They ask the teacher to expand or clarify when they are confused. If there isn't time to clarify during class time, they do it immediately after class or they do it during the teacher's conference hours. As Creators, these students actively listen to understand.

Choose today to master active listening in class and out of class. You'll be amazed at how much more you'll begin to hear.

> *If there is any one secret of success, it lies in the ability to get the other person's point of view and see things from his angle as well as your own.*
>
> Henry Ford

Journal #21

In this journal entry you will have an opportunity to practice active listening. With practice, active listening will become a habit that will strengthen your relationships and support your success.

First, take a deep breath and relax. Realize that relaxation enhances your ability to clear your mind for effective listening.

To focus your mind, recall the four steps of active listening:

1. Listen to understand (not to respond).
2. Clear your mind of expectations and remain silent.
3. Reflect (restate) the speaker's thoughts and feelings.
4. Ask the speaker to expand or clarify.

1. Write a conversation between you and your Inner Guide (IG). Let your IG demonstrate the skills of active listening. Label each of your IG's responses with the listening skill it uses: silence, reflection, expansion, or clarification.

Let this conversation explore one of your present difficulties as you pursue your goals and dreams. Remember, your IG, as a good active listener, will add nothing new to the conversation. Below is an example of how your dialogue might sound:

Me: I've been realizing what a difficult time I have asking for assistance.
IG: Would you like to say more about that? **(expansion)**
Me: Well, I've been having a rough time with math. I know I should be asking more questions in class, but there's something about having to ask for help . . . I don't know, I guess I feel dumb when I can't do it myself.
IG: You seem frustrated that you can't solve the math problems without help. **(reflection)**
Me: That's right. I've always resisted that sort of thing.
IG: What do you mean by "that sort of thing"? **(clarification)**
Me: I mean that ever since I can remember, I've had to do everything on my own. When I was a kid, I used to play alone all the time.
IG: Uh huh . . . **(silence)**
Me: I never had anyone to help me as a kid. And I don't have anyone to help me now.
IG: So, no one is available to help you? Is that how it seems? **(reflection)**
Me: Well, I guess I could ask Robert for help in math. He seems to really know what he's talking about.
IG: You seem hopeful that Robert might help you. Is that right? **(reflection)**
Me: Yes, but it also seems kind of scary to ask him.
IG: What's scary about asking him? **(expansion)**

Continue your dialogue until the conversation feels complete. Remember to label each comment by your IG with the listening skill it is using.

2. Write a paragraph or more explaining what you learned during this conversation with your Inner Guide.

Relax (clear your mind and be silent), think of an important problem that you'd like to discuss with a good listener, and write a dialogue with your Inner Guide as the active listener.

Are you an effective communicator? Do you know the key communication skills that Creators use to strengthen their relationships?

■ ■ ■ ■ ■ 22. **Communicating Effectively**

One more way to strengthen a relationship is to **send** effective communications. But, given the complexity of the communication process, it's amazing that anyone ever sends an effective message.

Consider how communication works. Suppose I want to tell you about an experience that I've had. My total experience consists of 1) what I believe happened, 2) my thoughts about what I believe happened, and 3) my feelings about what I believe happened. To effectively communicate this total experience, I must translate this experience into words and then speak them to you.

Now it's your turn. You listen to my words and interpret my meaning as best you can. But here's the problem: You have never had my exact experience. The only way you can make meaning from my words is to filter them through your own previous experiences, thoughts, and feelings, all of which are different from my own. Words, then, form a shaky bridge between our two realities. And Victim language makes communication even less effective.

Once a human being has arrived on this earth, communication is the largest single factor determining what kinds of relationships she or he makes with others and what happens to each in the world.
Virginia Satir

How Victims communicate

According to family therapist Virginia Satir, the two most common patterns of ineffective communication are **placating** and **blaming**. These are the favorite voices of the Inner Critic and Inner Defender.

Placating: Victims who placate place themselves below others. They protect themselves from the sting of criticism and rejection by saying whatever they think will gain approval. Picture them on their knees, looking up with a pained smile, nodding and agreeing on the outside, fearfully hiding their true thoughts and feelings within. "Please, please *approve* of me," they beg as their own Inner Critic judges them unworthy. Satir estimates that about 50 percent of people use placating as their major communication style.

Learning to perceive the truth within ourselves and speak it clearly to others is a delicate skill, certainly as complex as multiplication or long division, but very little time is spent on it in school.
Gay and Kathlyn Hendricks

Blaming: Victims who blame place themselves above others. They protect themselves from wounds of disappointment and failure by making others responsible for their problems. The reasoning of the blamer seems to be, "I will feel better about myself if I can make you feel worse about yourself." Picture them glowering above you, a finger jabbing furiously in your face. Their Inner Defender snarls, "*You never . . . You always . . . Why do you have to . . . ? Why don't you ever . . . ? It's your fault that . . .*" Satir estimates that about 30 percent of people use blaming as their major communication style.

Placating and blaming keep Victims from developing mutually supportive relationships, making the accomplishment of their dreams more difficult.

How Creators communicate

Leveling: What, then, is the communication style of Creators? Satir calls it leveling. Leveling is characterized by a simple, yet profound, communication strategy: **telling your truth.**

Creators tell their truth without false apology or excuses, without harsh criticism or blame. Leveling requires a strong Inner Guide and a commitment to honesty. That's why leveling takes the courage of a Creator.

Creators use a number of communication strategies that assist them to level with others. By leveling, they nurture greater trust and respect in all of their relationships. Here are five strategies that enhance leveling:

1. Communicate purposefully. Creators express a clear purpose even in times of upset. If a Creator goes to a professor to discuss a disappointing grade, she will be clear whether her purpose is 1) to increase her understanding of the subject, 2) to seek a higher grade, 3) to criticize the teacher's grading ability, or whatever. By knowing her purpose, she has a way to judge the success of her communication. The Creator says purposefully, *When I saw my grade on this essay, I was very disappointed. I'd like to go over this essay with you to learn how to improve my next essay.*

2. Communicate specifically. Creators recognize that no one else has had their experiences, so they support their opinions with specific reasons. They offer the four E's of good support: Experiences, Examples, Explanations, and Evidence. The Creator offers her idea or opinion, then offers specific support: *I believe that good communication skills are the key to strong, healthy relationships. Let me tell you about a personal <u>experience</u> that supports my belief.... Let me give an <u>example</u> that illustrates what I mean.... Let me <u>explain</u> why I believe this is true.... Let me offer some <u>evidence</u> to prove my claim.*

3. Communicate honestly. When their feelings are negative or their opinions unpopular, Creators express them with candor. The Creator says honestly, *I'm angry that you didn't meet me in the library to study for the sociology test as you agreed.*

4. Communicate empathetically. Creators are keenly aware of their audience. They use words that their listeners know. They define concepts that might confuse their listeners. They answer important questions even before their listeners ask. The Creator says empathetically, *I learned a really great strategy in college today called "active listening." First, let me tell you what "active listening" means.*

5. Communicate responsibly. Because responsibility lies within, Creators express their personal responsibility with I-messages. An I-message allows

Say what you have to say, not what you ought. Any truth is better than make-believe.
Henry David Thoreau

I messages are self-responsible statements that express what one sees and hears, how one feels on the basis of that interpretation, and what one wants.
John Bradshaw

Creators to take full responsibility for their reaction to anything another person may have said or done. An effective I-message has four elements:

A statement of the situation: *When you . . . .*

A statement of your reaction: *I felt/thought/decided. . . .*

A request: *I'd like to ask that you . . . .*

An invitation to respond: *Will you agree to that?*

Below are some examples of I-messages. Notice that none of them placates or blames. In each one, the speaker takes full responsibility for his or her actions, thoughts, and feelings. Each speaker levels with his or her listener.

When you use that tone of voice in speaking to me, I get furious. It reminds me of the way my mother talked to me when I was five years old. I'd like to request that you stop using that tone of voice with me. Are you willing to do that?

At the beginning of the semester, you told us that our grades in this course would be based on essay tests. Now you're saying that we'll have only true/false tests, and I feel cheated. I much prefer essay tests because I think I can better show what I've learned. If I'd known you were going to give true-false tests, I would have switched to a different section, but now it's too late. I'd like you to keep your commitment and give us only essay tests. Will you do that?

I'm trying to tell you something that is very important to me, and you keep changing the subject. I'm beginning to think that you aren't interested in what I'm telling you. Is that accurate?

As one last illustration of these communication patterns, let's compare three different responses to the same situation.

You feel sick one day and decide not to go to your history class. You phone a classmate, and she agrees to call you after class to tell you what you missed. But she never calls. The next time you go to the history class, the teacher gives a test that was announced on the day you were absent. After the test, your classmate apologizes for not calling you. She was really swamped with work, she says. What response do you choose?

Placating: *Oh, don't worry about it. I know you had a lot on your mind. I probably would have failed the test anyway.*

Blaming: *You're the lousiest friend I've ever had. After making me fail that test, you have some nerve even talking to me.*

Leveling: *I'm angry that you didn't call. I realize that I could have called you, but I thought I could count on you to keep your word. If we're going to be friends, I need to know if you're going to keep your promises to me in the future. Are you?*

Notice how the leveling response is the only one of the three that both addresses the issue *and* nurtures a healthy relationship of equals. The Creator puts herself neither beneath others by placating nor above others by blaming. Rather, she levels by stating honestly what she thinks and how she feels. Others can trust that they know where they stand with a Creator. In a firm, honest, and caring way, she draws her boundaries: *This is acceptable to me; this is not acceptable to me. Now that you know, which do you choose?*

If you would like to communicate more effectively, start talking like a Creator. Start leveling.

I speak straight and do not wish to deceive or be deceived.
Cochise

Journal #22

In this journal entry you will have an opportunity to experience the contrast between effective and ineffective communication styles. As you become a better communicator, you will find that your relationships will become stronger and more mutually supportive.

First, take a deep breath and relax.

To focus your mind, recall the ineffective communication styles used by Victims: **placating** and **blaming**. Also recall the effective communication style used by Creators: **leveling.**

An I-message is a key ingredient of leveling. An I-message contains some or all of the following ingredients:

1. An objective description of a situation.
2. What you have chosen to think and feel about the situation.
3. A request made of the other person.
4. A check for the other person's agreement with the request.

1. Write three responses to the teacher described in the following situation. Respond to the teacher once each by 1) placating, 2) blaming, and 3) leveling. For an example of this assignment, refer to Section 22 (page 114).

Situation: You register for a course required in your major. It is the last course you need to graduate. When you go to the first class meeting, the teacher tells you that your name is NOT on the roster. The course is full, and there are no other sections of the course being offered. You've been shut out of the class. The teacher tells you that you will have to postpone graduation and return next semester to complete this required course.

Remember, in each of your three responses, you are writing what you would actually say to the teacher — first as a placator, second as a blamer, and third as a leveler.

2. Write what you have learned about placating, blaming, and leveling. How are these styles similar, how different? Which style have you used most in your life? What is your intention from now on? Be sure to use the four E's (Experiences, Examples, Explanation and Evidence) to support your viewpoint. You might want to write one paragraph about each of the three communication styles.

Relax, think, write.

Chapter 6

■ ■ ■ ■ ■ ■ ■ ■ ■

Despite all my efforts to create success in college and in life, I may still find myself off course. Now is the perfect time to recognize and address the obstacles to my success that lie within me.

Succeeding from the Inside Out ■ ■ ■ ■

I am choosing habit patterns and core beliefs that support my success.

Successful Students . . .

1. . . . **recognize when they are off course.**

2. . . . **identify their self-defeating habit patterns of behavior, thought, and emotion.**

3. . . . **identify their limiting core beliefs** about the world, other people, and themselves.

4. . . . **revise their outdated Scripts,** revising their self-defeating habit patterns and their limited core beliefs.

Struggling Students . . .

1. . . . unconsciously wander through life unaware of being off course.

2. . . . remain unconscious of their self-defeating habit patterns of behavior, thought, and emotion.

3. . . . remain unconscious of their limiting core beliefs.

4. . . . unconsciously persist in making choices based on outdated inner Scripts, finding themselves further and further off course with each passing year.

Are you aware of being off course in any of your life roles? Do you know how you got off course?

◼◼◼◼◼ 23. **Recognizing When You Are Off Course**

Take a deep breath, relax, and consider your journey so far.

You began by accepting personal responsibility for creating your life as you want it. Next, you chose personally motivating goals and dreams that gave purpose and direction to your life. Then, you created a self-management plan and began taking effective actions. Lastly, you developed mutually supportive relationships to help you on your journey.

Despite all of these efforts, you're probably still a little off course. Perhaps a lot off course. Maybe you're off course in college, in a relationship, in your job, or somewhere else in your life. Somewhere along the path you took a wrong turn.

Once again, you have an important choice to make. You can listen to your inner self-talk blaming, complaining, and excusing. Or you can ask your Inner Guide to find answers to important questions such as . . .

If you're human, you've set goals like losing weight (or saving money, or calling your parents more frequently, etc.), and haven't accomplished those goals. Why not?

John Hanley

- *What choices do I make that sabotage my success?*
- *What keeps me from cooperating with my own best interests?*
- *How can I consistently make wise choices that will keep me on course to a rich, personally fulfilling life?*

The mystery of self-sabotage

Throughout life, each of us needs to make periodic checks to see if we are still on course. When you find yourself off course, you aren't alone. Self-sabotage has probably been committed by every human being who's set off on a journey to a better life.

Consider Jerome. Fresh from high school, Jerome had a dream of owning his own accounting firm and earning at least $60,000 a year by his thirtieth birthday. He set long-term goals of getting his college degree and passing the CPA (certified public accountant) exam. He set short-term goals of passing all of his college courses with A grades. He developed a written self-management system. He created personal rules to support his success. He demonstrated interdependence by starting a study group. But at semester's end, the unthinkable happened: Jerome failed Accounting 101!

Wait a minute, though. Jerome's Inner Guide has more information. You see, Jerome skipped his accounting class three times to work at his part-time job. On another day, he didn't go to class because he was angry with his girlfriend. Then he missed two more classes when he got the flu. He was late five times because it was difficult to find parking on campus. Jerome regularly put off doing his homework until the last minute because he was so busy. He didn't hand in one important assignment because he got confused. He stopped going to his study group after the first meeting because . . . well, he wasn't quite sure why. As the semester progressed, he felt growing anxiety about the final exam. He stayed up all night cramming, then went to the exam exhausted. During the test, his mind went blank.

Haven't you, too, made choices that worked against your goals and dreams . . . against your very image of who you are and who you want to become? Haven't we all! We take our eyes off the path for just a moment, and some invisible force comes along and bumps us off course. By the time we realize what's happened — if, in fact, we ever do — we can be miles off course and feeling miserable.

What's going on around here, anyway?

Unconscious forces

One of the great psychological discoveries of this century is the existence and power of unconscious forces in our lives. We now know that experiences from our past — perhaps all the way back to our birth — linger in our unconscious minds long after our conscious minds have forgotten them. As a result, we're being influenced daily by old experiences that we don't even recall.

Research by Dr. Wilder Penfield of the Montreal Neurological Institute offers evidence that our brains may record nearly every experience we have ever had. Dr. Penfield performed brain surgery on patients who had had local anesthesia but were otherwise fully awake. During the operation, he stimulated brain cells using a weak electric current. At the moment that his patients received this tiny jolt of electricity, they reported reexperiencing long-forgotten events in vivid detail.

Dr. Penfield's work and that of others suggest that what we hold in consciousness is but a tiny fraction of the information actually stored in our minds. In other words, not only are we unaware of our many stored memories, we're also unaware of their powerful influence over our present lives.

If many of the forces that get us off course are unconscious, how can we even know they exist? By analogy, the answer appears in a fascinating discovery in astronomy. Years ago, astronomers developed a mathematical formula to predict the orbit of any planet around the sun. Yet one planet, Uranus, failed to follow the predicted orbit. Astronomers were baffled as to why Uranus was "off course" until the French astronomer Leverrier proposed an ingenious explanation: There must be a planet beyond Uranus, a planet that could not be seen with the telescopes of the time. The gravitational pull of that invisible planet, Leverrier believed, was the force pulling Uranus off course. When stronger telescopes were invented, Leverrier was proven correct. Astronomers could now see a previously invisible planet beyond Uranus. So it was that Leverrier predicted the existence of the planet Neptune long before it could be seen from earth.

Like planets, we all have invisible forces that tug at us every day. For us, these invisible forces are not in outer space; they exist in inner space, in our unconscious minds. As with Uranus, the first clue to the existence of these unseen forces is the recognition that we are off course. Victims seldom admit when they are off course; instead they deny it, make excuses, blame others, or give up. By contrast, Creators learn to recognize and acknowledge when they are off course.

So, where are you off course in your life today? What goals and dreams are you moving away from instead of toward? Until you recognize where you are off course today, you have little hope of making the necessary course corrections that will get you where you want to be tomorrow.

I learned that I could not look to my exterior self to do anything for me. If I was going to accomplish anything in life, I had to start from within.
Oprah Winfrey

Journal #23

In this journal entry you will have an opportunity to recognize where you are off course in the quest for your goals and dreams. Remember, everyone gets off course at some time, but only those who recognize they are off course can take steps to get back on course. This discovery is the first step toward creating success from the inside out.

1. Have your Inner Guide (IG) write a memo to you about your progress (or lack of progress) toward each of your major goals and dreams.

In this memo, let your Inner Guide evaluate your life roles with total honesty and objectivity. Remember, as we said in Journal #7, a life role is any function to which you regularly devote large amounts of time and energy — employee, student, spouse. Have your Inner Guide tell you objectively whether or not you are on course to your goals and dreams in each life role. Your Inner Guide can do this by answering three questions:

1) What important goals have you established in each life role?
2) Why are these goals important to your dream?
3) Are you currently on course or off course in your quest for these goals and dreams?

Here is the beginning of a memo that Jerome's Inner Guide might have written him during the semester that Jerome failed Accounting 101:

Date: October 15
To: Jerome
From: Your IG
Re: Are you on course?
It is time to be honest about whether or not you are on course to your goals and dreams. I will evaluate each of your life roles and tell you how you are doing in each of them.

1. LIFE ROLE — Accounting Student. *Your short-term goal this semester in Accounting 101 is to get an A. This A is an important step toward your long-term goals of graduating and passing the CPA exam. Achieving these goals is essential if you are to reach your dream of owning your own accounting firm and earning $60,000 or more per year by your 30th birthday. Presently your average in Accounting 101 is a D. I have to conclude that you're presently far off course in this role.*

2. LIFE ROLE — Employee . . . etc.

This journal entry provides a true Quadrant II activity: taking a nonjudgmental inventory of where you are in the pursuit of your goals and dreams. You can't make a course correction until you know where you are. Your Inner Guide can assist you to discover exactly that.

Relax, think, write.

focus questions   Are you aware of any habit patterns in your life that get you off course? Do you know how these habit patterns developed?

■ ■ ■ ■ 24. Identifying Your Self-Defeating Patterns

Once you realize where you're off course, the next step is to figure out how to get back on course. Unfortunately, the forces pulling us off course are often just as invisible to us as the planet Neptune was to Leverrier and his fellow observers of outer space.

As observers of inner space, psychologists today seek to identify what they can't actually see: the internal forces that divert human potential into human misery. Many psychological theories have been offered to explain how our invisible inner worlds get us off course. In various theories, these unconscious inner forces have been given many names: ego defenses, conditioned responses, programs, inner maps, mental tapes, outdated rules, frozen realities, blind spots, schemas, and lifetraps, to name a few.

We first make our habits, and then our habits make us.
John Dryden

The term we'll use to describe our unconscious patterns and beliefs is one coined by Eric Berne, the creator of a mode of counseling called Transactional Analysis. Berne called our invisible inner forces **Scripts.**

In the world of theater, a script is the set of directions telling an actor what words, actions, and emotions to perform on stage. When the actor gets a cue from others in the play, he doesn't make a choice about his response. He simply responds as his script tells him. Performance after performance, he reacts the same way to the same cues.

Responding automatically from a dramatic script is one key to being a success as an actor. However, responding automatically from a *life* Script is one key to being a failure as a human being.

This psychological model suggests that by an early age (perhaps as young as seven) we have all written complete Scripts for our lives. From then on, we unconsciously use our Scripts to make many important decisions. As adults, then, we may be little more than actors and actresses unconsciously playing out the parts that we wrote as children.

A script for life

Scripts are comprised of two parts. Closest to the surface of our consciousness are the directions for how we are to behave, think, and feel as we play our dramatic role. **Behavior patterns** include such habitual actions as smoking cigarettes, always arriving on time, never asking for help, exercising regularly. **Thought patterns** include self-talk: *I'm too busy, I'm good at math, I always screw up, I can't write.* **Emotional patterns** include responding to life with consistent anger, excitement, sadness, or joy. Obviously, some habit patterns help us to stay on course whereas others knock us off course. When people know us well, they can often predict what we will do, say, or feel in a given situation. This ability reveals their recognition of our patterns.

Deeper in our unconscious lies the second part of our Scripts, our **core beliefs.** These beliefs are like the theme of a play, the ideas that motivate our actions, thoughts, and feelings. Early in life, we form core beliefs about the world (e.g., *The world is safe* or *The world is dangerous*), about other people (e.g., *People can be trusted* or *People can't be trusted*), and about ourselves (e.g., *I'm worthy* or *I'm unworthy*). We're seldom aware of our core beliefs; nonetheless, these unconscious judgments dictate what we consistently do, think, and feel.

> *A psychological script is a person's ongoing program for his life drama which dictates where he is going with his life and how he is going to get there. It is a drama he compulsively acts out, though his awareness of it may be vague.*
> Muriel James and Dorothy Jongeward

> *Parents, deliberately or unaware, teach their children from birth how to behave, think, feel, and perceive. Liberation from these influences is no easy matter.*
> Eric Berne

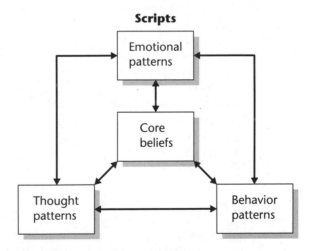

Scripts have a very practical purpose: We devised them to automatically direct us away from painful experiences such as hunger, pain, fear, shame, and loss of love, and guide us towards pleasurable experiences such as food, comfort, safety, approval, and love. Like instincts, our Scripts help us as children to meet our needs and to survive in a complex and often painful world. Unlike instincts, we can become conscious of our Scripts and rewrite the ones that limit our success, as we will see later.

How we create our Scripts

No one knows exactly how we write our Scripts. There are, however, a number of reasonable explanations. One contribution to our Scripts seems to be **how others respond to us.** Imagine, for example, a childhood scene. You're two years old. You're feeling lonely and hungry, and you begin crying. Your mother hurries in and picks you up. "There, there," she croons. "It's all right." She hugs you, feeds you, sings to you. You fall asleep full and content. If this happens often enough, what do you suppose you'd decide about the world, about other people, about yourself? You'd be likely to invent core beliefs such as, *The world is kind. People will comfort me and help me get what I want. I am lovable.* In turn, these beliefs would dictate your actions, thoughts, and emotions. With positive beliefs such as these at the core of your scripts, very likely you'd develop self-supportive behavior patterns (e.g., asking for what you want), optimistic thought patterns (e.g., *"I bet if I ask enough people I can get help."*), and positive emotional patterns (e.g., joy and harmony).

The most important lesson we learn in life is what creates pain for us and what creates pleasure.

Anthony Robbins

Now imagine the same childhood scene with a different response. You cry but no one comes. Your needs are ignored. You start screaming louder and louder, but still no one comes. Finally you give up hope that anyone will ever respond. Now imagine that this disappointment happens to you often. At some point, you may decide on core beliefs such as, *The world doesn't care about me. People won't help me. I'm not important.* What actions, thoughts, and feelings would likely result from core beliefs such as these? You could very well develop passive behavior patterns (e.g., not asking for what you want), pessimistic thought patterns (e.g., *"No one will ever help me."*), and negative emotional patterns (e.g., anxiety and anger).

What the mother sings to the cradle goes all the way down to the coffin.

Henry Ward Beecher

Now, imagine this same scene one more time. What if, as you're crying for attention and food, an adult storms into your room, screams, "Shut up!" and slaps your face? It won't take many experiences like this to convince you of core beliefs such as, *The world is a dangerous and painful place, People will hurt me, I'm unlovable!* And so you may develop defensive behavior patterns (e.g., immediately fighting or fleeing at the first sign of danger), defensive thought patterns (e.g., *"People are out to get me."*), and defensive emotional patterns (fear and rage).

As children we try to manipulate the responses of the world around us as best we can. What gets our needs met, what doesn't? What gets us food, what gets us a slap? What earns us love, what costs us love? We quickly learn ways to minimize our immediate pain and maximize our immediate pleasure.

Second, we seem to write our Scripts not only from what others do, but from their words as well. As we begin to understand language, **the words that significant adults say to us also shape our Scripts.** What did they say about the world: Is it safe or dangerous? What did they say about other people: Can they be trusted or not?

And, perhaps most important, what did important adults say about us? Psy-

"Mother, am I poisonous?"

chologists have a term for qualities that tell us how we "are" or "should be." These labels are called **attributions.** Common attributions we may have heard as children include *be good, be quiet, be funny, be obedient, be rebellious, be nice, be devoted, be stupid, be cute, be helpful, be athletic, be pretty, be tough, be a hard worker, be independent, be dependent, be a fighter, be invisible, be sexy, be shy, be dominant, be competitive, be unavailable, be smart, be messy, be emotional, be confident.*

Psychologists also have a term for the qualities that tell us what we "are not" or "should not be." These labels are called **injunctions.** Common injunctions include *don't be yourself, don't talk back, don't feel, don't depend on others, don't brag, don't think, don't cry, don't grow up, don't be close to others, don't ever leave your parents, don't ask for what you want, don't say no, don't say yes, don't get angry, don't trust, don't love yourself, don't lose control, don't be happy, don't be weak, don't believe in yourself, don't exist.*

A friend of mine has a seven-year-old daughter. Every time she shows him school work, he says, "You sure are a smart young lady! You have a wonderful mind!"

By contrast, one of my students once brought her preschool-age son to class. The little boy kept humming, and twice his mother told him to be quiet. Finally, she grabbed a fistful of his shirt, jerked him close to her face, and snarled, "I told you to shut up, you stupid little brat."

Two kids. Two different Scripts being written by their parents' words. *I'm a*

Children often become what their parents tell them they are.

Thomas Gordon

smart young lady. I'm a stupid little brat. What were *you* told years ago about who you are and who you are not? Chances are, your choices today are making those words come true.

A third way that we may have written our Scripts is by **observing the behavior of significant adults.** Children observe, *What did my role models do? If it's right for them, it's right for me.* When children play, we see them trying on adult behaviors, conversations, and emotions. It doesn't take Sherlock Holmes to figure out where they learned them.

One more way that children seem to write their Scripts is **in response to physical, mental, and emotional wounds.** These wounds may create the most powerful Scripts of all. A child who is mocked when she offers her opinion may develop core beliefs and habit patterns to avoid forever the shame of speaking her mind. A child who is told to shut up when he is crying may thereafter deny himself any emotional response at all. A child who is abused or beaten when she reaches out for love may shut herself behind an invisible wall, hiding her vulnerability forever.

And so it is that we all come to have our unique Scripts — core beliefs and resulting habit patterns. At hundreds of choice points each day we unconsciously refer to our Scripts for guidance: *What similar experience have I had in the past? What actions, thoughts, or emotions did I choose back then? Did that choice increase or decrease my experience of pain? Did that choice increase or decrease my experience of pleasure? Oh, look, here's a response that seemed to work back then. I'll use it again now.*

This, then, is the good news about our unconscious Scripts: Their intention is always positive — always to minimize our pain, always to maximize our pleasure. Many of us made it through the mental, physical, and emotional pain of growing up with the guidance of the Scripts that we created in childhood. Some of us would not have survived without them.

But, as you might guess, there is bad news as well: When we unconsciously use outdated Scripts today, we often get off course. That's because the Scripts we developed in childhood seldom apply to the situations of our adult lives. Imagine an actor in a Broadway show who can't stop playing a role from a grade school play! Many of us do the equivalent of this in our lives every day.

In Journal #23 we identified where we are off course. That discovery suggests that some of our Scripts need revision. In order to revise our Scripts, we'll first need to identify the self-defeating patterns and limiting beliefs that are getting us off course. Because our self-defeating habits are closer to the surface of our consciousness, that is where we will look first. Let us examine our patterns of behavior, thought, and emotion. Our objective here is to identify any self-defeating habits that are getting us off course.

Examples of self-defeating patterns

Though **Scripts** are invisible, we can often see their influence in the patterns of our choices. Put a check next to any of the following **self-defeating patterns** of behavior, thought, and emotion that are true of you. These habits may reveal the presence of unconscious and outdated Scripts that are getting you off course. Listen to your Inner Guide and tell yourself the truth.

- [ ] 1. I act "nice" even when I don't feel like it.
- [ ] 2. I wonder if I am "college material."
- [ ] 3. I often get angry.
- [ ] 4. I watch a lot of television.
- [ ] 5. I believe that most people don't like me.
- [ ] 6. I am very much overweight or underweight.
- [ ] 7. I change jobs a lot.
- [ ] 8. I often turn in college assignments late.
- [ ] 9. I get physically or emotionally abusive of others when things don't go my way.
- [ ] 10. I worry excessively about doing things perfectly.
- [ ] 11. I can't stand to be wrong.
- [ ] 12. I think most of my classmates are smarter than I am.
- [ ] 13. I don't listen well.
- [ ] 14. I wait until the last minute to do important college assignments.
- [ ] 15. I think about suicide.
- [ ] 16. I do the opposite of what others ask or expect of me.
- [ ] 17. I miss more college classes than I should.
- [ ] 18. I criticize myself constantly.
- [ ] 19. I have a person in my life who treats me badly.
- [ ] 20. I don't participate in class discussions.
- [ ] 21. I often break commitments.
- [ ] 22. I am addicted to something (such as caffeine, alcohol, cigarettes, soft drinks, drugs).
- [ ] 23. I worry about doing or saying things "right."
- [ ] 24. I experience severe test anxiety.
- [ ] 25. I don't show my emotions.
- [ ] 26. I almost never ask for help.
- [ ] 27. I don't say or do what I really want to.
- [ ] 28. I doubt that I'm good enough.
- [ ] 29. I often side-talk or daydream in my college classes.
- [ ] 30. I never forgive anyone who wrongs me.
- [ ] 31. I sulk when things don't go my way.
- [ ] 32. I seldom do my best work on college assignments.
- [ ] 33. I am often sad.
- [ ] 34. I get grades that are below my potential.
- [ ] 35. I keep promising to do better in college, but I don't.
- [ ] 36. I get my feelings hurt easily.
- [ ] 37. I am a loner.
- [ ] 38. I doubt that I will get my college degree, even though I want it.
- [ ] 39. I am very critical of other people.
- [ ] 40. I am often late for classes.

Are you aware of any other self-defeating patterns — behavioral, mental, emotional — that belong to you?

Journal #24

In this journal entry you will have an opportunity to discover **self-defeating patterns** in your life that may reveal unconscious and outdated **Scripts**. You are about to embark on an exciting journey into your inner world! There you can discover the invisible forces that have gotten you off course. This information can assist you to get back on course to your goals and dreams.

1. In your journal, write a paragraph (or more) discussing one of your self-defeating patterns. Choose one from the list on the previous page, or identify one of your self-defeating patterns that is not on the list. Keep in mind that these behavioral, mental, or emotional patterns are probably visible evidence of your unconscious Scripts.

Remember to develop each paragraph by anticipating questions that someone reading it might have about your pattern. (Even you might have questions when you read your journal ten years from now.) For example, What exactly do you habitually do, think, or feel when caught in this pattern? When did this pattern start? What caused it? What impact has it had on your life? Use the four E's — Examples, Experiences, Explanation and Evidence — to develop each paragraph. For example, you might begin by writing . . .

One of my self-defeating patterns is a behavioral one: I am often late. I especially have a habit of arriving late for my college classes. For example, last Thursday I . . .

2. Repeat Step 1 for two (or more) additional self-defeating patterns. Try to write about all three kinds of patterns: behaviors, thoughts, emotions.

Relaxation is essential for getting in touch with the storehouse of experiences, thoughts, and feelings hidden away in your unconscious mind. As we begin to explore success from the inside out, you may wish to re-commit to relaxing fully before writing each journal entry.

Relax, think, write.

Are you aware of your most deeply held beliefs about the world, about other people, and about yourself? Do you know which of these beliefs limit your success?

■ ■ ■ ■ 25. Identifying Your Limiting Core Beliefs

Once in a writing class, I was explaining how to organize an essay when a student named Diana told me she didn't understand. She asked if I'd write an explanation on the blackboard.

Earlier in the class, we'd been talking about the differences between left-brain and right-brain thinking. We had discussed how the left side of our brain deals with logical, organized information, while the right side of our brain deals in more creative concepts and abstractions. "Sure," I said to Diana, "I hear your left brain crying out for some order. Let's see what we can do for it."

As I turned to write on the blackboard, she screamed, *"You have no right to talk to me that way!"*

I was stunned. I took a deep breath to compose myself. "Maybe we could talk about this after class," I said.

Later, we did talk. Diana was in her late thirties, a single mother of an eight-year-old daughter. Our conversation wandered for a while; then, Diana mentioned that she had always disliked school. In grade school, Diana had consistently gotten low grades. One day, when she was about twelve, she overheard her father and mother talking about her report card. "I don't know what we're going to do with Diana," her father said. "She's the *half-brain* of the family."

Ever since that day, Diana had disliked school. And no wonder! From her perspective, look at the pain that trying to learn had caused her: Teachers failed her, and her own father called her a half-brain.

So Diana accepted as a fact other people's belief that she couldn't think, that she couldn't learn. Then she developed patterns of behaviors, thoughts, and emotions that supported this belief. She often missed school, she told herself that school was a waste of time, and she got furious whenever anyone questioned her about schoolwork. When Diana barely escaped high school with a diploma, college wasn't even a consideration. She got a job that bored her, but at least she didn't have to think.

For nearly twenty years, Diana had heard her Inner Critic (sounding much like her father) telling her there was something wrong with her brain. Finally, another inner voice began to whisper, *Maybe. . . .* Then one day she took a big risk and enrolled in college.

"So what happens?" she snapped at me. "I get a teacher who calls me a *half-brain!*"

She was furious at me for the insult and at herself for putting herself in a situation where someone could insult her again.

"I ought to just quit college," she said.

[T]he responses that helped me survive my childhood are inappropriate, even dangerous, for me as an adult.
Walter Anderson

The limits I do experience are limits of belief, not limits of the human organism. I am limited because I believe I am limited.
Harville Hendrix

When an adult with a wounded inner child experiences a current situation which is similar to a prototypic painful event, the original response is triggered as well. . . . Something which is actually trivial or quite innocuous is reacted to with intense emotion. This is a case of responding to what isn't there on the outside because it is still there on the inside.
John Bradshaw

I used my best active listening skills: I listened to understand, not to respond. I reflected both her thoughts and her anger. I asked her to clarify and expand. I allowed long periods of silence, giving Diana time to think.

Finally, her emotional storm subsided. She took a deep breath and sat back. I waited a few moments. "Diana, I know you think I called you a 'half-brain.' But what I actually said was *left*-brain. Remember we had been talking in class about the difference between left-brain and right-brain thinking? I was talking about that."

"But I *heard* you!"

"I know that's what you *heard*. But that isn't what I *said*. I've read two of your essays, and I can see that your brain works just fine. But what really matters is what *you* think! You need to believe in your own intelligence. Otherwise, you'll always be ready to hear people accuse you of being a 'half-brain' no matter what they really said."

Diana had come within an inch of dropping out of college, of abandoning her dreams of a college degree. And all because of her Scripts from childhood. Diana's limiting core belief seemed to be, *I'm the half-brain of the family. I can't think.* Unless she changed that belief, she would continue to behave, think, and feel in ways that would prove herself correct.

Let me offer another example of the impact of a destructive script. Vernon was a student in a college success class that I taught in a large auditorium. During one class, we listened to a panel of four former students, each of whom had graduated with an extremely high grade point average. I'd invited these graduates back to the college to tell us about their very best success strategies as students. After each of the graduates had spoken, I urged students in the class to ask questions.

Just before the class ended, Vernon raised his hand, and I brought him the microphone. "Did any of you ever have trouble with procrastination?" he asked.

As the panelists looked at each other to decide who would answer the question, I joked to them, "Maybe you'd rather tell us about procrastination later."

A number of students in the class chuckled. Then one of the panelists answered Vernon. After a few more questions and answers, I dismissed the class.

The next day I got a call from the college vice-president. "One of your students says you mocked him in front of the whole class. He's going to drop out of school. What's going on?"

The student was Vernon. "Let me talk with him," I said. "I'll get back to you."

Sometimes we get lucky. Because of the panel, I'd had our media department video tape the class. I asked Vernon if he would be willing to watch the video and talk to me afterwards. He took the video to the library, returning about an hour later.

"You didn't say what I thought you did," Vernon admitted in disbelief.

"What did you think I'd said?"

"I couldn't hear you. I was too nervous. But everyone laughed. I thought. . . ."

Vernon paused. An eternity passed. ". . . I thought everyone was laughing at me."

"That must have hurt."

"But I asked such a stupid question. No one on the panel even wanted to answer it. Sometimes I say the stupidest things. I don't even know why I try."

Apparently Vernon's Inner Critic had drowned out my attempt at humor with its well-practiced self-judgments: *My question about procrastination is so stupid. Now the teacher's making fun of me, and the whole class is laughing at me.*

Vernon had a powerful and limiting core belief, something like: *Nothing I do or say comes out right. I'm worthless.* Despite having seen the videotape proving that no one had laughed at him, Vernon still dropped out of college. We cannot underestimate the power of our unconscious core beliefs. Vernon's outdated Script was even more powerful than reality!

> **Limited**
>
> I am riding on a limited express, one of the crack trains of the nation. Hurtling across the prairie into blue haze and dark air go fifteen all-steel coaches holding a thousand people.
> (All the coaches shall be scrap and rust and all the men and women laughing in the diners and sleepers shall pass to ashes.)
> I ask a man in the smoker where he is going and he answers: "Omaha."
>
> — *Carl Sandburg*

It's no wonder our core beliefs can make such a mess of our adult lives. They were decided upon by children! If you encountered a difficult situation in your life today, would you ask a child for advice? Yet that is exactly what we do when we react automatically from our Scripts.

Many of our core beliefs were created by a child who most of all wanted to escape pain and experience pleasure. Your child-self was a tiny soul in a huge, confusing, and often threatening world. It did the best it could to survive. Today, your child-self is alive within you, present as the author of your Scripts.

Outdated Scripts keep you from responding with the mature wisdom of who you are today. As long as you hang onto your unconscious and limiting core beliefs, you will never consistently choose actions, thoughts, and emotions that will keep you on course to your goals and dreams. The time has come to identify your limiting beliefs.

Among the deep unconscious beliefs everybody holds are beliefs about human potentialities and limitations — one's own, and other people's. These limits tend to be confirmed by experience, not because they are true but because they are believed.

Willis Harmon

Examples of limiting core beliefs

Scripts cause us to respond unconsciously and automatically to life's challenges. Victims unconsciously use outdated core beliefs — probably decided upon in childhood — to guide their important decisions in adulthood. By contrast, Creators continue the process of creating success from the inside out by identifying their outdated core beliefs.

Consider which self-defeating core beliefs below sound like the self-talk of your Inner Defender and Inner Critic. Check the ones that you believe. Any of these beliefs will limit your effectiveness both in college and in life.

The following core beliefs keep you from ACCEPTING PERSONAL RESPONSIBILITY:

- ☐ Taking charge of my life causes pain.
- ☐ I'm a Victim.
- ☐ I have no choice.
- ☐ I can't decide.
- ☐ I make lousy choices.
- ☐ It's not my fault.
- ☐ Someone else should decide.
- ☐ Others are to blame for my problems.
- ☐ Life is overwhelming.
- ☐ I'm not in control.

The following core beliefs keep you from DISCOVERING A MEANINGFUL PURPOSE:

- ☐ Wanting things causes pain.
- ☐ I don't know what I want.
- ☐ I never get what I want.
- ☐ I can't be what I really want to be.
- ☐ It's safer to think small.
- ☐ What I want isn't important.
- ☐ Other people deserve good things more than I do.
- ☐ Life is purposeless.

The following core beliefs keep you from TAKING PURPOSEFUL ACTIONS:

- ☐ Taking action causes pain.
- ☐ Nothing I do matters.
- ☐ It's easier to procrastinate.
- ☐ I've got too much to do.
- ☐ There isn't enough time.
- ☐ I'm disorganized.
- ☐ I'm lazy.
- ☐ I'm undisciplined.
- ☐ Obstacles always stop me.
- ☐ Quality doesn't matter, just get it done.
- ☐ Life is overwhelming.

The following core beliefs keep you from DEVELOPING MUTUALLY SUPPORTIVE RELATIONSHIPS:

- ☐ Having relationships causes pain.
- ☐ I don't need anyone else.
- ☐ Others should come first.
- ☐ I am weak if I ask for help.
- ☐ I can't depend on others.
- ☐ I better hold onto what I've got.
- ☐ Everyone's out for himself.
- ☐ No one really cares about me.
- ☐ Being independent is the best way to be.
- ☐ Getting close to someone is dangerous.
- ☐ People won't like the real me.
- ☐ People can't be trusted.
- ☐ Be nice no matter what.
- ☐ People always let me down.

The following core beliefs keep you from MAXIMIZING YOUR LEARNING:

- ☐ Thinking and learning cause pain.
- ☐ School is for jerks.
- ☐ Failure hurts.
- ☐ People won't like me if I'm too smart.

- [ ] Feeling is better than thinking.
- [ ] Thinking gets me in trouble.
- [ ] I can't learn.
- [ ] Women aren't logical.
- [ ] I have to be right.
- [ ] Curiosity gets me in trouble.
- [ ] I can't do math.
- [ ] I'm a lousy student.

The following core beliefs keep you from CREATING A POSITIVE EXPERIENCE OF LIFE:

- [ ] Feeling my emotions causes pain.
- [ ] I can't control my feelings.
- [ ] Playing is frivolous.
- [ ] Passion is wrong.
- [ ] I can only get what I want when I'm angry.
- [ ] Thinking is better than feeling.
- [ ] Showing emotion is a weakness.
- [ ] Men don't cry.
- [ ] I shouldn't feel good.

The following core beliefs keep you from BELIEVING IN YOURSELF:

- [ ] Being myself causes pain.
- [ ] I'm not good enough.
- [ ] I don't deserve to *have* what I want to have.
- [ ] I don't deserve to *do* what I want to do.
- [ ] I don't deserve to *be* what I want to be.
- [ ] I'll feel good about myself when I'm successful.
- [ ] If I fail, I'm a failure.
- [ ] Celebrating success is bragging.
- [ ] Promises are made to be broken.
- [ ] I'm no good at anything.
- [ ] Others are better than I am.
- [ ] I'm unacceptable.
- [ ] I'm not capable.
- [ ] I'm unlovable.
- [ ] I don't respect myself.
- [ ] I'm worthless.
- [ ] I don't deserve to exist.

Journal #25

In this journal entry, you will have an opportunity to identify some of the limiting core beliefs that you took on years ago as a child. People who identify their core beliefs are much better equipped to make wise choices as adults and to stay on course to their goals and dreams.

1. In your journal, write a paragraph about one of your limiting beliefs. Because core beliefs are usually unconscious, you'll be using one of your self-defeating patterns as a clue to the invisible belief that motivates it. In the paragraph, answer the following three questions:

A. **What is one self-defeating pattern that gets you off course in your life?** The pattern may be a habitual **behavior,** a habitual **thought,** or a habitual **emotion.** You can use one of the habit patterns that you discussed in Journal #24, or identify a new one. Explain the pattern fully: What do you habitually do, think, or feel? Give examples.

B. **What limiting core belief is probably causing this pattern?** For example, if your self-defeating pattern is to wait until the last minute to do important college assignments, what unconscious beliefs might you have about the world, other people, or yourself that support this habit? Don't worry about being wrong. What's your best guess? Do your beliefs include *I'm not college material* or *I can't get organized* or *I work best under pressure?* Explain your limiting belief as fully as you can.

C. **Where do you suppose you learned this limiting core belief?** Track this belief back as far into your childhood as you can. See if you can recall the time when you first started having this core belief. Describe your earlier experience as fully as you can. Diana, for example, recalled the time she overheard her father call her a "half-brain" as a possible source for her limiting core belief.

2. Repeat Step 1 two (or more) times. The more you expose your unconscious limiting beliefs, the more you are prepared to create your success from the inside out.

Relax, think, write.

The battles that count aren't the ones for gold medals. The struggles within yourself — the invisible, inevitable battles inside all of us — that's where it's at.

Jessie Owens
Winner of four gold medals
at the 1936 Olympics

Do you believe that people can make fundamental changes in who they are? If not, why? If so, how?

■ ■ ■ ■ 26. Revising Your Outdated Scripts

Let's sum up what we've said so far about creating success from the inside out.

First of all, being human, you probably find yourself off course today. Despite all of your good intentions and efforts, you have gone astray in one or more of your life roles. Some of your choices are moving you steadily away from (instead of toward) your goals and dreams.

Even if you can identify the specific choices that got you off course, you probably can't say for sure why you made some of them; the reasons are hidden somewhere in your unconscious mind. In that murky darkness, your mind has stored most (if not all) of your earlier life experiences along with your thoughts and feelings about those experiences. From this data, your unconscious mind has written life Scripts made up of your . . .

*Must I always be what I am? Can I really be more? **Can I begin again?** It may be the most difficult question we have to answer.*
Walter Anderson

1. Core Beliefs
2. Habit Patterns.

Core beliefs represent our best attempt to make sense of the world, of other people, and of ourselves. At a deep, unconscious level we may believe *I am a half-brain* or *I am capable of learning whatever I want.* Just as ancient astronomers were unaware of the invisible planet Neptune, we are probably unaware of our unconscious core beliefs. But just as the gravitational force of Neptune pulled Uranus off course, so do our core beliefs pull us off course.

Your core beliefs cause you to develop particular habit patterns: the behaviors, thoughts, and emotions that you regularly choose. Unlike your core beliefs, your habit patterns are easily accessible to your conscious mind. Still, we are often unaware that we are caught in self-defeating patterns that get us off course.

Together, your core beliefs and habit patterns comprise your Scripts. The purpose of your Scripts is to guide you away from pain and toward pleasure, as you define them. But they often backfire.

[B]ecause of our unique human endowments, we can write new programs for ourselves totally apart from our instincts and training.
Stephen Covey

Most of us have never updated the Scripts that we created years ago. As a result, our Scripts may be guiding us away from, not toward, our goals and dreams. The very Scripts that served us well as children are very possibly the reason we are off course as adults. That's because many of our underlying core beliefs are limiting us instead of empowering us. Many of our habitual behaviors, thoughts, and emotions are defeating us instead of supporting us.

In Journal #2 we defined responsibility as the ability to make choices that move us toward our goals and dreams without interfering with the ability of others to do the same. Because our Scripts dictate our choices, **our ultimate responsibility is to choose Scripts that best support our movement toward our goals and dreams.** Only with wisely chosen Scripts can we have, do, and be what we truly desire.

In other words, total success is created not only from the outside in, but from the inside out, too. Total success requires mastery of our inner world.

Understanding reality

When I was a college freshman, I had an instructor who drove students crazy by responding to nearly any belief we expressed with the same comment: *If you say so.*

"I don't have enough time to study, Professor." *If you say so.*

"I love math." *If you say so.*

"English is difficult." *If you say so.*

Back then, I thought he was one of the rudest people I had ever met. Today I realize that he was telling us one of the great truths of human experience: **Whatever I believe becomes my reality.** If I believe that I *don't* have time to study, that is my reality — so I won't find the time. If I believe that I *do* have time to study, that is my reality — so I will find the time.

Here is another way to express this idea: **Life is a self-fulfilling prophecy.** If I believe that I *love* math, I will love it — no matter what. If I believe that I *hate* math, I will hate it — no matter what. I will prove my belief correct.

This idea has also been said this way: **In your world, your word is law.** If I believe that English is *difficult,* it will be — for me. If I believe that English is *easy,* it will be — for me.

I live by my own beliefs. No matter what is going on "out there" in the world, I create my reality by what I believe "in here" in my mind.

My student Diana, for example, truly believed that she was a half-brain. So strong was her belief that she was actually able to hear words *(You're a half-brain)* that existed only in her reality. My student Vernon truly believed that he was the kind of person that people laugh at. So strong was his belief that he was able to hear mocking laughter that existed only in his reality. Each of us has a similar process by which we create our own version of reality. Then, by careful selection of our behaviors, thoughts, and emotions, we provide evidence that proves our reality to be correct.

I'm reminded of an explanation I once heard about how elephants are trained. A young elephant is attached by a chain to a stake driven into the ground. For days, the baby elephant vainly yanks at the chain, but the elephant is too small to pull free. After enough failures and enough pain, the elephant learns its lesson: The chain and stake are too strong. Years later, when the elephant has grown huge and powerful, it still stands passively when chained to the stake. Although the elephant could now easily pull the stake from the ground, it remains a prisoner of its outdated belief. This powerful animal *believes* that the stake and chain are stronger than it is, so it acts accordingly. The elephant may dream all it wants of freedom; its version of reality won't allow it to take the necessary actions . . . *even though the actions are perfectly within its ability!*

What beliefs do you have that chain you to outdated behaviors, outdated thoughts, and outdated emotions? These beliefs are keeping you from achieving your goals and dreams. These beliefs are hindering you from living a rich, personally fulfilling life.

Revise your outdated scripts

Until I realize that my core beliefs dictate my patterns of behavior, thought, and emotion, I remain a prisoner of my unconscious Scripts. Until I revise my Scripts, I'm likely to remain off course in some or all of my life roles.

That's why finding ourselves off course can be a blessing in disguise. Being off course offers clues about the invisible forces tugging at our lives. By identifying the self-defeating patterns of action, thought, and emotion that got us off course, we may be able to identify and revise the limiting core beliefs that sabotage our success.

We need not judge ourselves harshly for the Scripts we created as children. We did the best we could with our immature, limited understanding of the world, of other people, and of ourselves. As adults, however, we can choose the Scripts that guide our steps.

One of the great discoveries about the human condition is this: We are not stuck with our past. Armed with the power of our choices, we can re-create ourselves. By revising our outdated Scripts, we can get back on course and change the outcomes of our lives for the better.

Three of the most influential inner Scripts we hold are those that dictate how we think, how we feel, and how we perceive ourselves. Thus, we now turn to an in-depth examination and possible revision of the Scripts that create the quality of the experiences we have in our mind, heart, and spirit. For the rest of this book, we will consider how we can make fundamental changes in who we are and therefore dramatically improve the outcomes of our lives.

*It is a marvelous faculty of the human mind that we are also able to stop old programming from holding us back, any time we choose to. That gift is called **conscious choice.***
Shad Helmstetter

Journal #26

In this journal entry, you'll have an opportunity to begin revising your Scripts. By doing so, you take greater control of your life, increasing your likelihood of being successful.

1. Write a dialogue with your Inner Guide that will assist you to revise your Scripts.

In this dialogue, your Inner Guide will ask you the ten questions below. After you answer each question, let your Inner Guide practice active listening skills. In response to your answers, let your Inner Guide use . . .

1. **Silence**
2. **Reflection** (of your thoughts and feelings)
3. **Expansion** (by asking for examples, evidence, and experience)
4. **Clarification** (by asking for an explanation)

Ten questions from your Inner Guide

1. In what life role are you off course?
2. What self-defeating **behavior patterns** may have contributed to this situation?
3. What different behaviors could you choose to get back on course to your goal?
4. What self-defeating **thought patterns** may have contributed to this situation?
5. What different thoughts could you choose to get back on course to your goal?
6. What self-defeating **emotional patterns** may have contributed to this situation?
7. What different emotions could you choose to get back on course to your goal?
8. What limiting **core beliefs** (about the world, other people, or yourself) may be supporting the self-defeating patterns that we've been discussing?
9. What different beliefs could you choose to get back on course to your goal?
10. As a result of what you've learned here, what new behaviors, thoughts, emotions or core beliefs will you commit to adopting?

A sample of a possible dialogue appears below.

Relax, think, write.

Sample dialogue with your Inner Guide

IG: In what life role are you off course? [Question 1]

Me: I'm not too happy with what's going on in my role as friend.

IG: Would you say more about that? [Expansion]

Me: My goal is to create a better relationship with Barry. But that's not happening. In fact, I haven't talked to him in weeks.

IG: What self-defeating behavior patterns may have contributed to this situation? [Question 2]

Me: Well, I have to admit that I haven't called him for quite a while.

IG: Are there any other behaviors you can think of? [Expansion]

Me: I haven't tried to set up time to spend with him, either. That's all I can think of.

IG: What different behaviors could you choose to get back on course to your goal? [Question 3]

Me: I could call him and suggest that we set up a day to get together. I could also ask him how his back is doing. I know he's been having a lot of pain with his back.

IG: What self-defeating thought patterns may have contributed to this situation? [Question 4]

Me: When I think of calling him, I tell myself, "Hey, I almost always call him. He hardly ever calls me. When I call, he often says he was just about to call me, but I don't believe him anymore. It would be nice if he'd call me for a change. Also, when he tells me he's going to call me back about something we discussed, he seldom does."

IG: And when he doesn't call, what do you tell yourself? [Expansion]

Me: That he's not a very good friend if I have to do all of the calling.

IG: What different thoughts could you choose to get back on course to your goal? [Question 5]

Me: I could remind myself that he has a lot of problems with his back. And he has a wife and three kids that keep him really busy, and I don't. I could also remind myself that whenever we do get together we have a good time, and I know that he considers me as one of his best friends. I guess he's just going through a difficult time right now.

IG: So, you can see many reasons why Barry might not be calling you as often as you'd like. Is that what you're saying? [Reflection]

Me: Exactly.

IG: What self-defeating emotional pattern may have contributed to this situation? [Question 6]

Me: I know that when I don't hear from him for a while, I get angry. I guess I get angry when I start wondering if he's a real friend.

IG: So, you feel angry with Barry for not keeping in closer touch. Is there anything else that you're feeling? [Reflection and Expansion]

Me: I'm aware of a little sadness, too. Barry and I have been friends for more than ten years, way before he was married or had kids, or even had his bad back. I miss hanging out with him the way we used to.

IG: Sounds like you're feeling sad about that loss. [Reflection]

Me: Yes.

IG: That's certainly understandable. Still, I'm wondering what different emotion could you choose to get back on course to your goal? [Question 7]

Me: I guess it would be great if I could just be happy about the time we do spend together. I know he's not really avoiding me on purpose. He's just got a lot he has to take care of in his life right now.

IG: What limiting beliefs (about the world, other people or yourself) may be supporting the self-defeating patterns that we've been discussing? [Question 8]

Me: I have a belief that friends are going to abandon me. I think they're not going to really be there for me when I need them. I hate to ask people for help for just that reason. I worry that they'll say no. I guess sometimes I wait for other people to call me just so I can get proof that they haven't abandoned me.

IG: What different core belief could you choose to get back on course to your goal? [Question 9]

Me: I guess it would help for me to believe that my good friends are going to be there for me. If they're not there for me, then they weren't friends, anyway.

IC: As a result of what you've learned here, what new behaviors, thoughts, emotions or core beliefs will you commit to? [Question 10]

Me: I'll commit to calling Barry this week to see how he is. I'll also watch my emotional patterns, and if I start to get angry at him, I'll just remind myself of all the problems he has right now. I'll also remind myself that if I expect him to be a good friend when I need him, then I better be a good friend when he needs me — like he does right now. I also want to look at this belief that my friends are going to abandon me. It feels real, but the friends I have now haven't even come close to abandoning me. I think that must be an old belief that is still hanging on in my unconscious mind. I'm going to remind myself that my friends will be just as good a friend to me as I am to them. Oh, I just realized that I've never told Barry any of this. I think I'll also tell him how much I value him as a friend and how I feel when he doesn't call.

Chapter 7

■ ■ ■ ■ ■ ■ ■ ■

I'll need to learn many new ideas and skills to achieve my goals and dreams. As a Creator, I take full responsibility for learning important lessons from every experience I have.

Maximizing Your Learning ■ ■ ■ ■ ■ ■ ■

I learn valuable lessons from every experience I have.

Successful Students . . .	Struggling Students . . .
1. . . . **relearn how to learn,** reactivating the effective and joyful process they used as young children to learn valuable new information and skills.	1. . . . often experience frustration, boredom, and/or resistance when given the opportunity to learn new information or skills.
2. . . . **learn to course correct,** giving them the flexibility to revise faulty behaviors or beliefs that limit their effectiveness.	2. . . . hang onto ineffective behaviors or beliefs even when these get them off course.
3. . . . **learn from their mistakes,** realizing that a mistake often uncovers a positive option they didn't see.	3. . . . blame their mistakes on others or use the mistakes to beat themselves up with negative judgments.
4. . . . **learn from their failures,** seeing that within every defeat are the instructions for a future victory.	4. . . . blame others for their own failure or use the outer failure to confirm their core belief that they are a failure as a person.
5. . . . **learn from their obstacles,** understanding that most barriers to success are ultimately within them.	5. . . . allow obstacles to block their progress toward their goals.

Do you learn as effectively today as you did when you were a child? Do you enjoy learning as much as you did years ago? What could you do today to increase your learning in college . . . and in life?

■ ■ ■ ■ ■ 27. **Relearning How to Learn**

I think; therefore I am.

René Descartes

I think I think; therefore I think I am.

Ambrose Bierce

As infants, we're curious about everything we see, hear, smell, taste, or touch. Each day is shaped by curiosity and inquiry, by gathering and sorting, by discovery and insight. Each evening finds us transformed by our day's learning. Each morning finds us eager to renew our quest. No doubt about it: healthy children delight in discovery.

Sadly, somewhere on life's journey, the joy of learning flickers and, for many, goes out. Take a look at a college class through your instructors' eyes: Students slouch in back rows, postures challenging: "Go ahead . . . try to teach me." Other students sit up front, pens poised, body language brightly chirping: "Go ahead . . . tell me everything I have to know for the test." But neither defiance nor compliance will get these students a true education. Both approaches are merely adaptions made by learners whose spirits of personal inquiry have been wounded.

It is the immediate fun of learning that keeps us going day by day, especially when we are young and have so much to learn.

Dr. William Glasser

Many dispirited learners drop out of formal education. Others trudge through high school and even college. For them, graduating is like being released from prison, and many vow never again to enter a formal classroom. Their diploma represents endurance not learning. Seldom do they head off into the world excited by the prospect of life-long learning. They may know that Hamlet asked, "To be or not to be?" but they haven't a clue about how to answer that question for themselves.

What went wrong?

Most kids come to experience school as a place where they **must** *go; they experience learning as something that is seldom pleasant or fun; they experience studying as tedious work; and they see teachers as unfriendly policemen.*

Thomas Gordon

What happens to us between infancy and college? Why do so many of us replace joyful, effective learning styles with hostile resistance or blind conformity? Perhaps as a child we reached out an exploring hand only to have it smacked. Or we asked a question and were told to shut up. Or we heard someone we love call us a "half-brain" or "NTB" (Not Too Bright). Or we studied hard, took a test, failed, and were put in the "slow" group. Or we realized one day that the kids who got A's never questioned the teachers' opinions. In short, learning stopped being safe, fun, or personally valuable.

So, we adapted. Many "good" students simply figured out how to earn the external rewards of formal education — high grades, honor societies, special privileges, scholarships. What they learned ceased to matter so long as they got the proper rewards. For their part, many "bad" students just never figured out how to get these rewards, or else they decided that the rewards weren't worth the effort or the pain.

Thus, whether we got A's or F's in school, many of us developed patterns that minimized our learning, such as

- making grades more important than learning.
- accepting whatever teachers say.
- fearing or cheating on tests.
- disconnecting school from our "real" lives.
- missing or arriving late to classes.
- not participating or not paying attention in class.
- doing assignments poorly or not at all.
- blaming or crediting others for our grades.
- not asking questions we really care about.

Do any of these behaviors, thoughts, or emotions sound familiar? If so, know that these are the self-defeating patterns of defiant or compliant learners. Your Scripts about learning are limiting your ability to think and, thus, to develop your potential wisdom. As a result of your limiting scripts, college for you is not about learning; it is about decreasing the pain of your formal education while increasing your immediate pleasure. You have forgotten what you knew as a child: Learning is about thriving, not just surviving.

Learn to learn — again!

As a child, you were a masterful learner. Think of all you learned in just your first few years of life! Chances are, you haven't been that effective as a learner in years. *Oh no, you're wrong!* some of you may argue. *I get good grades.* But getting good grades doesn't mean you're learning. A's are often the result of memorizing, not learning. Many students simply cram to pass a test, then they forget everything. True learning is demonstrated only by using your new information and skills to create a richer, more personally fulfilling life. That's the way you learned as a child.

And that's the way you can learn again. You can relearn the effective process of learning that you used so effectively as a child. First, you need to regain lost core beliefs: *Life is for learning. Learning is fun. I can learn anything I need to know to achieve my goals and dreams.*

If you readopt these beliefs, you will develop patterns of behaviors, thoughts, and emotions that will make them true. Remember, you create your own reality. Why not make your reality one in which you maximize your learning?

We are all permanently enrolled in the University of Life. Your college experience is merely one course at good old U. of L. Every relationship you have is a course; your job is a course; your health is a course. Wherever you are, whatever you are doing, school is always in session. Every experience you have is offering you the opportunity to learn the wisdom you need in order to live an extraordinary life.

In class one day, a student admitted that she had recently cheated on a history test. In our discussion, Chris's Inner Defender at first justified her behavior by saying that she wanted to be a pediatrician so what difference did it make if she knew history? Further, she blamed her history teacher for not making the course interesting.

To her credit, Chris agreed to explore this situation to see what greater lesson she could learn from her cheating. She asked herself questions such as, *What goals and dreams do I want to achieve? Can I get all that I want without help? Will I ask for help? What am I afraid of? Will I allow my fear to keep me from learning what I need to know to achieve my goals and dreams? What will I learn from this experience that will assist me to live a richer, more personally fulfilling life?*

In her journal, Chris wrote, *I learned a valuable lesson from really looking at my decision to cheat. The road to becoming a pediatrician will be long and difficult. I better learn to ask for help when I'm confused, or I'll never become a doctor. In fact, I'll probably never have many of the things I want in my life. I'm going to start asking for help!*

The University of Life continually tests us in our weakest subjects. Chris' cheating only *seemed* to be about a history test. In truth, Chris was being tested about how she was going to live her life — Would she choose independence or interdependence? Would she choose self-doubt or self-confidence? She was being given another chance to update her Scripts.

When we finally realize that every experience we have contains life's essential lessons, we'll begin to learn what's required to reach our goals and dreams. What we need is a Script that guides us to consistently ask one essential question of every experience: **What's the lesson here for me?**

The process of learning

People who believe in their ability to learn and who enjoy discovery can master virtually any subject by following the same learning process that they used as children. Try these three steps and see if you don't greatly improve your learning both in college and in life.

Step 1. Ask Creator Questions: Exceptional college students are curious. They maximize their learning by continually asking Creator questions. They ask questions in nearly every class. They schedule conferences with teachers in which they ask additional questions. Before reading a textbook, they preview the pages and turn chapter headings into questions; then they seek answers to their questions as they read. Successful students write effective reports and essays by asking and answering important questions about the subject. They form study groups where they ask and answer more questions. In preparation for exams, they predict possible test questions and answer them. If they don't know what to ask about a subject, they ask, "What questions *should* I be asking?"

Have you noticed that each section in this book begins with focus questions? Have you also noticed that journal entries ask you questions to answer? If you

"If I may, Mr. Perlmutter, I'd like to answer your question __with__ a question."

wondered why, now you know: You have been practicing the mental behavior of an exceptional college student. You are learning to listen to the Creator questions of your Inner Guide.

Asking Creator questions is not only valuable for excelling in college. It's the key to learning how to live a rich, full life. It's no accident that the root word of "question" is "quest." What important questions will you need to answer to achieve the quest for your goals and dreams?

The quality of your questions will determine the quality of your answers. And the quality of your answers will determine the quality of your life. Victims ask questions such as, *Why is it so hard to get what I want?* This question is merely a complaint in disguise. It diverts energy away from action. By contrast, Creators ask questions such as, *What can I do differently to get what I want?* Notice how this question accepts responsibility for improving results and begins a search for effective actions. Many struggling people get off course simply because they fail to ask themselves Creator questions.

The important thing is not to stop questioning — never lose a holy curiosity.
Albert Einstein

Step 2. Gather Relevant Information:
To answer our important questions, we need relevant information, lots of it. Everyone is constantly absorbing information, but struggling students seldom consider the quality of the data they are dumping into their brains daily. What, for example, is the value of infor-

mation gained while watching 30 hours of television each week or while listening to classmates complain about a teacher?

Successful students gather relevant information in many ways, and they learn which learning styles work best for them. They figure out if they learn best by what they see, or hear, or do. They discover what time of day they learn best. To gather information, they attend classes regularly. They have numerous conversations with teachers and classmates about their subject. They read textbooks, two or three times if necessary. They look for and read related materials on their own. They visit support labs. They do homework problems. They learn the unique vocabulary of the subject. They take notes on lectures and readings. They write journal entries. In short, they immerse themselves in the data of this unfamiliar subject. Many people struggle in college (and in life) simply because they don't gather enough relevant information to answer their questions (assuming they even have questions).

Step 3. Discover Empowering Answers: Struggling students often think their task is to memorize all of the information they gather. Sometimes we do have to memorize, but don't confuse memorizing with learning. Learning occurs when you answer personally important questions, causing change and growth. Memorized information is soon forgotten unless it's relevant to an important issue or desire in our life. Learned information is immediately used to change our behaviors, our thoughts, our emotions, or our deepest beliefs. As a result, true learning is worth the effort (even the pain) because it changes our Scripts and empowers us to stay on course to our goals and dreams.

Once you've gathered enough relevant information, don't memorize. Instead, relax. Review your questions, then ponder your information. Don't try to get it all at once. Take frequent breaks. Work on something else for a while. Come back and review your questions and data again . . . and again. Sleep on it. Relax and review again. All the while, your unconscious mind will be performing its magic: automatically sorting and organizing the random bits of information into meaningful answers to your questions. If you trust the learning process, your mind will invent empowering answers that will astound you.

The term some people apply to this process is critical thinking. Critical thinkers do more than memorize, they ask high quality questions and discover empowering answers. They *make meaning*. That is why they are Creators.

College introduces us to new and important questions, the relevant information, and the empowering answers that great learners throughout the centuries have explored. To learn what others have discovered about the physical world we take courses like biology or geography. To learn what has been discovered about societies we take classes like sociology or anthropology. To learn about ourselves, we study subjects such as psychology or literature. Good teachers help you make the connection between their subject and your life. Successful students make this connection on their own.

Just as the best college classes challenge us to make meaning from our studies, the University of Life invites us to consciously make meaning from every experience we have.

It's well documented that the best way to have ideas is first of all to immerse yourself in a subject for longish periods — like months or more — in which you study intensely, and then step away and do something else — go for a holiday, go out dancing, or something like that. Very often ideas come in this sort of incubation period.

Francis Crick
Winner, Nobel Prize
for Medicine

The most important attitude that can be formed is that of the desire to go on learning.
John Dewey

Journal #27

In this journal entry, you'll have an opportunity to explore your personal relationship with the process of formal learning. By understanding the Scripts about learning that you have developed in school, you can discover how to become a better student in college . . . and probably in life as well.

1. In your journal, divide a page into three columns. Label the three columns: TEACHER, PAIN, PLEASURE. Beginning with your most recent year of formal schooling, list as many influential teachers as you can recall going backwards through college, high school, junior high school, middle school, elementary school, grade school, kindergarten, preschool. In column two, write any pain you can recall experiencing with each teacher. In column three, write any pleasure you can recall experiencing with this teacher. For example:

Teacher	Pain	Pleasure
Dr. Sparks, English IV	*I tried to be creative by writing a literature paper in the style of the author. Sparks gave me an F. His only comment was, "Next time, do it straight."*	
Mr. Luciano, HS Algebra		*He told me I have a natural talent in math.*

2. Write a history of your formal education.

After reviewing what you wrote in Step 1, pick out three or more school experiences that had a profound influence on you as a learner. Write about each one in a fully developed paragraph. In each paragraph include . . .

1. What happened (record the details of each experience as if it is a scene from the story of your life).
2. How you felt about the experience (such as sad, happy, angry, proud).
3. What you learned from the experience (the belief that you formed about yourself and your ability to learn).

End this history of your formal education with a concluding paragraph in which you evaluate your effectiveness as a learner today. What areas of learning are you good in, poor in? How do you feel about yourself as a learner? How do you feel about being in college? Are you confident, or do you have doubts and insecurities? Are you more confident in some areas of learning than in others? Do you seek out or avoid situations where you will have to think and learn? (Feel free to use your own Creator questions; these are merely suggestions.)

Have fun as you write this history of yourself as a learner. The purpose here is to become conscious of your Scripts about thinking and learning, especially in a classroom learning environment. It is another step toward revising the outcome of your life from the inside out. You might begin, *My very first significant memory about learning occurred in. . . .*

Relax, think, and write.

focus questions

Are you aware how often you get off course because of ineffective habit patterns and outdated beliefs? Do you know how to change your habit patterns and beliefs to get back on course?

■ ■ ■ ■ 28. Learning to Course Correct

Each time I approach a strange object, person, or event, I have a tendency to let my present needs, past experience, or expectations for the future determine what I see.

Sam Keen

One evening, while at a restaurant, I went to the restroom. I pulled on the door handle, but it didn't budge. *Someone must be in there,* I thought. After a few minutes, no one had come out, so I tried again. This time I tried pushing on the door. Still, it wouldn't open, so I waited a few more minutes, my irritation growing. *What inconsiderate jerk would take so long in a public restroom!* Aggravated, I yanked on the door handle again, rattling it loudly. Still no response. I was standing there fuming when a waiter walked up, took hold of the door handle, slid the door to the left, and, with a dramatic wave of his arm, beckoned me to enter the empty bathroom.

Whoops.

How many times in our lives are we this ineffective? In the face of a problem, we repeat the same behaviors with disappointing results. We continue to think thoughts that fail to solve our problem. We generate emotions that serve only to create a negative experience rather than solve our problem. And, underneath these self-defeating patterns lies a limiting core belief (like my unquestioned assumption that doors swing only in or out). Had I changed my self-defeating patterns or my limiting belief, I could have solved my problem in an instant. Who knows how long I might have remained off course had not a teacher (cleverly disguised as a waiter) arrived to show me how to course correct?

Here's a problem for you: Look at the three stars in the margin; then draw *one straight line* that touches all three stars.

Notice how you go about solving this problem:

★   ★

★

- **What are you doing?** Do you immediately begin drawing lines to seek a solution . . . or sit back trying to think of a solution . . . or turn the page to look for the answer . . . or keep reading without attempting to solve the puzzle? . . . or what?
- **What are you thinking?** Do you think, *This is great, I love challenges like this* . . . or *I hate puzzles like this* . . . or *This is impossible* . . . or *Oh, I already know the answer* . . . or *Who cares?* . . . or what?
- **What are you feeling?** Do you feel excited by the challenge . . . or frustrated by the difficulty of the puzzle . . . or irritated by the request . . . or depressed by your inability to solve it immediately? . . . or what?

- **What are your unconscious core beliefs?** This puzzle is easy to solve, but most people have unconscious beliefs that keep them from seeing the answer. What belief is keeping you from solving this simple problem?

If your present habit patterns and beliefs aren't working, you'll have to make a course correction to solve this problem. The same is true of life. When you face a problem and your present answers aren't working, you need to do, think, feel, or believe something different. In other words, you need to make a course correction.

The enemies of course correction are our present self-defeating patterns and our insistence that our beliefs are right. The allies of course correction are our flexibility and our courage to change.

For flexible and courageous learners, there are three essential steps in making course corrections: test your answers, heed feedback, and consciously revise the answers that get you off course.

Step 1. Test Your Present Answers: In college, teachers give tests to find out if students are on course or not. Many students don't cooperate with these tests. Instead they resist. They put off preparing for them. They experience anxiety. They may even try to cheat. They may see these tests as barriers to their success. They are wrong. Only by testing ourselves can we possibly know if we are on course or off course. Resisting a test is like refusing to look at a road map for fear of finding that we're traveling in the wrong direction. When we resist a test, we're saying, "Leave me alone. I don't want to know if I'm on course or not."

Instead of resisting, Creators cooperate with tests. In fact, Creators constantly test themselves. As a result, they seldom avoid the tests given by others. They may even look forward to them. Test anxiety turns into excitement, and the urge to cheat disappears. They understand that no one achieves lofty goals and dreams without being tested.

Successful students constantly test themselves by thinking up and answering their own examination questions. In class, they volunteer answers to their teachers' questions. Outside of class, study group members test each other. Creators treat each opportunity to answer questions as a dress rehearsal for final exams and a way to be sure they are on course.

College instructors test us occasionally. The University of Life tests us often. Begin looking at the small problems that life gives you as if they are pop quizzes. Consider the bigger challenges as major exams. If you have a problem, simply realize that you are enrolled in a course called Relationship 101, Money 110, Employment 202, or Health 125. Expect that the U. of L. will keep testing you in this subject until you learn the answers necessary to master it. Then life will promote you to another course and begin testing you in that area. The point is, there's nowhere on this planet that you can escape being tested, so you might as well cooperate and learn as much as you can from your tests.

One student, Daryl, was having difficulty keeping up with all of his commitments. "It's like I'm on a treadmill that keeps going faster and faster. I don't have enough time to do everything I have to do. I've got five classes, a part-time job,

The capacity to correct course is the capacity to reduce the differences between the path you are on now and the optimal path to your objective — between your present path and your critical path.

Charles Garfield

A feedback mechanism registers the actual state of a system, compares it to the desired state, then uses the comparison to correct the state of the system.

Horace Freeland Judson

It is the capacity for receiving feedback information which enables the organism continually to adjust its behavior and reactions so as to achieve the maximum possible self-enhancement.

Carl Rogers

and I'm on the basketball team." What Daryl didn't understand was that the University of Life had enrolled him in Self-Management 201, and the course was testing him daily. In a class discussion, Daryl's classmates offered him nearly a dozen ideas; each suggestion required that he spend some time taking Quadrant II (important but not urgent) actions to get his life back in balance. For instance, one student suggested that Daryl analyze exactly what he was doing with his time for one week to see where he might be wasting precious minutes. To every suggestion, Daryl kept saying, "Yes, but. . . . I don't have time to do that. I'm too busy." After a while, Daryl's resistance became obvious. He was determined to keep doing what he had been doing. As a result, Daryl was flunking Self-Management 201, and this failure was influencing every part of his life — his classes, his job, his sports, his relationships. His whole life was suffering because he was stuck in his old ways of self-management. He refused to test his present habit patterns and beliefs to see if they needed changing.

In what areas of your life are you stuck off course because you, too, resist testing your present actions, thoughts, emotions, or beliefs?

Step 2. Heed Feedback: Feedback is any information that tells you whether you are on course or off course.

The world bombards us with valuable feedback every day. Sadly, many of us ignore it. At first, feedback will knock on our door. If we don't heed it, the feedback will begin pounding on our door. If we ignore it long enough, the feedback may break down the door and create havoc in our lives. This havoc might look like failing out of school or having a heart attack. There is usually plenty of feedback long before the failure or the heart attack if we will only heed it.

Victims typically resist feedback that indicates they are off course: Instead of listening, they get angry, ignore the message, blame the messenger, deny the truth, throw a tantrum, complain, cry, or give up and wallow in self-pity. Dramatic? Yes. Effective? No. None of these responses gets a Victim back on course.

Why is it that our Victim-self is so reluctant to heed valuable feedback? Perhaps it's because we have so often experienced feedback as negative judgments about who we are. In truth, feedback has nothing to do with our value as a person. Criticism is only another person's opinion about whether or not we are on course.

Teachers not only provide you with an opportunity to learn; in addition, they are also your feedback machines. They are like an air traffic controller telling a pilot, *You're on course, on course . . . whoops, now you're off course, off course . . . that's right, now you're back on course.* Better teachers offer more accurate and more easily understood feedback. Successful students heed their teachers' feedback and use it to get back on course: They read every comment their teachers offer on assignments; they understand the message in their test scores; they request a clarification of anything they don't understand; they ask for additional feedback from classmates, other teachers, or mentors.

In life, heeding feedback looks much the same: Creators listen objectively to what others (bosses, friends, lovers, spouses, parents, even strangers) have to say about them. One of the benefits of college is that we are often exposed to peo-

Honest criticism is hard to take, particularly from a relative, a friend, an acquaintance, or a stranger.
Franklin P. Jones

Negative feedback means that the current approach is not working and it is up to you to find a new one. We learn by trial and error, not by trial and rightness.
Roger von Oech

[B]eing criticized is not really a threat to you or harmful in any way. You may begin to perceive criticism as valuable feedback which may help you improve your performance.
Ken Keyes

ple of great diversity who offer feedback of a kind that we have probably not experienced before. We meet people who are older or younger than we are, people from other states and countries, people of other races and cultures, people with other religious and political beliefs. If we are open to their ideas as feedback, we may hear just the ideas we need to get us back on course.

Additionally, Creators look for feedback in the results they've created in their lives: a broken relationship, a job promotion, ill health, or a serious depression are all valuable feedback if we will listen. Someone once said that a heart attack is nature's way of telling us to slow down. People who learn to heed more subtle feedback can make important course corrections early enough to avoid an impending disaster.

Creators also heed feedback from their intuition as well. Your intuition can provide you with important information from your unconscious mind about how to solve problems. Once, when I was pondering what I could do to create more happiness in my life, I had two dreams: In one dream, I was a waiter at a banquet, happily serving people food; in the second dream I was throwing a baseball for two young boys to catch. My dreams, I decided, were feedback telling me that I could create more happiness in my life by giving more service to other people. I tried, and it worked.

Step 3. Revise Your Answers: After testing your answers and heeding feedback, the last step of course correction is revising your old answers where necessary. Victims hate to give up their old self-defeating patterns and limiting beliefs. Creators willingly revise Scripts that push them off course.

For example, one problem every college student has to face is, "How do I write effectively?" The answer that many students bring with them from high school is, "Get right to the point." By this, they usually mean writing a few abstract ideas as the entirety of an essay. Writing college assignments allows students to test whether or not this answer will keep them on course in college. Feedback from teachers (grades and comments) will most likely indicate that they are off course when they "get right to the point." College teachers expect effective writing to include sufficient and well-organized support for abstract ideas. (By the way, adding the four E's — Examples, Experience, Explanation and Evidence — is a great way to add support for an abstract idea.)

Now, the question is: Will the students revise their old answers? Will they change from the old thought of "getting right to the point" (which may, in fact, have kept them on course in high school) to the new thought of "adding suffi-

---

| Summer Words for a Sister Addict |

the first day i shot dope
was on a sunday.
        I had just come
home from church
          got mad at my mother
cuz she got mad at me.   u dig?
          went out.shot up
behind a feeling against her.
        it felt good.
gooder than dooing it.   yeah
          it was nice.
i did it. uh. huh.   I did it   uh huh.
i want to do it again.   it felt so gooooood.
        and as the sister
        sits in her silent/
        remembered/high
        someone leans for
        ward gently asks her:
            sister.
            did u
            finally
        learn how to hold yr/mother?
and the music of the day
          drifts in the room
to mingle with the sister's young tears
        and we all sing.

— *Sonia Sanchez*

My contemplation of life and human nature in that secluded place [prison] had taught me that he who cannot change the very fabric of his thought will never be able to change reality, and will never, therefore, make any progress.
Anwar Sadat

cient, well-organized support for abstract ideas" (which is necessary to stay on course in college)? Students who learn how to revise their old patterns and beliefs have a greater chance of excelling in college and in life.

The courage to change

Being human, all of us are off course in some areas of our lives. With course correction, we can learn what we need to know to get to our goals and dreams. But here's the challenge: Course correction requires change, and change demands courage.

In order to change, we need to let go of what we have now and embrace something new in the hopes that it will improve our lives. Our habits have gotten us this far, so we are reluctant to let them go. The problem is that the very patterns that got us where we are often prevent us from going further.

True wisdom requires the courage to revise our answers when they no longer serve our success. Life asks us to change, and change, and change a thousand times again. Only by changing can we do, think, feel, and believe what is necessary to stay on course.

What is important is to keep learning, to enjoy challenge and to tolerate ambiguity. In the end there are no certain answers.

Martina Horner
President, Radcliffe College

Journal #28

In this journal entry, you'll have an opportunity to explore course correction in your life. People who are successful are willing to exchange old ways of doing, thinking, feeling, and believing for newer, even more effective ways. Creators have the courage to change!

1. Write about a major course correction that you have made some time in your life.

A course correction changes the direction you are headed in one of your life roles. Some course corrections send you in a positive direction, others in a negative direction. What course corrections have you made that affected the quality of your life?

Examples of major course corrections include: getting married or divorced, entering or quitting college, starting or stopping an addiction, beginning or ending an exercise program, changing jobs or careers, adopting a child, moving to a new location, and changing a belief about yourself, other people, or the world.

Develop your journal entry by asking and answering Creator questions such as . . .

- What was I doing before I realized that I was off course?
- What feedback did I get that I was off course?
- What course corrections did I consider?
- What course correction did I choose?
- What actions, thoughts, feelings, and/or beliefs did I have to change?
- What challenges did I face in trying to change?

Did you figure out how to connect the three stars with one straight line? If you were stumped, what limiting belief kept you from solving this problem? Did you assume that you were restricted to a pen or pencil with a narrow point? You weren't. In fact, the solution is to use a writing implement (such as a large crayon) with a point wide enough to cover all three stars. Simply draw one straight line that covers all of them. Once you change your limiting belief, solving the problem is easy! How many other problems could you solve in your life if you mastered the creative art of course correction?

- What difficulties did I experience as a result of my change?
- What benefits did I experience as a result of my change?
- What additional changes could I make in this area of my life?

2. Write about one of your life roles that is currently crying out for a course correction. Remember to ask and answer Creator questions.

Relax, think, and write.

focus questions   Do you know what a mistake *really* is? Do you know how to profit from the mistakes you will inevitably make?

■ ■ ■ ■ 29. Learning from Your Mistakes

Everyone makes mistakes. We all know that. But what is a mistake?

We make hundreds of choices daily, maybe thousands. Each choice has one of three effects on our lives. Some choices move us toward our goals and dreams. Some choices leave us right where we are. And some choices move us away from our goals and dreams.

When Victims make a decision that moves them away from their destination, their Inner Critics point the finger of judgment inward, saying, *It was my fault. I'm to blame.* Then their Inner Defenders immediately point the finger outward, blaming others and excusing themselves. This inner chorus of blaming and defending distracts Victims from the reality that they did have other choices. They just didn't see them.

Here, then, is a nonjudgmental way to think about a mistake:

A mistake is a choice *that gets us off course from our dreams when a choice existed that could have kept us on course to our dreams.*

No blame. No excuses. Our choices either lead to desired results or they lead to undesired results. This is the way your Inner Guide sees it.

Everyone makes mistakes, but Victims repeat theirs. Over and over. Worse, they often judge themselves for having made the mistake or they judge others for having caused them to make the mistake.

By contrast, Creators learn from their mistakes. As a result, they seldom repeat them. Also, they resist judging themselves or others for their mistakes.

The following choice evaluation process can help you profit from past mistakes. To illustrate the five-step process, let's look at how it helped a student named Tina. Tina was a twenty-three-year-old wife and mother who dreamed of becoming a buyer in the fashion industry. To achieve her dream, she needed a college degree.

Step 1: What Choice Did I Make That Got Me Off Course?   "I've missed my night class two weeks in a row," Tina acknowledged.

A man may make mistakes, but he isn't a failure until he starts blaming someone else.
John Wooden

Humans have learned only through mistakes.
Buckminster Fuller

Step 2: What Did I Make More Important Than Taking a Step Toward My Goals and Dreams?

"I waited until my husband came home from work so he could take care of our baby. When he works overtime, he doesn't get home in time for me to get to school. Surely you don't expect me to make this class more important than my baby?"

"So," I said, ignoring Tina's Inner Defender, "last Monday, you made taking care of your baby until your husband got home more important than coming to class."

"Right."

Step 3: What Other Choices *Could* I Have Made?

"I didn't have any other choice."

"I understand that at this moment you don't see another choice. But if you *were* able to see another choice, what would it be?"

"Well, maybe I could have brought my baby to class," Tina said, her Inner Guide starting to cooperate.

"Great. That's one option. What else?"

"I could have asked the day care center to keep my baby later than usual. I already know they don't want any kids there after 5:30, but maybe they would have made an exception just this once. Or, I could. . . ." She paused.

"Yes. . . ?"

"Well, my sister has a baby, too. She's not working or going to school right now, and she lives near me. Maybe she would have watched the baby until my husband got home. I could watch her baby when she wants to go out on the weekend."

"Great! So you did have other options. You could have brought your baby to school, you could have asked the day care center to keep your baby later, and you could have asked your sister to watch your baby until your husband got home."

"I like the last one. My baby will be fine with my sister."

"So, it looks like missing class was a mistake. After all, you did have other choices that would have moved you toward your goals."

Step 4: Is My Original Choice Part of a Pattern in My Life?

"Well, I guess it is. I don't like to ask other people for help."

"And you don't ask other people for help because. . . ?"

"I guess because I'm afraid they'll say no."

"It sounds as though you make avoiding rejection more important than getting help and getting what you want. Is that right?"

"I guess I do."

Step 5: What Did I Learn?

"I learned that I don't have to miss class so often," Tina said. "I learned that I can ask my sister to babysit. Also, I have more choices than I thought I did. I learned that I don't always have to choose between taking care of my baby and getting my degree."

"Great. Anything else?"

"Sometimes I don't ask for things because I'm afraid of being rejected."

"Great. Anything else?"

"Nope. I think that's it."

Now, you may not have a baby as Tina did. And you may not be missing classes, either. But if you're making choices that lead you away from your dream when better choices exist, you're making mistakes, too.

Many Victims put themselves in an "either/or" mind set. *Either I meet this need or I meet that need. But I can't possibly have them both.* The choice evaluation process shows you that often you can have them both. When you explore your options with the choice evaluation process, you will often see that you can create much more in life than you ever thought possible. Additionally, this process gives you a way to identify limiting patterns that get you off course from your goals and dreams.

With practice, Creators begin recognizing their mistakes closer and closer to the moment of choice. A man I know denied for more than ten years that he is an alcoholic, despite losing his wife, being fired from his job, and going bankrupt. Finally, after a decade of denial, he listened to his Inner Guide, evaluated his choices, and recognized that his drinking was a serious mistake. He decided to stop making alcohol more important than his relationships, his career, and even his life. He joined Alcoholics Anonymous, stopped drinking, and during the next five years pieced his life back together. He found a new job, got remarried, and regained his self-respect.

At a party one night, he decided that he could handle a glass of wine. One glass led to many more. On the way home, he drove off the road, and when he regained consciousness, he found himself upside down and badly bruised, but still alive. Lying there in a ditch, still groggy from wine, he evaluated his choice to drink again and recognized immediately that he had made a mistake. With that recognition, he was able to correct his mistake and resume his sobriety within hours (instead of years) after his mistake. Perhaps the next time that he considers drinking alcohol he'll realize his mistake even before he takes the first sip.

So, when you make a mistake, don't abuse yourself or others with judgment. Judgement keeps you off course. Judgment keeps you from learning from your mistakes. And Judgment keeps you from seeing that blessings sometimes come disguised as mistakes. Instead, profit from your mistakes: Learn your lesson and get right back on course.

Journal #29

In this journal entry you will have an opportunity to learn from a past mistake by applying the choice evaluation process. People who profit from their mistakes can minimize their misery while achieving much more in their lives than they ever thought possible.

1. Use the choice evaluation process to examine a choice you made that got you off course. Write the five questions and your answers in your journal.

Remember: **A mistake is a *choice* that gets us off course from our dreams when a choice existed that could have kept us on course to our dreams.** Think of a choice you made regarding your family, college, friends, job, a love relationship, or anywhere else in your life and how this choice got you off course. This choice might have been a broken commitment in this course or elsewhere in your life.

STEP 1: What choice did I make that got me off course?
STEP 2: What did I make more important than taking a step toward my goals and dreams? (What did I do instead?)
STEP 3: What other choices *could* I have made? (Make a long list.)
STEP 4: Is my original choice part of a pattern in my life? (Do I often think, act, feel, or believe as I did in this situation?)
STEP 5: What did I learn?

2. Write a paragraph (or more) exploring your thoughts and feelings about evaluating your choices and learning from your mistakes. As before, you will probably benefit from first writing a list of Creator questions to answer.

Everyone makes mistakes. What matters is what you do after you make a mistake. Victims listen to their Inner Critic and Inner Defender; then they repeat the mistake over and over. Creators listen to their Inner Guide, find better options, and learn valuable lessons from every mistake.

Relax, think, write.

focus questions   Do you know what a failure *really* is? Do you know how to transform a failure into one of your greatest teachers?

■ ■ ■ ■ 30. Learning from Your Failures

Every man's got to figure to get beat sometime.

Joe Louis
Former heavyweight
boxing champion

During final exam period one semester, I heard a painful shriek come from the nursing education department office. A second later, a woman charged out of the office, screaming, flailing papers in the air, and stumbling down the hall. A cluster of concerned classmates caught up to her at the end of the hall. I could hear them desperately trying to comfort the wailing woman. "It's all right. You can take the exam again next semester. C'mon, it's okay. Really." She leaned against the wall, eyes closed. She slid down the wall until she sat in a limp heap, surrounded by consoling voices. Later, I learned that she had dropped out of school.

At the end of another semester, I had the unpleasant task of telling one of my hardest-working students that she had failed the proficiency exams. She would have to repeat the course. Her husband had left her during the semester, so I was particularly worried about how she would handle this additional bad news. We had a conference, and as soon as I told her the bad news, I began consoling her. I assured her that I knew how hard she'd worked, that she had come very close, that I was confident she would pass next time, that I hoped she wouldn't let this news get her down. After quietly listening to my encouragements, she said, "You're taking my failure pretty hard. Do you need a hug?" Before I could respond, she plucked me out of my chair and gave me an encouraging hug. "Don't worry," she said, patting my back. "I'll pass next semester," and sure enough, she did.

Everyone fails something. A failure is what our Inner Critic calls it when our efforts have not yet created our desired outcomes. A failure is a setback, not a life sentence — unless we believe it is. A critical element of our success is how we respond to our failures in life: What do we **do?** What do we **think?** How do we **feel?** As always, our responses are guided by our deepest **core beliefs** about ourselves, about other people, and about the world. Our failures can destroy us or they can teach us the greatest lessons life has to offer. The choice is ours.

Learned helplessness is the giving-up reaction, the quitting response that follows from the belief that whatever you do doesn't matter.
Martin Seligman

Learned helplessness

Psychologist Martin Seligman has spent many years studying how people respond to failure. Failure, he's found, is tough on everyone. He compares it to being punched in the stomach. The punch will hurt and maybe even knock a person down. Some people get back up. Others stay down for the count. Folks who stay on the floor typically believe that nothing they try will make any difference. So, they quit.

Mind you, these people are not necessarily any less capable than other people, but they *believe that they are helpless in the face of defeat.* And so, they are. Their belief becomes their reality.

I don't mind the failure, but I can't imagine that I'd forgive myself if I didn't try.
Nikki Giovanni

Seligman says people quit when they believe that the causes of their failures are **permanent, pervasive,** and **personal.** For example, the woman who failed her nursing exams may have explained her defeat to herself by saying, *Oh, no, I'll never pass these exams!* (permanent), *I screw up everything I do* (pervasive), and *I'm so stupid* (personal). These, of course, are the self-judgments of her Inner Critic. The Inner Critic's harsh self-appraisal brings a Victim to her knees and she quits.

The student who accepted her English 101 failure so gracefully must have been listening to very different inner voices. According to Seligman, her inner conversation probably attributed her failure to causes that were **temporary, specific,** and **impersonal.** She may have explained her failure to herself by thinking, *Okay, I failed, but I know I can do better next semester* (temporary — she can improve the situation in the future), *I'm doing fine in my other courses* (specific — the problem is limited to this one area of her life), and *I'll be able to do better when I'm not so upset about my husband leaving me* (impersonal — she doesn't falsely make some flaw in herself the cause of the problem). This version of reality allows a person to stand up, brush herself off, and get back on the path. My sense is that her Inner Guide also added, *And I'll do better next time because I'll learn from my failure and do something different.*

What can we learn from failure?

Failure is one of the master teachers in the University of Life. Most of us enroll in its courses many times during our lives, and we always learn something. The question is, What do we learn?

The research of Seligman and others shows that failure teaches many people to doubt their ability to go on. These people *learn* to feel helpless. They become Victims of their circumstances.

By contrast, other people learn to stand back up when failure knocks them down. This lesson allows them to focus on their destination rather than their problems, to keep going instead of quitting. In short, learning perseverance (instead of helplessness) teaches people the self-discipline they need to stay on course. They become Creators of their circumstances.

Earlier, you read the story of Luanne, the student who passed English 101 in her sixth try. Luanne could very well have quit after any of her five "failures," but somehow she had learned to persevere. Luanne's experience demonstrates that **you have not truly failed until you quit.** As long as you keep going there is the possibility of success. Some people need only one try to succeed; some people need many. Perseverance is a critical ingredient of success.

But Luanne didn't succeed just because she persevered. She succeeded because she was willing to learn a new way to overcome her obstacles and to change what she had been doing for five previous semesters. She was finally willing to revise her Scripts so she could change her results in the outer world.

The role call of the world's successful people is full of "failures" who would not quit. R.H. Macy failed seven times before his department store in New York became immensely profitable. Henry Ford didn't taste success in the automobile industry until he had experienced going broke five times. Winston Churchill failed the sixth grade on his way to becoming prime minister of England. Albert Einstein didn't learn to read until he was seven. Babe Ruth struck out 1,330 times in addition to his 714 home runs. Walt Disney went bankrupt before building Disneyland. Abraham Lincoln lost six elections for various political offices before being elected the sixteenth president of the United States of America.

Failure isn't a life sentence; it's temporary . . . if you say so. Failure doesn't pervade your whole life; it pops up here and there . . . if you say so. Failure isn't an indictment of your personal worth; it's an opportunity for course correction . . . if you say so.

Your Inner Guide knows that failure is merely feedback. Failure simply means that so far you haven't reached a goal or dream. When you fail, life is giving you a choice. You can keep doing what got you the failure. You can quit. Or you can learn from your failure, pick yourself up, and try something new. What's your choice?

Journal #30

In this journal entry, you'll have an opportunity to examine what you've learned from a past failure. When you learn to benefit from a failure, you have employed one of life's great teachers as your personal tutor. What you learn from a failure can propel you to successes you would not otherwise have achieved!

1. Write a list of failures that you have experienced in your life. Remember, a "failure" is what your Inner Critic calls those times when you haven't created your goals or dreams exactly on schedule. Consider failures in school, jobs, relationships, sports, diets, travel, addictions, commitments, parenting, or other parts of your life.

2. From your list in Step 1, choose one of your failures that has been a great teacher. Write a list of ten or more questions that an interested person might want you to answer about this failure. Invent Creator questions that will help you learn whatever lesson this failure has to teach you. (See examples in the left-hand margin.)

3. Write an interview with yourself about this failure, emphasizing what you learned from the experience. Let your Inner Guide ask you the Creator questions that you wrote in Step 2. Allow your Inner Guide to be an active listener by asking you follow-up questions that help you to explore your answers in more depth. Label the questions and comments of your Inner Guide with "IG." Label your own comments with "ME."

For example, your interview might begin . . .

IG: What is one of your most significant failures?
ME: Certainly one of them would have to be getting fired from my job two years ago.
IG: What happened?
ME: I can remember it like it was yesterday. My boss came up to me and handed me an envelope. He stood there looking at me with the strangest look on his face, almost like he was looking at someone about to be shot by a firing squad.

I felt a shiver go through my body. "What?" I asked.

"This isn't working," he said. "Here's a check for two weeks' pay. That will hold you over until you get a new job." Then he turned and walked away without another word.

I stood there holding that envelope, and I started thinking about what I was going to do now. I guess that was what hit me the most. What in the world am I going to do now?
IG: How did you feel right then? . . .

Relax, think, write.

POSSIBLE QUESTIONS:
What did you tell yourself when you "failed"? What did you do? How did you feel? Did your thoughts or feelings change later? Do you have any regrets about what you did? Did this event remind you of any experience you had as a child? What did other people say about what had happened? What advice did they give you? Who was your greatest supporter during this challenge? How would you handle the situation differently today? Do you see any self-defeating patterns in the way you responded? Do you recognize any limiting beliefs that surfaced during this situation? Did you respond more as a Victim or a Creator? If this experience had been designed by a master teacher to teach you an essential lesson about life, what do you suppose that lesson would be? How will you live your life differently as a result of what you learned?

What is the greatest obstacle standing between you and your goals and dreams? Do you know how to learn the life-changing lesson that this master teacher is presenting to you?

▪ ▪ ▪ ▪ ▪ 31. Learning from Your Obstacles

One of the ways that the University of Life tests us is by placing an obstacle in the path to our goals and dreams. Victims typically let their obstacles block their success. Creators let their obstacles (as well as their mistakes and failures) teach them valuable lessons.

What is in your way?

[G]rowth depends upon the presence of difficulty to be overcome by the exercise of intelligence.

John Dewey

Visualize for a moment your greatest goal or dream as a student. Picture its accomplishment off there in the distance. Now, see all the obstacles that stand between you and your destination. For now, you don't need to worry about a way past these barriers. For now, all you need to do is see them.

Here's a list of common obstacles. Check the ones that you see in your way.

☐ Lack of time	☐ Fear
☐ Self-doubts	☐ Pessimism
☐ Lack of money	☐ Lack of knowledge or skill
☐ Procrastination	☐ Depression
☐ Poor physical health	☐ Shyness
☐ Lack of help	☐ Self-judgment
☐ A person	☐ Too much competition
☐ Disorganization	☐ Too many responsibilities

Remember to look across the river first and remind yourself of your dreams. Then, look down at the river and figure out how to conquer the alligators that stand between you and your dreams.

John Hanley

You may think that you are alone in having a major obstacle. Not so. Problems are the human condition. The question is not *whether* you will face obstacles. The question is, what will *your* particular obstacles look like? More important, how will you deal with them? And, perhaps most important, what will you learn from them? If you let them, your obstacles will be some of your greatest teachers about life and success. Otherwise, they will become your excuses for failure. As always, you get to choose.

A Victim blames his failures on his obstacles: *How can I possibly succeed? I have so much in my way! I have no money. Where am I supposed to find the time? Nobody will help me. Look at what my mother and father did to me. I'm too shy. See all my competition. I don't stand a chance!*

Everyone is dealt a problem in life. Mine is missing four fingers.

Jim Abbott
Professional baseball player

A Creator views his obstacles as teachers and learns from them: *Dealing with my obstacle has been a wonderful opportunity for me to grow. I'm learning to be more conscious. I'm improving my ability to make wise choices. Problems don't scare me the way they used to, and I'm learning valuable new information and skills. By learning from my obstacles, I'm becoming more of the person I want to be.*

What personal qualities do you need to overcome your obstacle?

An obstacle can teach you about the personal qualities you need more of in order to move past it. Do you need to be more bold, more disciplined, more self-forgiving? Do you need to be more organized, more optimistic, more confident?

If there is a quality you would like more of, you can add it to your personal affirmation created in Journal #9. (If you've stopped saying your affirmation daily, you can choose to begin again today.) Remember, the qualities in your affirmation express the qualities that you are nurturing in yourself. Repeating your affirmation every day reminds you about the powerful inner resources you have available to support your success. In this way you can begin transforming your self-defeating thoughts into empowering beliefs.

What actions do you need to take to overcome your obstacle?

Your obstacle can also teach you which purposeful actions will move you past it. You can add these actions to your personal rules for success (Journal #13). You might even want to make a thirty-two-day commitment to turn one of these actions into a habit. (If you've stopped doing your thirty-two-day commitment from Journal #14, you can choose to begin again today.) You can schedule these purposeful actions in your written planner (Journal #15). You can raise your standards of what you expect of yourself (Journal #16). You can visualize yourself taking these new actions (Journal #17). You could request assistance (Journal #19).

The most creative and evolved people we know are those who use every situation as an opportunity to learn about themselves. Openness to learning is a hallmark of evolution.
Gay and Kathlyn Hendricks

Richard dreamed of earning a college degree, yet he was considering dropping out of school. He said that his obstacle was lack of time: *There just aren't enough hours in a day to accomplish all I have to do.* When he decided to view his obstacle as his teacher, Richard learned that lack of time had *always* stood between him and his goals and dreams. Telling himself that he didn't have enough time had caused him to abandon nearly every dream he had ever had.

Now, looking closer, Richard realized that time was only the surface issue, the excuse his Inner Defender trotted out to disguise the deeper issue. Below Richard's time problem lay a core belief that he wasn't worthy of a college degree . . . or worthy of any personally meaningful accomplishment. Richard's Inner Critic, with its limiting beliefs about his intelligence and value as a human being, was the real obstacle. Dropping out of school wouldn't solve that problem. His problem would merely follow him to his next goal or dream. It was time to put this obstacle behind him. When he finally let his obstacle teach him, Richard learned a lesson with the potential to alter the outcome of his whole life.

I have learned that success is to be measured not so much by the position that one has reached in life as by the obstacles which he has overcome while trying to succeed.
Booker T. Washington

At the moment that you see your obstacles for what they really are — your teachers — they lose their power to stop you. In fact, what you learn from them can get you to your dreams even sooner.

Now it's time to pull together all of the elements of this chapter and consider how we can dramatically improve how we think and learn.

Revise your Scripts about learning

In my first semester in college, I took calculus. By the third week, I was lost. Somehow I stumbled through the next twelve weeks and managed to escape with a D. I was positive that I would never pass the second-semester calculus course, so it was with dread that I viewed the university's graduation requirement of two semesters of math.

To solve my problem, I asked a Victim question: *How can I avoid taking any more calculus?* (A Creator question would have been: *What can I do to regain the math confidence and skills I had in high school so I can pass the second semester of calculus?*)

In answer to my Victim question, I discovered that I could take a one-semester statistics class and fulfill the math requirement. By the third week of statistics, however, I was once again lost. My belief in my math ability totally shattered, I wandered farther and farther off course. Just when I was positive that I had no prayer of passing, fate stepped in. The day after the final exam, my professor had an emotional breakdown and was institutionalized. It turned out that he'd kept no records for the class (bless his heart), so university officials decided to give everyone in the class a C. The good students were furious. I, of course, was thrilled! I would never have to take another math class for the rest of my life.

Wrong.

Have you ever noticed how your unresolved issues have a way of lying in wait for you, then ambushing you when you least expect them? Some years later, I enrolled in a graduate program in psychology and found that I was again required to take statistics.

In the first class, the professor announced, "You're going to work in study teams of three people. Each team will have at least one person who is strong in math, and this person will tutor the other two people." Each of us had to decide then and there if we were a "one" (strong in math), a "two" (average in math), or a "three" (weak in math).

I was tempted, of course, to label myself a three. But by then I had learned about life being a self-fulfilling prophecy. Perhaps, I pondered, I'm only weak in math because I think I am. What if I revised my Scripts?

When the teacher asked for ones I raised my hand. Soon I was joined by a two and a three, and my study group was formed. I heard my Inner Critic screaming at me: *FRAUD.* My Inner Guide countered: *You were good in math in high school. You can learn what you need to know to pass this course.*

On our first take-home quiz, I received the lowest score on our team, a fifty-five. As the "one" for our team, I was supposed to teach the other two students what they hadn't understood. *What a joke,* my Inner Critic mocked. I wound up asking the one-student on another team for help, then bringing her answers back to my team.

At the end of that class session, the teacher once again asked us to assign ourselves numbers. *You can move up or down,* he said. *It's up to you.* Inside I felt a clash: My Inner Critic kept pointing at my outer reality: *You scored a fifty-five! Face it, you are a math dunce.* My Inner Guide countered: *Tens of thousands*

Habits of thinking need not be forever. One of the most significant findings in psychology in the last twenty years is that individuals can choose the way they think.

Martin Seligman

If you once had a bad experience with numbers, your mind may have decided to keep you away from anything having to do with numbers by evoking anxiety whenever you approach the subject. So here you are, ten, twenty, thirty or more years later, still telling yourself that you can't do math and making it impossible to give it a chance. Much of the mind's "natural" programming consists of such self-imposed limitations that keep you from realizing your potential and from feeling good about yourself.

Bernie Zilbergeld and Arnold A. Lazarus

of people have learned statistics; certainly you're as smart as some of them. You can do it.

When the teacher called for "ones" to nominate themselves, I once again raised my hand. Was it my imagination, or did my teammates give me funny looks?

That next week, I changed my study habits. I read the assignment four times. On the fourth time, I got a glimmering of what it was about. I experienced an almost physical sensation, as if my brain cells were rearranging themselves to account for this new perception. During that week, I spent more time than before solving the problems, checking and rechecking them. When I got back my next quiz, my score was in the seventies, surpassing one of my teammates. I was able to teach her a few concepts, and I learned a few myself from our third member. At the end of the class meeting, I again declared myself a one.

In the days that followed, I once more revised my study habits. Not only did I read the text and solve the problems, I got on the phone with a friend (a high school math teacher) who explained some of the things I didn't understand. I created an affirmation (*I am a confident, intelligent, hardworking man, and I love math!*), which I repeated to myself again and again. My next quiz score moved into the eighties, and somewhat more confidently I once more claimed my status as a one. My outer reality was looking more and more like my inner reality.

The following week, in addition to my reading, problem solving, and phone conferences with classmates and my tutor, I began my semester project. I had feared the project when I first heard about it, but now I felt a quiver of excitement. What a great opportunity to apply what I was learning and to prove that I was, indeed, mastering statistics. My quiz grade that week moved into the nineties. That week I had a great time tutoring my two teammates.

Perhaps you can see where this story is heading. Yes, I got an A in that statistics class. And I learned something even more important than statistics. I learned that I can revise my Scripts about learning math . . . and about anything else. It's unlikely that I will ever take another math class, but if for some reason I do need to learn more math to support a goal or dream, I believe that I can. I have developed behaviors, thoughts, and feelings to support that belief. I now associate mathematics more with pleasure than with pain. I no longer feel helpless when I think about learning mathematics. I now believe that I can learn whatever I need to know to achieve my greatest goals and dreams.

Teach your answers to someone else

Here's one last suggestion about maximizing your learning: approach learning with the consciousness of a teacher rather than the consciousness of a student. This shift is actually very simple to make. Just decide that within twenty-four hours of learning any significant new information or skill, you will teach it to someone else.

To do so, you must learn the subject so well that you can simplify it to its essence. As a result, you will learn the information and concepts even better

What you're thinking, what shape your mind is in, is what makes the biggest difference of all.

Willie Mays

Any effective teacher will tell you that if you share your knowledge with others, the very act of trying to help someone understand a new concept will increase your own understanding. The teacher generally learns more than the student.

Hyrum W. Smith

yourself. Think of your journals as your effort to teach your ideas to someone else, and you will find that your level of mastery of success strategies will soar.

Journal #31

In this journal entry you will have a choice. You can choose to learn important lessons from one of your obstacles. Or you can recall a time when your process of learning got abused. Either choice offers an opportunity for you to revise your Scripts so that you can maximize your learning.

Unless your instructor tells you otherwise, choose only one of the two journal steps below. Pick the one that you think would produce the greatest improvement in your ability to learn.

1. Have your Inner Guide interview one of your biggest obstacles and write out their dialogue. Your Inner Guide can ask the following questions and more:

- Obstacle, what is your name?
- Why are you such a challenge for me?
- How have I attempted to overcome you in the past?
- How have you defeated my attempts to overcome you until now?
- What personal qualities will I need to get beyond you?
- What different actions will I need to get beyond you?
- What different thoughts will I need to get beyond you?
- What different emotions will I need to get beyond you?
- What different beliefs (about the world, other people, or myself) will I need to get beyond you?
- What important lesson have you come to teach me?

Have your Inner Guide demonstrate effective listening skills, including asking your obstacle to expand or clarify its answers (using the four E's: Experience, Examples, Evidence, Explanation) where appropriate. Label each comment with IG (Inner Guide) and OB (Obstacle).

OR . . .

2. Write a letter to someone in your life who has caused you pain about learning. This person might be a former teacher, school principal, parent, grandparent, coach, spouse, brother, or sister . . . anyone who wounded your ability to learn effectively. In this letter, tell the person what he or she did, how it affected you, how you feel about it, and how you are overcoming this injury today.

On the next page is a letter that Diana wrote to her father, the man who had called her a half-brain. Diana's father had been dead for five years when she wrote her letter, but expressing her pain and anger helped Diana heal and move past an ancient injury that was hindering her ability to learn.

Relax, think, write.

*Ultimately, there's only one answer to the question of what's standing in my way: **me, myself, and I.***
Joyce Chapman

Dear Dad,

I miss you a lot, and I know that you still live in my heart. As a child, I used to think you were everything. I liked everything you did. When you lifted your car hood, I was there watching you fix your car. When you shaved your face, I watched you. When you came home from work, I was the first person to greet you at the door with "Hi, Daddy!" I liked to laugh at you and with you. When I couldn't get my mother to see things my way, I always came to you to help me out. Usually you did help me out.

The greatest disappointment you gave me in my life is to say I was too dumb to go to college. I was so angry at you because you were the one person in my life I thought believed in me. I thought the sun and moon revolved around you. I didn't know until recently I was still carrying the pain of that moment. I've never forgotten when I walked into the conversation you were having in the kitchen with my mother telling her that I was too dumb to go to school. I remember when I heard it how I wanted to curse you out and how hurt I was to hear that this man that I had given my trust and love to had no confidence in me. All I wanted was to make you proud of me.

Daddy, I can forgive you because that only proved to me that you didn't know me at all. I understand why you felt the way you did when I reflect back to my childhood. Especially in the fourth grade. That's the year I failed. That's the year I was having a hard time with a teacher who was very strict on me. She hampered my ability to effectively do my work. She gave me below average grades in most of my subjects. In those days you never questioned my teacher. You just accepted her decision that I was slow. Her opinion of me stuck with you for my whole life. I was labeled in fourth grade because you believed in what a teacher said of your child. You never asked me about her, so if I got a bad report card the reason in your mind was that I wasn't smart, even though my older sister was also on the verge of failing.

It's strange, when I think about it, but since my older sister failed, I thought it was no big deal if I failed too. But it really was because she didn't lose her smarts. I did. Everyone seemed focused more on my failure. My failures were always highlighted, even in my adulthood, so much so that I'd forgotten that my older sister also failed until this very moment as I write. No one even talked much about her failure. There are a lot of questions I could ask about that, but Daddy, I let all that go. I am not going to let it ruin the fun times we had.

I still miss you, Dad. I still love you. I forgive you because I understand why you felt the way you did. I am no longer living for you, Dad, but I am living for myself. I am not trying to prove anything to anyone any more. I am just trying to live a life I can be proud of. I wish sometimes I could just sit back with you and talk about the fun times we had. Sometimes when I want you near I buy some of that cheap cologne you used to get, and I can smell my father being close to me. My memories of you are the ones of laughter and love. Daddy, I cried in class more than I cried for you when you died.

Love,
Diana

Chapter 8

■ ■ ■ ■ ■ ■ ■ ■

Creating worldly success is meaningless if I am not happy. That means I must take responsibility for creating the quality of my entire experience of life, in both my outer world and my inner world.

Creating a Positive Experience of Life ■

I create my own happiness.

Successful Students . . .	Struggling Students . . .
1. . . . **honor their emotions,** using them as a compass for staying on course.	1. . . . resist, distort, or exaggerate their emotions.
2. . . . **choose the content of their consciousness,** carefully deciding what thoughts will reside in their minds.	2. . . . take no responsibility for the quality of the thoughts that occupy their consciousness.
3. . . . **resolve incompletions in their lives,** freeing positive energy to pursue their goals and dreams.	3. . . . postpone taking action on unresolved issues in their lives, draining energy needed for positive pursuits.
4. . . . **create flow,** feeling happily absorbed in their choices of work and play.	4. . . . frequently experience boredom or anxiety in their lives.
5. . . . **develop involved detachment,** understanding that pursuing a futile quest only creates personal suffering.	5. . . . become addicted to their desired outcomes, creating misery for themselves when destiny doesn't cooperate.

What is the emotion that you experience most often? How can you become comfortable with all of your emotions?

■ ■ ■ ■ 32. Honoring Your Emotions

The heart has its reason which reason knows not of.

Blaise Pascal

Healthy emotions are a vital factor in creating our success in college and in life. Healthy emotions act as a compass. When we're headed toward our goals and dreams, positive emotions give us the energy to keep traveling in the right direction. When we drift off course, emotional distress alerts us that something is wrong. When we honor our healthy emotions, they help keep us on course to personally meaningful destinations.

Four of our primary emotions are anger, fear, sadness, and happiness. Each emotion has a different function. Healthy anger bears a message that we are being violated in some way. As we encounter a perceived injustice or threat, our brain signals the body to release hormones. These chemical changes fuel our anger, providing the strength to fight for what's important to us.

Happiness is the meaning and purpose of life, the whole aim and end of human existence.

Aristotle

Like anger, fear also causes the release of hormones that increase the body's strength, this time in preparation for flight. Healthy fear alerts us that we are in actual danger and generates the energy that we need for escape.

Healthy sadness overtakes us upon the loss of something dear. By fully grieving, we resolve the loss or disappointment, freeing us to move on with our lives. When we fail to acknowledge sadness, our creative energy may become frozen in the past, unavailable to us for pursuing our goals and dreams.

Happiness has been called the goal of all goals. After all, why do we pursue any goal or dream? Isn't it for the positive experience that it will create? Ultimately, we pursue our goals and dreams because we believe their attainment will make us happy, and happiness is our greatest reward for being on course.

There can be no transforming of darkness into light and of apathy into movement without emotion.

Carl Jung

Unfortunately, though, many adults don't have healthy emotions. Healthy anger may become destructive rage. Healthy fear may become immobilizing anxiety. Healthy sadness may become lingering depression. Happiness may become dulled, damaged, anesthetized. Unhealthy emotions are an unreliable compass on the journey of life. In fact, they may become a major obstacle.

What went wrong?

Just as our childhood experiences taught us what is safe to think, so they taught us what is safe to feel. In healthy families, everyone is free to responsibly express the full range of human emotions. In unhealthy families, however, emotions are often banned or distorted: *Don't you get angry with me, young lady. . . . You better stop that crying or I'll give you something to really cry about. . . . Stop all that laughing in there. . . . You don't really feel that way. . . . Well, if you're going to feel that way, I'm leaving.*

In these families, emotions are often contaminated not only by words but by negative examples as well: A parent flies into a rage whenever things don't go his or her way . . . or cowers and withdraws from the slightest conflict . . . or sobs at the smallest disappointment . . . or wallows in deep depression for days on end.

So, as children we learned from important adults which emotions are acceptable and which are not — which are safe and which are dangerous. If we're shamed, abused, or abandoned for expressing healthy emotions, we'll quickly revise our emotional Scripts. We'll adopt emotional habit patterns that are much less natural, but far safer in the world as we perceive it.

Many adults are still using the outdated emotional Scripts that they created as children. Having lost their natural compass for staying on course, they have great difficulty creating a positive experience of life. They respond to life with the emotional patterns they created as children, regardless of what may be present in their lives as adults.

Piano

Softly, in the dusk, a woman is singing to me;
Taking me back down the vista of years, till I see
A child sitting under the piano, in the boom of the tingling strings
And pressing the small, poised feet of a mother who smiles as she sings.

In spite of myself, the insidious mastery of song
Betrays me back, till the heart of me weeps to belong
To the old Sunday evenings at home, with winter outside
And hymns in the cozy parlor, the tinkling piano our guide.

So now it is vain for the singer to burst into clamor
With the great black piano appassionato. The glamor
Of childish days is upon me, my manhood is cast
Down in the flood of remembrance, I weep like a child for the past.

— *D.H. Lawrence*

From the earliest age most of us had our feelings — of curiosity, excitement, joy, fear, sadness, and, especially, self-protective anger — shamed. In order to defend against the painful feeling of shame, we learned to numb our feelings.
John Bradshaw

When you take full responsibility here and now for all of your feelings and for everything that happens to you, you never again blame the people and situations in the world outside of you for any unhappy feelings that you have.
Ken Keyes

Take responsibility for your inner experience

One day a student named Angela came to my office and exploded, "Doesn't Paul make you furious? He's always coming to class late. Then he wanders around looking for a seat, making all that noise so we can't even hear. He bangs his chair against the desk; then he drops his books on the floor. When he finally gets seated, he keeps turning the pages in his notebook . . . what is he looking for, anyway? Every time I say something in class, he groans and rolls his eyes like I'm some sort of moron. He's ruining the class for me!"

As Angela saw it, Paul was to blame for her discomfort in the class. But was he? In fact, other students in the class were unaffected by Paul's behavior. Some probably hadn't even noticed it. Believing as she did that Paul was *making* her feel bad, Angela was responding to his behavior as a Victim. Victims say, "**He** makes me furious . . . **He** infuriates me . . . **He's** ruining the class for me." Victims believe they have no control over their inner experience. Their happiness exists at the mercy of outside forces.

Creators understand that outside forces do not *make* them feel a particular emotion. Rather, it is their *perception* of what is going on outside of them that creates their inner experience. In other words, a person's choice as to how to view a particular event creates his or her inner experience.

This is great news, especially if you're having a lousy day or a lousy life. If you can cause gloom in your heart, you can make the sun shine as well. Psychologists have discovered that when you change your behaviors or your thoughts, you change your emotions as well. And when you change your emotions, you change the quality of your inner experience.

Perhaps you doubt that you can choose a positive experience of life. Consider, then, the extraordinary experience of Viktor E. Frankl. Frankl, a psychiatrist, was imprisoned in the Nazi concentration camps during World War II. In his book *Man's Search for Meaning,* Frankl relates how he and a few of the other prisoners were able to rise above their unspeakable suffering to create a more positive inner experience.

In one example, Frankl tells of a particularly bleak day when he was falling into deep despair. With terrible sores on his feet, he was forced to march many miles in bitter cold weather to a work site. There, freezing and weak from starvation, he endured the constant brutality of the guards as he worked. Frankl describes how he "forced" his thoughts to turn to another subject. In his mind he imagined himself "standing on the platform of a well-lit, warm and pleasant lecture room." Before him sat an audience pleased to hear him give a lecture on the psychology of the concentration camp. "By this method," Frankl says, "I succeeded somehow in rising above the situation, above the sufferings of the moment, and I observed them as if they were already of the past."

From his experiences and his observations, Frankl concluded that everything can be taken from a person but one thing: "the last of the human freedoms — to choose one's attitude in any given set of circumstances, to choose one's own way."

In this chapter, we will test the commonly held belief that outside circumstances control our emotions. We will explore how to choose the thoughts and attitudes that will help to create a positive experience of life. Heed the feedback you will encounter in your journals and perhaps you will discover a more empowering belief. We will begin by honoring the wisdom of our emotions.

Journal #32

In this journal entry, you'll have an opportunity to explore your present emotional patterns. Look for emotional patterns that support your inner and outer success, as well as those that do not. As you become more conscious of your emotional patterns, you will be better able to choose ones that support your creation of a positive experience of life.

1. Write an exploration of your past and present emotional life.

As you write, become conscious of your Scripts about emotions. Look especially for patterns of emotions that you automatically fall into when you aren't getting what you want in life. This exploration of emotional patterns is another major step toward revising the outcome of your life from the inside out.

Before writing, list some Creator questions that you can explore. For example . . .

- What am I feeling right now?
- What emotions show up most often as patterns in my life?
- What emotions are rare in my life?
- What was the primary emotion in my family as I was growing up?
- What emotions were absent in my family?
- How was I treated as a child when I expressed a particular emotion?
- How comfortable am I with the primary emotions of anger, fear, sadness, happiness?
- What other emotions such as guilt, resentment, shame, and contentment, show up in my life?
- Which of my emotions do I trust, which do I distrust?
- What are the emotions that I commonly feel in college? In relationships? On my job?
- Do I seek out or avoid situations where I may have an emotional reaction?
- How well do my emotional patterns currently serve me to stay on course?
- What changes would I like to make in my emotional life?

You needn't answer all of these questions to create an accurate examination of your emotional life. Rather, answer the questions that reveal the dominant emotional patterns in your life. Feel free to add your own Creator questions in addition to or instead of these questions.

Relax, think, and write.

People are about as happy as they make up their mind to be.
Abraham Lincoln

focus questions

Are you having a positive or negative experience today? This week? This life? Do you know how to create a more positive experience inside you no matter what is going on outside you?

■ ■ ■ ■ 33. **Choosing the Content of Your Consciousness**

There is nothing either good or bad, but thinking makes it so.
William Shakespeare

The mind is its own place, and in itself can make heaven of Hell, a hell of Heaven.
John Milton

A Zen parable tells about a monk who was walking along a thousand-foot cliff when he encountered a ferocious tiger. Acting quickly, the monk grabbed hold of a thin vine, swung himself off the cliff, and slid down a dozen feet. Dangling high above the dark and jagged rocks below, the monk looked up to see the snarling tiger poised hungrily at the edge of the cliff. Then the monk felt a strange vibration in his hands. Looking up, he saw a mouse chewing the vine. The monk looked at the hungry tiger, then at the waiting rocks below, then back at the mouse. He shook the vine, but the mouse kept on chewing. Then the monk noticed a small plant growing out of a crevice in the cliff. On the plant was one large, luscious red strawberry. The monk reached out a hand and picked it. Then he placed it in his mouth, savoring the wonderful sweetness of the fruit.

This parable beautifully illustrates the options available to us when we encounter adversity. First, we should take every possible action to improve our external conditions: The monk slid down the vine to escape the tiger; next he shook the vine to scare off the chewing mouse. In short, he did what he could to better his outer circumstances.

Sometimes, however, we can do nothing more to improve our external conditions. At that point, many people sink into despair. But we have another choice. Even in the midst of overwhelming adversity, we can choose the content of our consciousness. We can choose what we will think about: When a hungry tiger waits above and deadly rocks wait below, and a hungry mouse is chewing on our vine, we can still focus our attention on a delicious strawberry.

Cognitive psychologists suggest that our thoughts about an experience determine how we feel about it. If I think, *I'm being treated unfairly,* I'll create the inner experience of anger. If I think, *I'm in danger,* I'll create the inner experience of fear. If I think, *I have lost someone dear to me,* I'll create the inner experience of sadness.

What is actually happening in the outer world, then, is less important than what I *tell* myself is happening. If I change my thoughts about an event, I will change my emotional state of mind. In other words, **what I think about a problem is the problem.**

This view suggests a fascinating possibility. What if happiness is a choice? What if many of your negative experiences in life are simply the result of self-defeating thought patterns and limiting beliefs? What if you could create a more positive experience of life simply by choosing to think about events in a different, more positive way?

When you have done all you can to deal with life's challenges — the hungry tigers, deadly rocks, and gnawing mice — you still can choose your attitude. Here are six ways to choose the strawberry.

Find the Opportunity in a Problem: I was once talking to two fashion design majors about their career choice. The first student said, "I hate fashion design. There's too much competition." The second student said, "You're right! There *is* a lot of competition, and I love it! Competition makes me work even harder to do my best. It's the competition that's going to make me a success in fashion design." Same facts, different interpretation. One student sees a problem; another sees an opportunity. When you face a problem, ask yourself, "What's great about this? What's the opportunity here?"

But, you may object, *what about a heartbreaking loss like the death of someone I love? Simply changing the way I think about my "problem" will not make it go away!* Your objection, of course, is correct. Your loss will never "go away." It is both natural and essential that you fully honor your loss, express-

If you are pained by external things, it is not they that disturb you, but your own judgment of them. And it is in your power to wipe out that judgment now.

Marcus Aurelius

[W]e could say that most men in a concentration camp believed that the real opportunities of life had passed. Yet, in reality, there was an opportunity and a challenge. One could make a victory of those experiences, turning life into an inner triumph, or one could ignore the challenge and simply vegetate, as did a majority of prisoners.

Dr. Viktor E. Frankl

ing the depth of sadness you feel. Your grieving process may go on for a long while, but at some point you will need to make a choice: You can stay in your grief or, without forgetting your loss, you can decide to move on to a more positive experience of life. You can do this by making some changes in the way you see your loss. A woman in one of my classes shared that her son had died of AIDS. After grieving his death for more than a year, she decided to become a nurse so that she could care for the children of other mothers. This compassionate woman had not forgotten her son or her sadness; rather, she had found a beautiful life mission that was destined to bring comfort to many other grieving mothers. Creators like this woman assume that they can find some good in even their most painful life circumstances.

Focus on the Positive: In the 1980s, American Benjamin Weare was held hostage in Lebanon. For the first six months he was kept blindfolded and chained to a radiator. Then his blindfold was removed, but he remained chained to the radiator for ten more months. When Weare was finally released after sixteen months of being chained to a radiator, he was asked how he had endured his imprisonment. He explained that every day he had run his fingers along the chain that bound him, and, with every link, he reminded himself of one positive thing in his life.

Focusing on the positive doesn't mean ignoring reality. It means that you identify the problem and do what you can to improve your situation, but when there's nothing more you can do, you turn your attention to what's positive in your life.

Reflect on your present blessing, of which every man has many; not on your past misfortunes, of which all men have some.
Charles Dickens

Choose What You Allow In Your Mind: Whatever you invite into your mind each day becomes the content of your consciousness. What television shows and movies do you watch? What books do you read? What music do you listen to? What people do you associate with? What conversations do you participate in? These choices will greatly influence your positive or negative experience of life.

Ask Positive Questions: Change your question and you change your focus. Change your focus and you change the quality of your inner experience. Victims often ask negative questions such as *Why does everything always go wrong in my life?*

Creators ask positive questions such as *What can I learn from this problem? What's perfect about this difficulty? What will I do differently next time? What's great about my life right now?*

Appreciate Your Blessings: Be grateful for what you have rather than upset by what you don't have. I once taught a Vietnamese man who wrote a heartfelt essay about his experiences of growing up near Saigon during the Vietnam War. I asked him to read his essay to our class. He graphically related the terror of daily bombings, his aching hunger because of the scarcity of food, his grief at watching people — including his younger sister — die all around him, and his constant fear that he might not survive the day. After he had finished reading his essay, silence enveloped the classroom. Finally a woman said, "I thought I had it bad growing up on the streets of New York. Compared to you, I was blessed."

Choose Positive Self-Talk: Psychologist Albert Ellis believes that many negative emotions are the result not so much of what happens to us as what he labels **"stinkin' thinkin'."** Stinkin' thinkin' causes people to feel depressed and helpless. These negative emotions often lead to self-defeating actions or to no actions at all. As a result, people wander off course. Then a negative cycle has been created: negative thoughts lead to negative emotions, which lead to negative behaviors, which cause negative outcomes, which reinforce the negative emotions, . . . and so it goes around and around. This self-defeating pattern is one reason why people with negative self-talk seldom achieve their potential.

An experiment by Martin Seligman with three hundred freshmen at the University of Pennsylvania shows how self-talk affects college grades. Before the semester began, college personnel predicted each student's future grade point average based upon their Scholastic Aptitude Test (SAT) scores and high school grades. Seligman also tested each of these incoming freshman to determine if their self-talk was optimistic or pessimistic. Later, Seligman found that students who earned grades significantly better than predicted used optimistic self-talk, whereas students who earned grades significantly below their predicted scores used pessimistic self-talk. These results are consistent with other studies that show optimistic people doing better than pessimistic people not only in school, but at work, in sports, and even in politics.

The critical moment of choice in self-talk comes immediately after an undesirable event: What do you tell yourself is the cause of the problem? Pessimists, as we noted in our discussion of failure, explain problems as being **permanent, pervasive,** and **personal.** We can make valuable use of this awareness as we encounter any negative experience. By way of illustration, imagine what you might say to yourself after the following undesirable experience: You go to a scheduled appointment with your sociology teacher to review a research paper that you're working on, but he isn't there. You wait half an hour, but he never shows up. First, listen for pessimistic thoughts about the **permanence** of the adversity: *I'll never be able to get help from this teacher; he's never around.* Second, listen for pessimistic thoughts about the **pervasiveness** of the adversity, comments that suggest that this particular problem overflows into other areas of your life: *No one cares about other people's problems any more.* And third, listen for pessimistic thoughts about the **personal nature** of the problem, thoughts that irrationally make the problem your fault: *He doesn't want to help me because I'm not as smart as other students.*

These sorts of pessimistic explanations are seldom based on reality. More likely, your stinkin' thinkin' reveals the self-defeating thoughts and limiting beliefs that make up part of your outdated Scripts. As such, these statements simply voice the automatic comments of your Inner Defender and Inner Critic.

Once you recognize your pessimistic self-talk, the next step is to prove it wrong. Your Inner Guide can use any or all of the following approaches to dispute stinkin' thinkin':

- Prove the accusations wrong by offering contrary evidence: *In fact, my sociology teacher called me last week to see if I needed help with my research paper, so I guess he doesn't dislike me.*
- Offer a positive explanation for the problem: *He may have had a last-minute crisis, so he couldn't stay to meet with me.*
- Question the importance of the problem: *Even if it's true that he's never around, I can still go to the Writing Center to get help.*
- Offer a practical plan of action to solve the problem: *It's true that I haven't been good in sociology up until now. But, I'm going to read my assignments two or three times, attend every class, take good notes, and create a study team. I'm determined to improve my work in sociology.*

Think of what you would do if you were on trial for a crime that you didn't commit. How would you prove the accusations wrong? What would you say to counter the irrational charges leveled against you by the prosecution? In a like manner, transform your Inner Guide into a world-class lawyer and have it dispute your own Inner Critic's prosecution of you.

If all else fails, you can simply distract yourself from your negative thoughts. When you find yourself obsessing on negative thoughts, simply tell yourself, "STOP!" Then replace your negative thoughts with something positive: watch a funny movie, tell a joke, recall your goals and dreams, think about someone you love.

The next time something unpleasant happens in your life, remind yourself that you are in charge of what you choose to think. You can let your automatic, negative thoughts stay. Or you can evict them. As a Creator, you are responsible for the content of your consciousness. And the content of your consciousness determines the quality of your inner experience of life.

Journal #33

In this journal entry, you'll have an opportunity to practice choosing the content of your consciousness. When you learn to choose the quality of your thoughts, you will greatly improve your ability to create a positive experience of life.

To focus your mind, think of a recent problem (adversity) that you have encountered, one about which you feel bad.

1. Write a dialogue between your Inner Critic (IC) and your Inner Guide (IG).

Let your Inner Critic find fault with you for your recent problem or adversity. Let its comments represent the kind of criticism that you might automatically think as you explain the cause of a problem to yourself. Being a true pessimist,

It's your thoughts and only yours that are making you feel terrible; you're the only person in the world who can effectively persecute yourself.
Dr. David Burns

*It is the mind that maketh good or ill,
That maketh wretch or happy, rich or poor.*
Edmund Spenser

© Chronicle Features, 1982

"You know, we're just not reaching that guy."

Larson 7-4   ©Chronicle Features, 1986

"I hate this place."

your Inner Critic should make comments that describe the problem as permanent, pervasive, and personal.

Let your Inner Guide dispute the stinkin' thinkin' of your Inner Critic. Do that by countering each criticism with a rebuttal that

- proves the criticism wrong by offering contrary evidence.
- offers a different explanation for the problem.
- questions the importance of the problem.
- offers a practical plan of action to solve the problem.

For example, the beginning of your dialogue might sound like this:

IC: *Well, your son got suspended from school today. That certainly proves that you're a lousy parent.* (The problem is personal.)

IG: *It's true that Robert was expelled from school today, but I don't see how that proves that I'm a lousy parent. In fact, my older two children never had any problem with school. Both of them are doing well in college today.* (Offers contrary evidence.)

IC: *Not only is Robert getting in trouble, but you have dozens of unpaid bills. Your whole life is falling apart.* (Your problems are pervasive; they are everywhere.)

Choosing the Content of Your Consciousness ■ **175**

IG: *Well, it's true that I do have bills to pay, but I just got a raise at work, and if I budget well I can have my bills paid off by the end of the year.* (Offers a practical plan of action to solve the problem.)

IC: *This is the second time that Robert has been suspended. He's going to be a heartache to you for the rest of your life.* (The problem is permanent; it will never go away.)

And so on.

2. Write a paragraph (or more) about what you have learned while exploring the content of your consciousness. Don't forget to anticipate and answer your readers' questions.

Relax, think, and write.

focus questions

What important action have you been postponing? What old grudge are you hanging onto? What would happen to the quality of your inner experience of life if you performed that important action or released that old grudge?

■ ■ ■ ■ 34. Resolving Incompletions

Why don't you tell Paul how you feel?" I asked my student, Angela, after she'd told me how angry she was at her classmate.

"I don't know. . . . I don't think I should."

"But, Angela, you're furious at Paul. You said you're not enjoying the class. And my guess is that you're not learning much, either. If you don't tell Paul that you're angry, then who's *really* ruining the class for you?"

"Why don't *you* say something to him? You're the teacher."

"And you're the one who's angry. You're the one who'll benefit from leveling with him. Remember how we worked on I-messages? *Hey, Paul, when you come to class late and make a lot of noise, I lose my concentration and I get angry. Would you be willing to be more quiet?* Maybe Paul doesn't even realize that he's bothering you."

"I don't know. . . . Couldn't you just say something to Paul without mentioning me?"

I wasn't surprised at Angela's reluctance to express her anger. She was a quiet, meek person whose whole manner cried out, *Go ahead, step on me. I won't do anything about it.*

She had an opportunity here to do something different, to revise her self-defeating emotional pattern. By expressing her anger, she could not only solve this particular problem, she could also learn how to express her anger in other situations where she felt violated. Instead, she chose to say nothing to Paul, to simmer in her anger, to leave the issue incomplete.

Why do we have so much to learn about feelings? Part of the problem is the lack of education and practice. After all, compared to math and science, how many hours of your schooling were devoted to teaching you about your feelings and how to express them?

Gay and Kathlyn Hendricks

But, something within the human mind hates an incompletion. The mind wants to create a **gestalt** — an experience of wholeness, of completion. Think of each of your incompletions as a burden that your mind carries as you move through life. Carrying one or two small burdens is relatively easy. But add a few more incompletions, especially some big ones, and great amounts of energy are necessary to lug them through your daily activities. If the incompletions are big enough or numerous enough, they may take so much energy that you have none left over to live a positive life.

Angela's pent up anger toward Paul needed completion or it would continue to drain her of positive energy. Every time she came to class, the heavy burden of her unexpressed anger weighed down on her. Your incompletions will do the same to you. Consequently, an effective way to bring more positive energy to your life is to identify and resolve your incompletions.

Outer-world completions

You may be draining your positive emotions by leaving something undone in your outer world. Stop procrastinating and turn your positive energy loose. Do something to resolve your incompletions!

Here are some examples of incompletions that can exist in different areas of life. Check areas where you have incompletions. You'll have an opportunity to address them further in your journal entry.

- [ ] **Relationships:** You're hanging onto a bad relationship, you owe someone an apology, you're keeping a painful secret, you're withholding telling someone how you feel.
- [ ] **Work:** An important project remains undone, you're still waiting to receive a raise that was promised you months ago, you haven't asked a colleague to help you and you know you need the help, your desk or work area is disorganized, you're hiding a mistake you made.
- [ ] **College:** You have important assignments that you haven't completed, you're avoiding a required course, you keep postponing applying for the financial aid that you need, you haven't studied for an upcoming test, you're confused in a class and you haven't asked the teacher for help, you're behind in your reading.
- [ ] **Health:** You keep ignoring a pain in your body, you continue with an addiction you've been promising yourself to quit, you keep putting off losing the weight that bothers you, you postpone starting an exercise program, you keep using eyeglasses that don't help your vision any more.
- [ ] **Finances:** You keep stacking unpaid bills on your desk, your financial records remain horribly disorganized, you keep postponing the creation of a budget, you hope the IRS won't notice your unpaid back taxes, you find out that you overpaid a bill and do nothing to recover your money,

---

Harlem (A Dream Deferred)

What happens to a dream deferred?
Does it dry up
like a raisin in the sun?
Or fester like a sore —
And then run?
Does it stink like rotten meat?
Or crust and sugar over
like a syrupy sweet?

Maybe it just sags
like a heavy load.

Or does it explode?

— Langston Hughes

If you can't sleep, then get up and do something instead of lying there and worrying.
Dale Carnegie

Nothing so fatiguing as the eternal hanging on of an uncompleted task.
William James

you put off resolving a bad credit rating you got years ago, your check-book remains unbalanced.

☐ **Possessions:** For months now your car has been hard to start in the morning, every time you enter your bedroom you notice that it needs painting, a faucet has been dripping for more than a year, you have a closet full of clothes that you never wear.

☐ **Dreams:** You've stopped taking actions on one of your most important dreams.

Nagging incompletions such as these will spoil your inner experience of life. The solution: move into Quadrant II. Take an action that is important and yet not urgent. I recall three incompletions in particular that caused me long-term distress. In each case, I had sunk into a dark mood, yet I resisted making a positive choice for months or even years. When I finally acted, my experience of life improved dramatically. One time I ended a relationship that had been empty and unfulfilling for more than two years; another time I quit a job that paid well but which I hated; a third time I stopped postponing my dream and sat down to write this book. As soon as I took these positive actions, I got back on course to what I truly wanted, and my mood immediately lightened.

Inner-world completions

Some incompletions can't be resolved with an external action. You may have exhausted every outer-world action you can think of to resolve these nagging situations, with no success. You have still another choice. You can decide to complete these experiences inside of you.

Perhaps you resent a teacher for failing you, or a parent for abusing you, or a friend for betraying you, or a brother for stealing from you, or an employer for firing you, or a spouse for cheating on you. In each circumstance, you have a choice. You can listen to the blaming and criticizing of your Inner Defender while you righteously hold onto your resentments toward others, or you can listen to your Inner Guide and courageously let go of your judgments.

If you decide to relinquish your judgments, the key is **forgiveness.** You hold the power to forgive others for the crimes you perceive them to have committed against you, to close the case in your mind, and to move on.

Wait just a minute, you may object, *I can't forgive what they did to me. I was deeply wronged. I really was victimized. They don't **deserve** to be forgiven for the horrible things they did to me!*

This argument misses the point of forgiveness. The question is not whether *they* deserve forgiveness, the question is whether *you* deserve the benefits of forgiveness. The reason for forgiveness is primarily to improve *your* life, not theirs. You are the one who is poisoned daily with your own resentment. In many cases, the other people don't even know about your resentment — and even if they do, they may not even care. No, we don't end our prosecution to free others. We close the case to free ourselves of the heavy burden of judgments.

Oh, no, you may counter, *I can't forget what was done to me. I could get my-self right back in that same situation. Then I'd have to go through all that pain again!*

Again, not the point. Forgiveness is not forgetting. You learn from your experience, and you take every precaution to prevent its recurrence. Then, you forgive and move on.

Well, that might be fine for others, comes a rebuttal, *but I've been so terribly wronged that in my case forgiveness is impossible!* Then consider Zalinda Dorcheus. In his book *One Person Can Make a Difference,* Gerald Jampolsky tells the story of Ms. Dorcheus, whose son was shot to death by a man named Michael. After years of bitterness, Zalinda Dorcheus forgave Michael. She even assisted him to earn parole, escorting him out of prison when he was released.

"I was destroying myself through my hate and bitterness," Dorcheus explained. "My body was falling apart, and it seemed to me that all the hate inside me was attacking my own body. . . . My forgiveness was as much for me as it was for Michael. It was the only way I could survive." Through the inner completion provided by her forgiveness, Zalinda Dorcheus was able to rescue her life from negativity.

To be candid, I don't know that I could forgive a person who killed someone I love, but Zalinda Dorchcus' extraordinary example certainly makes it seem more possible to forgive lesser offenses.

Most people hold judgments not only against others but against themselves as well. Their Inner Critic eloquently condemns them for their mistakes, failures, and personal defects. If we listen to the nonstop criticism of our Inner Critic, we will be racked with guilt, shame, and inferiority, hardly the ingredients of a positive experience of life.

Unrelenting self-judgment only burdens us with negative emotions that linger long after our lesson could have been learned. Self-forgiveness is the antidote to self-judgments. I can forgive myself for my actions, thoughts, or emotions that led to mistakes or failures: *I forgive myself for losing my temper with my boss and getting fired.* I can also forgive myself for the judgments I held against myself that brought me pain: *I forgive myself for judging myself as a horrible person for getting fired.* Self-forgiveness is not an excuse to repeat a mistake or an undesirable behavior. Rather, self-forgiveness releases me from the pain I am creating in the present and frees me to move into the future with greater understanding and compassion for myself.

Forgiveness is a sign of positive mental health. Victims look backwards with judgment to a painful past they cannot change. Creators forgive so they can move forward to a positive future unburdened by resentment and negative judgments. What is stopping you from moving into forgiveness? What would your life be like if you stopped judging yourself or others? What if you learned the lesson of your grievance but let go of the grievance itself? What if you were no longer bound to the past by negative judgments of yourself and others?

For that matter, what if you were no longer bound to the past by any incomplete business in your life? How much would you improve your positive experience of life if you resolved all of your incompletions, both in the world and in your heart?

[T]he evidence is overwhelming that if we can learn to understand and forgive ourselves, our behavior tends to improve. However, if we remain relentlessly self-condemning, our behavior (like our self-esteem) tends to worsen.

Nathaniel Brandon

Living life as an art requires a readiness to forgive.

Maya Angelou

Journal #34

In this journal entry, you'll have an opportunity to explore areas of your life where incompletions exist. You can then decide which, if any, you want to resolve. Each time you resolve an incompletion, you lay down a burden that you have been carrying. You feel lighter and your energy is freed to create a more positive experience of life.

1. Write a list of incompletions that exist in your outer world. These are things you need to do but have been postponing. To jog your thoughts, refer back to the text for examples of common outer-world incompletions.

2. Choose one of your most energy-draining incompletions (from Step 1). Write a paragraph (or more) that presents your plan to resolve this incompletion.

To resolve this incompletion, don't forget the possibility of using some of the strategies you have learned in earlier journals. For example, you may wish to schedule an action in your written self-management plan. Or you may wish to make a thirty-two-day commitment to begin nibbling away at a large incompletion.

3. Write the following pair of sentence stems ten or more times.

I RESENT _____ FOR. . . .

I FORGIVE _____ FOR. . . .

Each time you write the pair of sentences, fill in both blanks with the name of the same person (someone in your life, including yourself). For example . . .

I RESENT my father FOR running out on our family.
I FORGIVE my father FOR running out on our family.

I RESENT myself FOR dropping out of college.
I FORGIVE myself FOR dropping out of college.

You may use the same person for as many pairs of sentences as you wish.

4. Write a letter of forgiveness to one of the people you mentioned in Step 3.

Tell the person fully what he or she did that you resent and how you felt about it. Offer the person your forgiveness. Don't overlook the possibility of writing a letter of forgiveness to yourself. You can choose to lay down the burden of your judgments forever.

Relax, think, and write.

What are you doing when you feel most happy and alive . . . when you become so absorbed that time seems to disappear? How can you create more of these peak experiences in your life?

■ ■ ■ ■ 35. Creating Flow

When you study people who are successful as I have over the years, it is abundantly clear that their achievements are directly related to the enjoyment they derived from their work. They enjoy it in large part because they are good at it.

Marsha Sinetar

For centuries, explorers of human nature have wondered: How do people create periods of natural happiness and peace of mind? Psychologist Mihaly Csikszentmihalyi has called these highly positive periods of time **flow states.** His studies offer insights about how we can consciously choose happiness.

Csikszentmihalyi believes that the key to creating flow lies in the interaction of two factors in consciousness: the challenge a person *perceives* himself to be facing and the related skills he *perceives* himself to possess. Note that the inner experience is created by the person's *perception* of both the challenge and his skill level. Once again, we're reminded that the quality of our inner experience is dependent upon what we *believe* to be true.

Let's consider examples of three possible relationships of skill level and degree of challenge. First, when a person's perceived skill level is higher than the perceived challenge, the resulting state of consciousness is **boredom:** Imagine how bored you'd feel if you took an introductory course in a subject in which you were already an expert.

Second, when a person's perceived skill level is lower than that needed to meet the perceived challenge, the resulting emotional state is **anxiety:** Imagine how anxious you'd feel if you took an advanced mathematics course before you could even add and subtract.

Third, when both the individual's perceived skill level and the perceived challenge are about equal, the inner experience is one of **flow:** Imagine one of those extraordinary moments when you lost yourself in the flow — maybe writing a challenging essay about a subject you had researched thoroughly, or playing a sport you love with a well-matched opponent. A few years back, the Phoenix Suns beat the Chicago Bulls in triple overtime during the National Basketball Association Championships. Some observers called it the greatest professional basketball game ever played.

CREATING FLOW

Skill level HIGH — Challenge level LOW = Boredom

Skill level LOW — Challenge level HIGH = Anxiety

Skill level and Challenge level EQUAL = Flow

Never continue in a job you don't enjoy. If you're happy in what you're doing, you'll like yourself, you'll have inner peace. And if you have that, along with physical health, you will have had more success than you could possibly have imagined.

Johnny Carson

Afterwards, Charles Barkley of the Suns said that he'd been so involved in playing that whether his team won or lost became irrelevant. Barkley was describing the feeling of flow. **In flow, participating in the activity is its own reward — the outcome doesn't matter.**

Activities with certain qualities, according to Csikszentmihalyi, are likely to create a flow experience:

• These activities have specific goals and clear rules about how to achieve the goals.

- The challenge in these activities can be adjusted up or down to match our skill level.
- They offer us clear feedback about how we're doing.
- These activities have the capacity to screen out distractions and therefore maximize our absorption in them.

Violinist Nadja Salerno-Sonneberg has found her source of flow in creating music. "Playing in the zone is a phrase that I use to describe a certain feeling on stage, a heightened feeling where everything is right," she says. "By that I mean everything comes together. Everything is one . . . you, yourself, are not battling yourself. All the technical work and what you want to say with the piece comes together. It's very, very rare but it's what I have worked for all my life. It's just right. It just makes everything right. Nothing can go wrong with this wonderful feeling."

To paraphrase the words of philosopher Joseph Campbell, flow occurs when you follow your bliss.

Work and flow

Get happiness out of your work or you may never know what happiness is.
Elbert Hubbard

When do you suppose a typical working American experiences the most flow? After work? On the weekends? On vacations? If these are your guesses, you'll be surprised by what Csikszentmihalyi found: typical working adults report experiencing flow on their jobs three times more often than during free time.

If you want to create a positive experience of life, engage in work that appeals to your natural inclination, your inborn desires. It's hard to be depressed when you wake up every morning excited about your day's work. It's hard to be excited if you don't love the challenge.

Carolyn, a twenty-year-old student, was often gloomy. She was studying to be a nurse, but that was the career her mother wanted for her. Carolyn's dream was to dance.

Part of us — perhaps our Inner Defender — will do anything to keep the peace, to stay safe, to make things a little more pleasant in the moment. "If I even mention dancing, my mother goes off," Carolyn confided. "It's not worth it to fight her."

Do you know that disease and death must needs overtake us, no matter what we are doing? . . . What do you wish to be doing when it overtakes you? . . . If you have anything better to be doing when you are so overtaken, get to work on that.
Epictetus

Another more spirited part of us — probably our Inner Guide — hangs onto our dreams. That spirit urges us to strive for what we truly love.

Which part will you heed? It's an important choice. Remember, responsibility is the ability to meet your own needs without interfering with the needs of others. There was no one depending on Carolyn but Carolyn. She had responsible options besides giving up her dream. She could drop out of college and get a job to pay her bills while pursuing her dancing career. She could complete her nursing degree and then work as a nurse while pursuing her dancing career. Neither choice would interfere with her mother's life, and both would responsibly move Carolyn toward her dream.

The last time I saw Carolyn (about a year after our conversation about her dream of dancing), I asked her what she was doing.

"I'm still in nursing," she said.

"Any dancing in your life?"

"I've sort of stopped thinking about that."

As best I could tell, Carolyn had abandoned her bliss.

Have you? Let's revisit your written goals and dreams. Are you headed for a career that represents your bliss? Is this the work that you would choose if you had absolutely no restrictions? Do you love this work enough to do it for free?

For the next couple of decades at least, you'll probably spend more than one third of your waking hours at work. Needless to say, your career choice will greatly affect the quality of your inner experience of life. You don't have to settle for just a paycheck. You can do what you love.

I spent more than a year doing work I disliked, and I know how quickly my inner experience turned sour. I woke up many mornings with a stomachache. I lived for weekends, but by Sunday afternoon I began to dread Monday morning. Finally, I heeded my depression and sought work where I was happy. I urge you — follow your bliss. This may require self-discipline to get you through the education or training necessary to qualify you to do what you love. This choice of experiencing short-term pain for long-term pain, you will recall, is the essence of mature decision making.

Play and flow

What do you do when you're not working? People who successfully create a positive experience of life have a knack for having fun. They stay connected to the little kid inside of them. They make time to play.

Effective self-management includes planning time for recreation. True **re-creation** is a Quadrant II activity and deserves time in your weekly written plan. Schedule time to go dancing, play basketball, learn a new computer game, play an instrument, watch a movie, play cards, ride a horse, go shopping, plant a garden, put together a puzzle. . . . What do you love to do?

Be open to spontaneous play as well. Tell a joke at lunch. Skip along the sidewalk between classes. Crawl around the floor with a baby. Go to a matinee. Call a friend you haven't talked to in years and talk like Donald Duck.

Don't put off having fun because money is tight; play for free. Go to a park. Write a poem. Throw a frisbee. Play chess. Climb a mountain. Read a novel.

Notice what activity is missing in these lists of playful recreation: television. If you watch a lot of television, you should know what Csikszentmihalyi found in his study of flow. Students reported experiencing flow five times more often while doing homework than they did while watching TV. Television, he discovered, relaxes your mind, but it also lowers your alertness, mental focus, satisfaction, and creativity. Certainly there are entertaining and educational shows on television. But, the longer you watch television in one sitting, the more you become passive and the further you move away from experiencing flow.

One more point remains to be made about the benefits of creating flow in work and play. Not only does flow improve your inner experience, it promotes your professional and personal growth. Each time you test your present skills against a new challenge, your skills improve. To create flow the next time, you

Whatever you are by nature, keep to it; never desert your line of talent. Be what nature intended you for and you will succeed.

Sydney Smith

Angels can fly because they take themselves lightly.

G.K. Chesterton

[F]low activities lead to growth and discovery. One cannot enjoy doing the same thing at the same level for long. We grow either bored or frustrated; and then the desire to enjoy ourselves again pushes us to stretch our skill, or to discover new opportunities for using them.

Mihaly Csikszentmihalyi

need to increase the difficulty of the challenge, which, in turn, offers an opportunity to improve your skills once again. Over time, by creating flow, your skills of working and playing become world class, and this growth adds even more happiness to your life.

Journal #35

In this journal entry, you'll have an opportunity to explore how to create more flow in your life. The more flow you create day to day, the more positive will be your inner experience of life.

1. Write a list of activities that you love to do. These are the activities that have the potential to create flow in your life.

2. Write about work and flow in your life.

Think about past or present work experiences. Explore the inner states of consciousness (particularly boredom, anxiety, flow) that you experienced or are now experiencing on these jobs.

Then consider the work experiences that you have planned for your future: What sort of work are you preparing for in college? What do you honestly believe will be your inner experience of doing this work day after day . . . year after year? Is there some other career that you believe would create a more positive experience for you? Are there any changes you want to make in your career plans?

3. Write about play and flow in your life.

Recall times in your life in which you created a flow experience while playing. Describe the activity and your inner experience of it. What recreational activities have you never tried but think would give you a flow experience? What changes might you want to make in how you spend your recreational time?

What other Creator questions could you ask to more fully explore your relationship with work, play, and flow?

Relax, think, and write.

I think the foremost quality — there's no success without it — is really loving what you do. If you love it, you do it well, and there's no success if you don't do well what you're working at.

Malcolm Forbes

focus questions What hopeless desires are you holding on to that are causing you misery? What would happen to your inner experience of life if you simply let them go?

■ ■ ■ ■ 36. Developing Involved Detachment

If there's one thing we can count on in life, it is this: We won't achieve every goal and dream that we desire. Some disappointment is inevitable. The job I want goes to someone else. The person I love doesn't have the same feelings for me. The college course I need to pass I fail. The car I crave costs too much. The part I want in a play is won by another. The university I long to attend turns me down.

Even when we do get what we want, there's something else we can count on: What we have sometimes slips away.

I get fired from my job. My spouse divorces me. I flunk out of college. My health gives way to sickness. I cost my team a victory with a last-second mistake. My best friend moves to Europe. My business goes bankrupt.

That's the trouble with having goals and dreams, your Inner Defender complains. *When you don't get them, you feel miserable. Maybe the people who don't dream are the smart ones.*

To address this concern wisely requires a shift in perspective. Once again the issue that matters isn't what's going on *outside* us; rather, it's what's going on *inside* us. The pain we experience isn't caused by our pursuit of a goal or a dream. It's created by our attachment to the outcome. Even when we can't change what's going on outside us, we can still change what's going on inside us.

The way, then, to increase our positive experience of life isn't to give up dreaming. The way is to **develop involved detachment.** Pursue your goals and dreams with both total commitment to success and total detachment from results. How can this be? Think of the way a lioness stalks her prey. Crouched low, eyes focused, muscles twitching, her whole being concentrates on one goal. But what if she misses? Does she stand there depressed and miserable as the zebra scampers off? Does she spend days offering excuses, blaming the shifting wind, complaining that zebras don't play fair? Does she let that failure ruin her day? Her year? Her life? Hardly. A moment later she's got her eye on that antelope over there. *That's* involved detachment.

Here are five effective ways to develop involved detachment:

1. Focus on the Process, Not the Outcome. Your Inner Critic expects you to reach every goal, to achieve every dream. But your Inner Guide knows this truth: *All you can do is your best.* Consistently giving your best effort not only maximizes your chances of achieving your goals and dreams, it can also minimize your misery if you fail. You can only control what you can do. To expect any more is stinkin' thinkin'. When you've done all you can to achieve a goal, the outcome then belongs to destiny.

2. Maximize Your Options. The more choices you have in times of trouble, the happier you are likelier to be. With options in your life, you'll rarely be devastated by one blow of bad fortune. If you apply for one job and don't get it, you're set up for misery. If you apply for ten jobs and you don't get one, you still have nine other possibilities to lift your spirits. Another illustration of the value of seeing options occurred when I met a friend for lunch. He had been depressed for months after his wife left him for another man, but on this day he couldn't have been more cheerful.

"What gives?" I asked.

"I thought I'd never love again," he said. "But driving through town today, I started noticing how many beautiful women there are in the world. Suddenly, life is looking a whole lot brighter."

3. Change Addictions into Preferences.

Victims *have* to achieve a desired goal or dream in order to feel good. Like addicts, they allow for no other options. If they get exactly what they want, they are happy for the moment. If they don't get what they want, they are miserable. Creators have a healthier outlook. They certainly *prefer* to achieve their goals and dreams, but (like lions) they aren't going to sink into misery and depression if they don't. A Victim says, *I have to have a date for New Year's Eve.* A Creator says, *I'd prefer to have a date for New Year's Eve.* A Victim says, *I should have lost ten pounds last month.* A Creator says, *It would have been nice if I had lost ten pounds last month.* Don't misunderstand. These Creators are just as committed to their goals as are the Victims, but the Creators are far less addicted to a particular outcome. They know when to let go of an unattainable goal. As a result, their emotions remain far more balanced and much more positive.

4. Stop Pretending to Know What's Best.

We humans display a certain arrogance when we get upset at the way events turn out. How do we, with our limited perspective of life, pretend to know what's best? The truth is, what looks like a mistake, failure, or disaster today may very well be a blessing tomorrow. Haven't you had something "terrible" happen to you, then some time later said to yourself, "Thank goodness that happened or I wouldn't be where I am today"? In *The Road to Successful Living,* Louis Binstock tells a story about the American artist James McNeill Whistler that illustrates this idea perfectly. Young Mr. Whistler was a student at West Point preparing for a career as a soldier when his chemistry teacher asked him a question about silicon. Whistler stood and began his answer by saying, "Silicon is a gas." (It's not.) The teacher immediately told him to sit down. Only a few weeks later, Whistler was discharged from West Point, which must have greatly upset the young student. Years later, however, long after he had become a successful painter, Whistler enjoyed recalling his fateful mistake in chemistry class thusly: "If silicon had been a gas, I would have been a general." Whenever we appear off course from our present destination, we may, in fact, be on course to something even better. We just have to be willing to detach from our first desire and embrace something new that may be even better.

5. Accept, Learn, and Move On.

Being attached to an outcome we're unable to create brings on emotional distress. When you have unsuccessfully exhausted every option you can think of to achieve a goal, there are only three wise things to do: Accept what is, learn your lesson, and ask, "What's next?"

I saw this principle illustrated while waiting for a plane at Chicago's O'Hare Airport. Two men rushed up to a locked gate door. The taller of the men screamed at an airline employee, "Our connecting flight was late. Open the door and let us on the plane. We have to make that flight!"

"I'm sorry, but I can't do that, sir," the employee replied.

"I can see the plane," the shorter man said, looking out a window. "It's just sitting on the runway."

"I know, sir, but I'm not allowed to let you out there once the plane has de-

Addictions always cause unhappiness sooner or later. Preferences never do.

Ken Keyes

Always fall in with what you're asked to accept. Take what is given, and make it over your way. My aim in life has always been to hold my own with whatever's going. Not against: with.

Robert Frost

parted the docking area. I can get you on another flight that leaves in about an hour."

The taller man began screaming again, waving his umbrella all about. The shorter man looked out of the window at the plane, looked back at his companion who was shouting at the airline employee, shrugged his shoulders, sat down, and took out a book. For the next hour, the taller man hollered at one airline employee after another. Then, still red-faced with anger, he stormed aboard the next plane. The shorter man closed his book, stretched leisurely, and calmly boarded as well. Both men had achieved the same result, but clearly one, by accepting the reality of his situation, had created a much more pleasant experience for the hour they both had to wait.

The next time that life deals you a bad hand, remember that you always have a choice about how you respond. You can go into a fury about the unfairness. Or you can calmly accept your cards, play the hand as best you can, learn what you can, and then say, "Next."

When we learn to be totally involved in creating our goals and dreams yet totally detached from the outcomes, we have taken a major step toward creating a more positive experience of life.

Now it's time to combine all of the strategies in this chapter and see how we can create a more positive experience of our lives by changing our Scripts.

Revise your scripts about feelings

I once had a student named Bill, a man who wore a permanent scowl on his face. He seemed constantly angry, forever looking for a fight. Early in the semester, he protested that the homework assignments were too long. Later on, when I gave no assignment one day, he was furious that he wasn't getting the instruction he had paid for. He was angry that our class wasn't using a book that another teacher required, so I suggested that he was welcome to buy it in the college bookstore. He came back irate that the book was so expensive. Once, when another student cried while reading her journal out loud to a partner, he became enraged with me for "making her sad." It became apparent that Bill's automatic pattern was to respond to his discomfort with anger.

Simultaneously, a theme that constantly arose in Bill's journal was loneliness. He was baffled by one failed relationship after another. I told him that I experienced his constant anger as a barrier that kept me at a distance. I suggested that he might consider if his anger was scaring other people away as well. Angrily, he acknowledged that it was. Ironically, the anger pattern that Bill had probably created for protection as a child was now causing him a great deal of pain as an adult.

Suppose that, like Bill, we do become aware of a self-defeating emotional pattern in our Script. What can we do to revise it?

The initial step is to understand that we are each responsible for our own feelings. No one *makes* us feel a particular emotion. My emotions are coming from inside me, not from outside me. When I keep experiencing the same nega-

Be willing to have it so. Acceptance of what has happened is the first step to overcoming the consequences of any misfortune.

William James

The trick is to realize that after giving your best, there's nothing more to give. There's no shame in losing. As long as you gave it your best. Win or lose the game is finished. It's over. It's time to forget and prepare for the next one.

Sparky Anderson
Manager, Detroit Tigers

It is one of the most puzzling facts of life that we seem to keep repeating the same self-destructive patterns over and over.

Jeffrey E. Young
and Janet Klosko

tive emotion again and again, awareness of this self-defeating pattern alerts me to the probable existence of an old emotional wound that is still affecting my life. If I can rediscover that old wound, I may be able to revise the patterns or the core beliefs that the wound created.

I suggested that Bill track his emotional pattern of anger back to its source: When had he first felt this way in the past? What happened back then to contaminate his present emotional response? What past wound was his present pattern protecting him from reexperiencing?

Bill recalled being the smallest boy in his neighborhood, and he was always picked last for all the games. He remembered one day when one of the team captains said he'd rather pick no one than pick Bill. Bill got angry even as he pictured himself standing there alone watching everyone else play.

What we need to realize is that beneath our anger is almost always a painful wound that needs attention. Not surprisingly (given his pattern of anger), Bill refused to acknowledge the hurt he was feeling as he recalled this childhood rejection, but if you get in touch with some sadness as you rediscover an old wound, know that the feeling is perfectly natural. You might even experience some tears. This is appropriate, even helpful. Feeling the sadness allows you to become conscious of your past emotional wounds and offers you the opportunity to begin changing their influence on you as an adult. The tears can't harm you, but bottling them up within you for years can.

If I can track down an original painful event, I have various options for revising my Script. I can address the original pain and create a more supportive memory by . . .

> *The greatest discovery of my generation is that human beings, by changing the inner attitudes of their minds, can change the outer aspects of their lives.*
>
> William James

- vividly recalling the original scene unfolding not as it really happened but as I wish it had happened.
- adding my adult self to the scene to comfort and protect my child self as I wish someone had done years before in the original event.
- writing a letter to the other person(s) involved, telling them how hurt, angry, or afraid I was at what they said or did; then I can forgive them and resolve this incompletion in my emotional past.
- disputing the relevance of this old wound to my present life.

> *I learned many years ago that the genuinely happy people I meet are not happy because they have had only good fortune. I know that they are choosing their attitude.*
>
> Dr. Bernie Siegel

The intention of each of these approaches is to interrupt the outdated pattern of a present stimulus and my automatic emotional response from the past. If I can revise this self-defeating pattern, then I can free myself from reacting to a present event as if it were the past event. Instead, I can learn to pause for a second between a stimulus and my response, and in that pivotal moment I can make a conscious choice that will move me on course to creating a more positive experience of life.

Journal #36

In this journal entry, you'll have an opportunity to choose one of two options for your journal entry. You can choose to work on developing involved detachment or revising a part of your emotional Scripts. Either will support you to manage your emotions more effectively.

Unless your instructor tells you otherwise, write only one of the following two journal entries. It's your choice. Pick the one that you think will best assist you to create a more positive experience of life.

1. Write a journal entry in which you explore detaching from a situation that is now creating disappointment or emotional pain for you.

To focus your mind, take a few moments to consider a situation about which you are unhappy. This situation doesn't have to be your greatest problem in life. It can simply be something bothersome.

Remember that effective communication answers the important questions someone might have about your topic. Before writing, make a list of questions that you will answer in your journal entry. Use the four E's (Example, Experience, Explanation, Evidence) in answering your questions.

Wherever appropriate, apply any of the five strategies presented in the text to create involved detachment:

- Focus on the process, not the outcome
- Maximize your options
- Change addictions into preferences
- Stop pretending to know what's best
- Accept, learn, and move on

OR . . .

2. Write a letter to someone in your life who has caused you pain, shame, doubt, or fear about expressing your natural emotions.

This person might be a parent, grandparent, teacher, school principal, coach, brother, or sister . . . anyone who wounded your ability to express your feelings naturally (even someone who is now dead). In this letter, tell the person what he or she did, how it affected you, how you feel about it, and how you are over-coming this injury today. See if you can bring yourself to express forgiveness for this person's words or actions.

Relax, think, and write.

Chapter 9

■ ■ ■ ■ ■ ■ ■ ■ ■

The foundation for achieving both outer and inner success is my strong self-esteem. I am responsible for making choices that will increase my belief in myself.

Believing in Yourself ■ ■ ■ ■ ■ ■ ■ ■ ■ ■ ■

I am acceptable, capable, admirable, lovable, and valuable.

Successful Students . . .

1. . . . **develop self-acceptance,** appreciating themselves despite any perceived personal shortcomings.

2. . . . **develop self-confidence,** feeling capable of achieving their greatest goals and dreams.

3. . . . **develop self-respect,** trusting themselves to pursue their goals and dreams with integrity and honor.

4. . . . **develop self-love,** seeing themselves as unconditionally lovable.

5. . . . **rediscover their self-worth,** realizing that they are, and have always been, worthwhile and valuable just as they are.

Struggling Students . . .

1. . . . judge themselves as unacceptable because of too many faults or too few talents.

2. . . . judge themselves as incapable of creating what they want in life.

3. . . . judge themselves as undeserving of admiration for how they live their lives.

4. . . . judge themselves as undeserving of being loved, either by themselves or by others.

5. . . . judge themselves as unworthy and lacking value as a human being.

Do you realize that the foundation of your success is your self-esteem? Do you know how to raise your self-esteem?

37. Developing Self-Acceptance

Roland was in his forties when he enrolled in my English 101 class. He was a stocky, soft-spoken man who quickly displayed a wisdom born of considerable life experience. I was perplexed when the first two assignments passed without an essay from Roland.

Both times, he apologized profusely, promising to complete them soon. He didn't want to make excuses, he said, but he was stretched to his limit: He was working evenings in an insurance office, and during the day he took care of his two young sons while his wife worked. "Don't worry, though," he assured me, "I'll have an essay to you by Monday. I'm going to be the first person in my family to get a college degree. Nothing's going to stop me."

But Monday came, and Roland was absent. On a hunch, I looked up his academic record and found that he had taken English 101 twice before. I contacted his previous teachers. Both of them said that Roland had made many promises but had never written an essay.

I called Roland, and we made an appointment to talk later in the week. He didn't show up.

During the next class, I invited Roland into the hall while the class worked on a writing assignment.

"Sorry I missed our conference," Roland said. "I meant to call, but things have been piling up."

"Roland, let me be straight. I talked to your other teachers, and I know you never did any writing for them. I'd love to help you be the first person in your family to earn a college degree, but you need to take an action. You need to write an essay." Roland nodded silently. "C'mon, Roland, I believe you can do it. But I don't know if *you* believe you can do it. It's decision time. What do you say?"

"I'll have an essay for you on Friday."

I looked him in the eye, raising my eyebrows as a question mark.

"Really," he said.

I knew that no matter what Roland said, his actions would reveal his core beliefs about himself . . . or his courage to risk a new behavior despite his beliefs.

At the heart of our core beliefs about ourselves is the statement I AM. . . . How we complete that sentence profoundly affects the quality of our lives. Fortunately, some of us learned from our parents and other influential adults that we are acceptable, capable, admirable, lovable, and valuable — even when our behavior is less than ideal. Sadly, however, some of us learned that it's painful to be ourselves. Early on, we adapted to what we believed our parents and other important adults asked of us. We cleverly fashioned ourselves into the person we thought would please them the most and displease them the least. We dis-

Coaches, teachers, business people and their consultants all agree on one point: you've got to believe in yourself and your ability to realize your goals.

Bernie Zilbergeld
and Arnold Lazarus

The foundation of anyone's ability to cope successfully is high self-esteem. If you don't already have it, you can always develop it.

Virginia Satir

owned aspects of ourselves that seemed unacceptable to them. We lost confidence in the abilities that they appeared to criticize. We deserted values that seemed in conflict with theirs. We stopped loving ourselves because we thought they didn't love us. Bit by bit, we abandoned our birthright: our unshakable trust that *I am a worthwhile human being just as I am.*

In place of our lost self, we constructed a counterfeit I AM, a false self. Our false self hides the parts of us that we have rejected, deserted, abandoned. We may automatically smile, concealing a fuming anger within. Or we may always insist on being right, cloaking a self-doubt deep inside. Or, like Roland, we may routinely make excuses, disguising a fear that we're incapable of doing what we must do to achieve our dreams. It isn't that people like Roland don't have what it takes to stay on course. Rather, they don't *believe* they have what it takes; therefore, they act as if they don't.

Self-esteem is the high-octane fuel that propels you to your dreams. It is the product of the core beliefs you hold about yourself. Do you approve of yourself as you are, accepting your personal weaknesses along with your strengths? Do you believe that you are capable of achieving lofty goals and dreams? Do you believe that how you live your life is admirable? Do you trust that you are unconditionally lovable? Do you believe that you are a worthy and valuable person just the way you are today? To the extent that you doubt these qualities, your beliefs will make it difficult (if not impossible) for you to stay on course to a rich, full life. Low self-esteem minimizes your ability to make wise choices and sentences you to a life of unfulfilled promise.

The good news is that self-esteem is learned, so anyone can learn to raise his or her self-esteem. This chapter is about how we can do just that.

Know and accept yourself

People with low self-esteem often had parents who found many things about them to criticize. As a result, these children often grow up believing that they have qualities about themselves that are unacceptable. Worse, they may learn to believe at a core level that they themselves are unacceptable.

People with high self-esteem know that no one is perfect, and they accept themselves with both their strengths and their weaknesses. Accepting their weaknesses doesn't mean being content with them. To paraphrase Reinhold Neihbur, Creators accept the things they cannot change, have the courage to change the things they can change, and possess the wisdom to know the difference.

To know themselves, Creators are willing to take an honest self-inventory. They acknowledge their strengths without false humility, and they admit their weaknesses without stubborn denial. They tell the truth about themselves.

By contrast, Victims typically deny their weaknesses (and sometimes even their strengths). As a result, their realities often clash with the realities of those around them. The Victim believes he's gotten a raw deal from fate; the Creator knows he's merely avoiding his weaknesses by complaining, blaming, and making excuses.

*Once we come to believe that we **are** this false self, **we do not know that we do not know who we are.** . . . Once the false self is created, the authentic self is frozen in past time. . . . I called this frozen self the **wounded inner child.***
John Bradshaw

We cannot change anything unless we accept it.
Carl Jung

AS SMART AS HE WAS, ALBERT EINSTEIN COULD NOT FIGURE OUT HOW TO HANDLE THOSE TRICKY BOUNCES AT THIRD BASE.

Creators have the courage to admit their personal weaknesses and will work to improve what they can. To do so requires the ability to set a goal for change, the self-management skills to create a plan for change, the wisdom to heed feedback during change, and — most of all — the courage to change.

Self-esteem is the reputation we have with ourselves.
Nathaniel Brandon

The Friday after my talk with Roland, he turned in his first English 101 essay in three semesters. His writing showed great promise, and I told him so. I also told him I appreciated that he had let go of his excuse that he was too busy to take action on his dream. From then on, Roland turned in his essays on time. He met with me in conferences about his essays. He visited the writing lab, and he did grammar exercises to improve his editing skills. When the English 101 exams arrived, he passed easily.

A few years later, Roland called me. In the meantime, he had transferred to a four-year university and was now graduating with a 3.8 average. He was going on to graduate school to study urban planning. But what he most wanted me to know was that one of his professors had asked permission to use one of Roland's essays as a model of excellent writing. "You know," Roland said, "I'd still be avoiding writing if I hadn't accepted two things about myself: I was a little bit lazy and I was a whole lot scared. Once I admitted those things to myself, I knew I could change."

Each of us is a unique package of strengths and weaknesses. The way your Inner Defender sees them, your weaknesses are someone else's fault. The way your Inner Critic sees them, your weaknesses prove there's something unacceptable about you as a person. The way your Inner Guide sees them, some of your qualities keep you on course, some get you off course.

When you start seeing yourself through the objective eyes of your Inner Guide, you can stop judging yourself, start accepting yourself, begin to change yourself, and get back on course to a rich, full life.

Journal #37

In this journal entry, you'll have an opportunity to explore the reputation you have with yourself — your self-esteem. As you become aware of how you have or haven't believed in yourself in the past, you can discover ways to improve your self-esteem in the future. This exploration of your self-esteem is another major step toward creating total success in your life from the inside out.

1. Write a history of your self-esteem.

As you write this history, recall how you've typically felt about yourself. Look especially for patterns of negative and positive judgments about yourself. Before writing, you may wish to list some Creator questions to explore in this autobiography. For example . . .

- What are my personal strengths and weaknesses: mental, physical, emotional?
- What do other people say are my strengths and weaknesses?
- What weaknesses do I accept, which do I judge about myself?
- How confident am I about undertaking new challenges?
- How courageous am I about taking positive risks?
- What am I afraid of?
- How do I demonstrate respect for myself?
- How well do I keep commitments to myself and others?
- How do I show love for myself?
- What do I do to nurture and take care of myself?
- How worthwhile do I believe myself to be compared to other people?
- What beliefs do I have about myself that weaken my self-esteem?
- What beliefs do I have about myself that strengthen my self-esteem?

Select and answer those questions above (or your own) that help you create an accurate history of your self-esteem. Which answers reveal the dominant patterns of beliefs that you hold about yourself? As you write, remember to use the four E's (Examples, Explanation, Experience, Evidence) to support your ideas.

Relax, think, and write.

In which areas of life do you feel self-confident? In which do you experience self-doubt? What can you do to increase your overall confidence?

38. Developing Self-Confidence

On the first day of one semester, a woman intercepted me at the classroom door.

"Can I ask you something?" she said. "How do I know if I'm cut out for college?"

"Do you think you are?" I asked.

"Well, I was in the Army for six years, and I did fine. I think I can make it in college," she said.

"Great," I said.

She stood there, still looking doubtful. "But . . . my high school counselor said. . . ." She paused.

"Let me guess. Your counselor said you wouldn't do well in college? Is that it?"

She nodded. "I think he was wrong. But how do I know for sure?"

Indeed! How *do* we know? There will always be others who don't believe in us, whether it's college, a career, or something else. What's important, however, is that we believe in ourselves. Self-confidence is the core belief that *I CAN.* It is the core belief that I can master any skills I need. It is the trust that I am capable of achieving my goals and dreams. It is the conviction that I am in control of my life.

Ultimately, it matters little whether someone else thinks you can do something. It matters greatly whether you think you can. Luck aside, you'll probably accomplish just about what you believe you can. In this section we'll explore three effective ways to develop greater self-confidence.

Create a success identity

Are you confident that you can tie your shoes? Of course. And yet there was a time when you couldn't. So how did you move from doubt to confidence? Wasn't it by practicing over and over? As a result of your unwavering efforts, you have successfully tied literally thousands of shoes during your lifetime. You built your self-confidence one small victory after another. As a result, today you have no doubts that you can successfully tie your shoes every time you try. By the same method, you can build a success identity in virtually any area of life.

The career of Nathan McCall dramatizes the creation of a success identity under the harshest of circumstances. In his book *Makes Me Wanna Holler,* McCall records his journey from a Portsmith, Virginia, ghetto where he lived a life of street crime, violence, and eventual prison, to his job with the *Washington Post,* where he created a new life as a successful and respected newspaper reporter. As you might imagine, one of McCall's greatest challenges on his journey was self-doubt. But he persevered, stacking one small success on top of another for years. After his release from prison, McCall went to college and studied journalism. Each day he accumulated small, confidence-building successes: a class attended, an assignment completed, a test passed. Each semester he logged more successes with each course he completed. Before long, he achieved one of his cherished goals: graduation. Then, he got a job with a small newspaper; a few years later, he joined a larger newspaper in Atlanta, Georgia. With each of these successes, McCall's self-confidence grew. But it was a six-year span of successes while working at *The Atlanta Journal-Constitution* that contributed most to McCall's growing self-confidence as a journalist.

During that period, he traveled in Europe with Atlanta's mayor Andrew Young. He wrote articles as they toured, wiring them back to his paper for publication. Later, he went to Miami, Florida, for a conference of black mayors and then attended a convention for the National Association of Black Journalists. He wrote numerous stories about city hall and soon became a bureau chief supervising two other reporters. Recalling his six years of accumulated successes, McCall wrote in his journal, "These experiences solidify my belief that I can do anything I set my mind to do. The possibilities are boundless." Boundless indeed! A few years later, this former street gang member and prison inmate had a book on the *New York Times* bestsellers' list.

Realistic self-confidence comes from a history of success, and a history of success comes from taking persistent, purposeful, effective actions over time. As we experience success in specific arenas of our life, self-confidence begins to seep into every corner of our life.

Supreme self-confidence is the core belief that we are capable of accomplishing any realistic goal that we set for ourselves. This belief becomes part of who we are. Even when we strike out, the next time we come to bat we still expect to hit a home run.

Celebrate your successes and talents

A friend showed me some school papers that his eight-year-old daughter had brought home. At the top of each page was a written comment such as, *Great work, Lauren. Your spelling is very good* and *I am proud of you, Lauren. You are good in math.* What made the comments remarkable is this: The teacher

I warm up for every match believing that I'm going to win. . . . And there's only one way to build that kind of confidence. That is to practice often enough and long enough. Deep down inside, you've got to know that you're capable.

Jimmy Connors

Success brings its own self-confidence.

Lillian Vernon Katz
Founder, Lillian Vernon mail order catalog

had merely put a check in the upper lefthand corner of each page; Lauren had added the comments herself.

At the age of eight, Lauren has much to teach us about building self-confidence: celebrate your successes and talents. It's great when someone else tells us how wonderful our victory is and how talented we are. But it's even more important that we tell ourselves.

One way to acknowledge success is with a daily success record kept in your journal. Another way is to create a success wall: Every day write a recent success on a 3 x 5-inch card and post it on a wall where you'll see it often. Soon your wall will be covered with reminders of your daily accomplishments: *Got an 86 on history test . . . Attended every class on time today . . . Exercised for 2 hours at gym . . . Started a study group for biology.* In addition to acknowledging your successes, you might want to celebrate them as well by rewarding yourself with something special — a favorite dinner, a movie, a night out with friends. No matter how you acknowledge yourself, be sure to hear it. Be an active listener and truly hear the proof of your capability.

We can also strengthen our self-confidence by visualizing our past successes. For example, as part of your preparation for an upcoming test, you could spend a few minutes relaxing and running a movie in your mind of a previous test that you passed. Victims often weaken their self-confidence by recalling past defeats. Creators build their self-confidence by revisiting their victories.

Stretch

Imagine a bubble around you. This bubble represents your invisible comfort zone. Each of us has one. Inside of our comfort zone lies all that is familiar to us: places, people, actions, thoughts, feelings, beliefs. Within our comfort zone, we know virtually all there is to know. That's why it's so comfortable. There are no surprises, no difficult tests, no personal challenges, no risks. There's also little growth.

Outside of your comfort zone there exists plenty of opportunity for growth. The problem is, it's scary out there. So we often have an important choice to make: comfort or growth.

Many people decide, *I'll just wait until my self-confidence improves; then I'll take a risk.* They have it backwards. First, they need to take a positive risk and experience some success; then they'll experience increased self-confidence.

What step toward your dream are you afraid to take? What would happen if you did it anyway? Remember, fear is an emotion warning you of a *perceived* danger. When there's real danger, fear can save your life. More often, however, we imagine the danger. Our thoughts create fear and we get stuck. As psychologist Fritz Perls once asked, "Who is stopping you but you?"

Recently I found myself standing beside a ten-foot-long bed of burning hot coals. A man I had met only a few hours before was inviting a group of us to walk across the coals in bare feet. It was a dark night, and the coals glittered red and orange in the blackness. The scorching heat made it uncomfortable to be closer than three or four feet from the coals.

Research studies show that people who have high self-esteem regularly reward themselves in tangible and intangible ways. . . . By documenting and celebrating their successes, they ensure that these successes will reoccur.
Marsha Sinetar

Life is a daring adventure, or nothing.
Helen Keller

Take calculated risks. That is quite different from being rash.
General George S. Patton

"It doesn't matter whether you believe you can walk on these coals or not," the seminar leader was telling us. "All that matters is whether you put one foot in front of the other. If you do, you'll get to the other side."

No way! I thought.

Then he took a couple of deep breaths, stepped a bare foot onto those coals, and quickly walked the glowing orange path to the other side. A few moments later another person did it. Then another. They stood on the other side of the coals, their faces alive with smiles. My mind ignored the evidence. I was still sure I couldn't do it.

A few more people crossed the coals successfully. Heart thumping, I stepped up closer to the coals. The air above them rippled with intense heat. I couldn't believe I was even thinking of doing this. I took a deep breath and took a step . . . then another, and two more, and suddenly I was on the other side. I waited for my feet to burst into flames. They didn't. I was fine. I looked back across the coals and thought, *That was a lot easier than it looked.*

My experience with the firewalk dramatizes that our biggest obstacles are often our own fears. We can let our fears stop us . . . or we can take a step and walk through our fears to success.

I urge you not to do a firewalk without an experienced leader. But you can do your own version. Simply identify some action that would benefit your goals and dreams, something you have feared doing, walk right up to it, take a deep breath, and do it.

When you get to the other side of your fear, you will have achieved many valuable benefits. You will have taken a purposeful step toward your goal or dream. You'll realize how often you've allowed your fears to stop you short of success. And finally, you will have made a major contribution to increasing your self-confidence.

If we all did the things we are capable of doing, we would literally astound ourselves.
Thomas A. Edison

Journal #38

In this journal entry, you'll have an opportunity to explore and increase your self-confidence. People with strong self-confidence take the steps necessary to achieve their goals and dreams, and they take these steps despite their fears.

1. Write a list of successes that you have created in your life. The more successes you list, the more you will contribute to your self-confidence. Include small victories as well as big ones.

2. Write a list of your personal skills and talents. Again, the longer your list, the more you will contribute to your self-confidence. What are you good at doing? Don't overlook talents that you use daily. No talent is too insignificant to acknowledge.

3. Write a list of positive risks that you have taken in your life. When did you stretch your comfort zone and do something despite your fear?

4. Write a list of purposeful actions that you have some fear about doing. Afterwards, look at your list. Ask yourself, what is the worst thing that could happen if I did these things? What is the best thing that could happen if I did them? Will I do them?

5. Write a paragraph (or more) assessing your self-confidence. Remember to think of Creator questions to answer. In what areas is your self-confidence the strongest? The weakest? What could you do to increase your self-confidence? What other intriguing questions could you answer about your self-confidence? Remember to use the four E's (Do you know them by now?) to answer your questions. Also use the information contained in your four lists to develop and support your ideas.

Relax, think, and write.

> *To believe is to become what you believe.*
>
> June Jordan
> Professor of Afro-American studies, University of California at Berkeley

Do you respect yourself for how you live your life? Do you know how you could raise your self-respect even higher?

▰ ◼ ◼ ◼ 39. Developing Self-Respect

This above all; to thine own self be true.

William Shakespeare

Self-respect is the core belief that I AM AN ADMIRABLE PERSON. If self-confidence is the result of *what* I do, then self-respect is the result of *how* I do it.

Two choices that build or tear down my self-respect are whether I live with integrity and whether I keep my commitments.

Live with integrity

The foundation of integrity is our personal value system. What is important to me? What experiences do I want to have? What experiences do I want others to have? Do I prize external acquisitions such as cars, clothes, compliments, physical beauty, travel, fame, or money? Or do I cherish inner qualities such as love, respect, self-worth, security, honesty, wisdom, self-control, and compassion?

Once we have a foundation of personal values, we create integrity by choosing words and actions consistent with those values. Sadly, I see many students like Roland, the man who hadn't written even one essay after two semesters of English. Their words say they value their education, but their actions indicate otherwise. They don't do their assignments, or they do mediocre work, or they don't attend classes, or they're usually late. They just don't behave in ways consistent with what they say they value. Inconsistency like this will tear at a person's self-respect. How can I truly respect myself if I say I value something but I don't take the necessary steps to achieve my goal?

You will always be in fashion if you are true to yourself, and only if you are true to yourself.

Maya Angelou

One of my own great integrity tests occurred years ago when I left teaching to find a more lucrative career. I was excited when I was hired in a management training position for a high-powered sales company. Graduates of this five-year training program were earning more than thirty times what I had earned as a teacher. I couldn't wait!

My first assignment was to hire new members of the company's sales force. When applicants answered a newspaper advertisement, I would give them an aptitude test that revealed if they had what it took to succeed in sales. The test was mailed off to be scored, and when the scores came back, the sales manager would tell me if the applicants had qualified. If so, they were offered a sales position working strictly on commission. Lured by dreams of wealth, most applicants signed on. Many of them left the security of a steady salary for the uncertainty of a commission check. Unfortunately, few of the new sales representatives lasted more than a few months. They sold to their friends. Then they floundered. Then they disappeared.

Integrity is acting in accordance with your deepest values without compromise.
A. Roger Merrill

Before long, I noticed an unsettling fact: No one ever failed the sales aptitude test. Just about the time that I realized this truth, I interviewed a very shy man who was a lineman for the local telephone company. He was only a year from early retirement, but he was willing to give up his retirement benefits for the promise of big money from sales. If ever there was someone wrong for sales, I thought, it was this man. I knew he would be making a terrible mistake to abandon his security for the seductive promise of wealth. Surely here was one person who wouldn't pass the aptitude test. But the sales manager reported that he, too, had passed. In fact, he reported, my telephone linemen had gotten one of the highest scores ever. The sales manager thumped him on the back as he reported the good news in person.

"How soon can you start?" the sales manager asked.

"Errr . . . well, let's see. It's Friday. I guess next week? If that's okay."

That night, after the sales manager had left, I went into his office and found the lineman's folder. I opened it and found the test results. His score was zero. The man had not even scored!

All weekend, my stomach felt as though I had swallowed acid. My self-respect sank lower and lower. My Inner Defender kept telling me that it was the lineman's choice, not mine. It was his life. Maybe he'd prove the aptitude test wrong. Maybe he would make a fortune. My Inner Guide just shook his head in disgust.

On Monday, I called the lineman and told him his actual score.

He was furious. "Do you realize what I almost did?"

I thought, *Do you realize what I almost did?* Two weeks later I quit. After that, my stomach felt fine.

Always aim at complete harmony of thought and word and deed.
Mohandas K. Gandhi

Each time you contradict your own values, you make a withdrawal from your self-respect account. Each time you live true to your values, you make a deposit. Here is a quick way to discover what you probably value: Ask yourself, *What qualities and behaviors do I admire in others? What qualities and behaviors do I despise in others?*

Now here's a quick way to see if you are living with integrity. Ask yourself, *Do I ever allow myself to be less than what I admire? Do I ever permit myself to be no more than what I despise?*

When you lack respect for yourself, look for where your life is out of alignment. In order to bring your life back into harmony, you must make a change. You need to revise your values, dreams, goals, actions, relationships, thoughts, emotions, or beliefs. You cannot stay out of alignment with what you hold sacred and still retain your self-respect.

Keep commitments

Now let's consider another choice that influences your self-respect and, therefore, your self-esteem. Imagine that someone has made a promise to you but he doesn't keep it. Then he makes and breaks a second promise. And then another and another. Wouldn't you lose respect for this person? What do you suppose happens when the person making and breaking all of these promises is YOU?

True, your Inner Defender would quickly send out a smoke screen of excuses. But the truth would not be lost on your Inner Guide. The facts would remain: You made commitments and broke them. This violation of your word is a major withdrawal from your self-respect account.

To make a deposit in your self-respect account, keep commitments, especially to yourself. Here's how:

- Make your agreements consciously. Understand exactly what you're committing to; say no to requests that will get you off course.
- Use Creator language: Don't say, *I'll try to do it.* Say, *I will do it.*
- Make your agreements important — write them down.
- Create a plan; then do everything in your power to carry it out!
- If a problem arises or you change your mind, renegotiate (don't just abandon your promise).

Do you keep your commitments? Here's some evidence: How are you doing with the commitment you made to your dream in Journal #8? How are you doing with your thirty-two-day commitment from Journal #14?

If you haven't kept these commitments (or any others), ask your Inner Guide, *What did I make more important than keeping my commitment to myself?* A part of you wanted to keep your agreement — why else would you have made it? But another, stronger part of you obviously resisted. Pursue your exploration of this inner conflict with total honesty and you may uncover a self-defeating pattern or limiting core belief. The choice-evaluation process in Journal #29 is great for this purpose. You may realize, for example, that you resist making or keeping commitments because deep inside you don't believe you are worthy of achieving your dreams. If you can revise this part of your Script, you'll keep more commitments to yourself and stay on course to your goals and dreams.

Keeping commitments often requires overcoming enormous obstacles. Rosalie was returning to college after dropping out a decade before. She had been pursuing her dream of a nursing degree when her new husband asked her to give up college to take care of his two sons by a former marriage. Rosalie had already waited years for her own children to graduate from high school before pursuing her dream of a nursing career. Reluctantly, she agreed to his request and deferred her dream once again. Now back in college ten years later, she had made what she called a "sacred vow" to attend every class on time, to do her very best on all work, and to participate actively. This time she was determined to get top grades all the way to her nursing degree.

Then, one night she got a call from her own son, who was now married and had a two-year-old baby. For the first time he told Rosalie that his wife was on drugs. That day his wife had bought two-hundred dollars worth of drugs on credit, and the drug dealers were holding Rosalie's granddaughter until the money was paid. Rosalie spent the entire evening gathering cash from every source she could. All night she couldn't sleep waiting to hear if her grandchild would be returned safely.

At six in the morning, Rosalie got the good news when her son brought the baby to her house. He asked Rosalie to watch the baby while he and his wife had a serious talk. Hours passed, and still Rosalie cared for the baby. Closer and closer crept the hour when her college classes would begin. She started to get angrier and angrier as she realized that once again she was allowing others to pull her off course. And then she remembered that she had a choice. She could stay home and feel sorry for herself, or she could do something to get back on course.

At about nine o'clock, Rosalie called her sister who lived on the other side of town. She asked her sister to take a cab to Rosalie's house, promised to pay the cab fare, and even offered to pay her sister a bonus to watch the baby.

"I didn't get to class on time," Rosalie said. "But I got there. And when I did, I just wanted to walk into the middle of the room and yell, 'YEEAAH!! I MADE IT!!'"

If you could have seen her face when she told the class about her ordeal and her victory, you would have seen a woman who had just learned one of life's great lessons: When we break a commitment to ourselves, something inside of us dies. When we keep a commitment to ourselves, something inside of us thrives. That something is self-respect.

This ability to persevere despite obstacles and setbacks is the quality people most admire in others, and justly so; it is probably the most important trait not only for succeeding in life, but for enjoying it as well.

Mihaly Csikszentmihalyi

Journal #39

In this journal entry, you'll have an opportunity to explore and strengthen your self-respect. People with self-respect honor and admire themselves not just for *what* they do but for *how* they do it. People with great self-respect are more likely to believe in themselves than those who find it difficult to admire themselves. Raise your self-respect and you raise your self-esteem as well.

1. Write a paragraph (or more) analyzing your present level of integrity. To do this, think first about your various life roles. Are there any in which you aren't living up to your deepest values? For example, in your role as a student, are all of your actions consistent with what you value in this role? If not, what changes could you make to bring your actions into alignment with your values?

2. Write a paragraph (or more) recounting a specific commitment that you kept despite difficult obstacles. Acknowledge your persistence and your commitment to overcome both the inner and outer obstacles between you and your goal.

3. Write a paragraph (or more) examining your present level of self-respect. How is the balance in your self-respect account? Is it high or low? Why is that? Propose a specific plan to raise your self-respect even higher. What could you do to improve your level of integrity? What broken commitments could you recommit to?

For each part of this journal entry, consider first writing a few questions that you could answer as you explore the issues of integrity, commitment, and self-respect. Remember, asking Creator questions leads to empowering answers. Use the four E's (Example, Experience, Evidence, Explanation) as you develop answers to your questions.

Relax, think, and write.

Do you love yourself? What can you do to love yourself even more?

I celebrate myself, and sing myself . . .
Walt Whitman

■ ■ ■ ■ 40. Developing Self-Love

Self-love is the core belief that I AM LOVABLE. It is the trust that, no matter what, I will always love myself and other people will love me as well.

Self-love is vital to success. Self-love empowers us to make wise, self-supporting choices instead of unconscious, self-destructive ones. Self-love enables us to continue taking purposeful action steps even when we don't feel like it. These wise choices create a rich, full life of both worldly achievement and inner happiness.

The human heart is always seeking love.
Virginia Satir

Adults who have difficulty loving themselves typically felt neglected or abandoned as children. Many grew up in families in which they felt unappreciated and unloved. What love they did experience was often little more than a short-lived reward for adapting to their parents' expectations and demands. For children who felt unloved, each new day meant a desperate search for something they could say or do to earn their parents' temporary approval.

As adults, they typically continue believing that self-love depends upon what they say or do. Self-love, they think, is conditional: *I'll love myself **after** I earn my degree, **after** I get a great job, **after** I marry the perfect person, **after** I buy my dream house. . . .*

Quite the contrary. Instead of success causing self-love, more often it is the other way around: *When I love myself, I'll earn my degree, get that great job, marry a wonderful person, buy my dream house. . . .* Without self-love, we are likely to slide off course and sabotage our fondest desires. On those occasions when we *do* achieve outer success without self-love, our victories will often feel empty: *Is **this** all there is?* Therapists' offices are filled with people who appear successful on the outside but who feel hollow on the inside.

Self-love is different from self-confidence. Whereas self-confidence is increased by accumulating successcs, self-love comes with no conditions. You are lovable simply because you exist. Self-love grows not by *what* you do; it grows by *how* you treat yourself as you live your life. Self-love thrives on self-nurturing actions, thoughts, and feelings.

We can fill the empty places in our hearts with self-love.

Developing a self-care plan

If we weren't loved as a child, it is hard to love ourselves as adults. We need to learn how.

First, we might ask ourselves, How do we know that other people love us? Isn't it by the way they treat us? Isn't it because they consider our welfare along with their own . . . make our wants and needs important . . . concern themselves with our success and happiness . . . treat us with kindness and respect even when our behavior makes us the least deserving? Don't we feel loved when others nurture the very best in us with the very best in them?

It was our parents' job to nurture us when we were children. Some parents did a great job, some didn't. Now that we are adults, we are responsible for continuing (or beginning) our own nurturing. We can become our own ideal parents by unconditionally loving the child-self within us. The more we care for ourselves, the more we will feel lovable.

Nurturing yourself begins with a conscious self-care plan. As you consider the following options for nurturing yourself, look for one or two changes you could make in your life that would increase your self-love.

Nurture Yourself Physically. The consequences of your choices about how to treat your body may not show up for months or years. People who love themselves make wise choices to nurture their bodies for a long, healthy life.

How is your diet? Creators are aware of what they eat and drink. The next time you're about to eat or drink something, ask yourself: *Is this what I would feed someone I truly loved?* Doing so will raise your consciousness and allow you to make wiser choices. Your college's health office can probably provide you with information on improving your diet.

Do you exercise regularly? Even moderate exercise at least three times a week helps most people stay stronger and healthier. Regular exercise is believed to strengthen the immune system as well as produce hormones that give us a natural sense of well being. Your physical education department can probably assist you to begin a safe, effective, and life-long exercise program.

Do you have habits that injure your body? Do you drink too much coffee,

If you are willing to learn to love yourself, you will have a far more dependable and continuous source of self-esteem.
Dr. Thomas Burns

When one has not had a good father, one must create one.
Friedrich Nietzsche

The extent to which we love ourselves determines whether we eat right, get enough sleep, smoke, wear seat belts, exercise, and so on. Each of these choices is a statement of how much we care about living.
Dr. Bernie Siegel

smoke cigarettes, drink alcohol to excess, take dangerous drugs? If so, you may wish to give up the immediate pleasure of such substances for the long-range improved health you will be affording your body. Substance abuse is misnamed. You are not abusing the substance — you are abusing yourself. All substance abuse is really self-abuse.

There are many other ways to nurture your body. Get enough rest. Swing on a swing. Have regular medical checkups. Get or give some hugs. Take a hot whirlpool bath. Laugh until your sides ache. See your dentist for a checkup and a cleaning. Go dancing. Give or get a massage. Do nothing for one hour. Stretch like a cat. Relax.

Nurture Yourself Mentally. How you talk to yourself — especially when you are off course — will influence your sense of self-love.

If you had a critical parent, you will very likely have a strong Inner Critic who dominates your thoughts with self-judgments. Whenever you begin to condemn yourself, stop. Replace your negative judgments with positive, supportive comments.

You may find it difficult at first to choose self-love over self-judgment. One way to help yourself make this important choice is to separate the doer from the deed. If you failed a test, your Inner Critic wants to label you a failure. But your Inner Guide knows you are not a failure; you are a lovable person who got an F on one test. Keep your self-talk focused on facts, not judgments. Stop allowing your Inner Critic to abuse you.

Deep self-love is the ongoing inner approval of who you are regardless of the outer results that you are presently creating. You are not your results. When you learn to love yourself even when you are off course, your self-esteem will soar.

Here are some other ways to nurture yourself mentally: Say your affirmation often, read a good book, ask a great question and seek the answer, learn new words, visualize your success, memorize your favorite poem, balance your checkbook, make a difficult decision, teach someone something that you value knowing.

Nurture Yourself Emotionally. The very times that you need self-love the most are often the times that you feel self-love the least. You may be feeling shame instead of self-acceptance, helplessness instead of competence, self-contempt instead of self-respect, self-loathing instead of self-love.

There is an antidote to your inner poison: **Replace your self-judgments with compassion.** Understand that you're doing the best you can. Develop compassion for the little child within you, the little child who desperately struggled to devise some way to be safe in a huge, confusing, and sometimes painful world. Realize that how you are with yourself as you go through difficult times — self-judging or compassionate — is what will continue to affect you long after the difficult times have come and gone.

I recall a student named Helen who judged herself unmercifully, especially for her shyness. She criticized herself for never participating in class, for her lack of friends in college, for being such a loner. One day we did the Wise-

Choice Process, and she identified many choices she had for making new friends. But she could never bring herself to actually do them. Her Inner Critic was having a field day with her failures.

In her journal she sought to exchange her self-judgments for compassion. She imagined her shyness as a string and followed it back through time. She revisited various scenes where her shyness had separated her from other children. Then she recalled an event she hadn't thought of in years. She was about four years old, and her aunt had come to take care of her while her parents went on vacation. One night Helen wet her bed, and the next morning her aunt was furious. She wrapped Helen in the urine-soaked sheets, took her outside, and tied her to a tree in the front yard. Hours later, the school bus drove up and dropped off the neighborhood children. They laughed at Helen and ran off.

I asked Helen what she would do today if she came across that little girl tied to a tree, wrapped in urine-soaked sheets. I suggested that she add this new ending to the movie in her mind.

In her revised ending, Helen went up to the little girl, untied her, wrapped her in a warm blanket, picked her up, and rocked her in her arms. Then she carried little Helen into the house and angrily told her aunt to get out. She bathed little Helen and dressed her in clean clothes. Next, she made little Helen her favorite sandwich — peanut butter and marshmallow cream — for lunch. Then she played with her and cared for her until her parents came home.

Helen found compassion for the part of her that was too scared to allow her reach out to others. She didn't make any friends while I knew her, but I noticed that she was less critical of herself, especially her shyness. My hope is that this step was her first of many toward putting her self-defeating shyness behind her.

When you find yourself in judgment of yourself, see if you can get in touch with the part of you that is hurting. Instead of automatically judging yourself harshly, find compassion for yourself, especially the little person within you who is doing the best he or she knows how to do.

If love is what is missing, then love is what is called for. Make a conscious choice to put self-love where there is self-judgment. Your act of self-love will help you to heal the wound of lost self-esteem. As your self-esteem grows stronger, you will find yourself making more and more choices that support, rather than sabotage, your greatest success.

Journal #40

In this journal entry, you'll have an opportunity to develop greater self-love. People who love themselves unconditionally typically accomplish more in their lives than those who judge themselves as unlovable. Additionally, people who love themselves experience an inner reserve of good feelings regardless of the outer circumstances of their lives.

Unless your instructor tells you otherwise, WRITE ONLY ONE of the following two journal entries. (Of course, you *could* choose to do both if you wanted to experience even greater self-love.)

Children who are not loved in their very beingness do not know how to love themselves. As adults, they have to learn to nourish, to mother their own lost child.
Marion Woodman

When there is no love put love and there you will find love.
Saint John of the Cross

1. Write a self-care plan to provide nurturing self-love for yourself.

In this journal entry, answer such Creator questions as . . . How loved did I feel as a child? How much do I experience self-love today? How do I express love to myself now? How comfortable am I about discussing the issue of self-love? What could I do today to nurture myself more physically? Mentally? Emotionally? Spiritually? What have I learned about myself and about self-love? As always, use these questions and/or any of your own, and the four E's to develop your answers.

OR . . .

2. Write two versions of an experience from your childhood in which you experienced physical, mental, or emotional pain.

A) In the first version, retell the painful experience just as you recall it happening.
B) In the second version, add yourself as an adult to the experience at the moment that it begins to get painful for your child-self. Let your adult greet your child-self and show loving compassion. Have the adult-you take care of that hurt child from long ago. Let the scene end perfectly with your child-self feeling fully loved, cared for, and protected. (For an example of this second version, review Helen's story in the text.)
C) Finally, let your Inner Guide step back and consider both scenes. Have your Inner Guide write its thoughts and discoveries as a result of what it has observed. What wisdom does your Inner Guide have to share with you now about the importance of self-love in your life?

Relax, think, and write.

Do you fully appreciate your value as a human being? What could you do to increase your sense of self-worth?

▮ ▮ ▮ ▮ ▮ 41. Rediscovering Your Self-Worth

Of all the judgments we pass, none is as important as the one we pass on ourselves.
Nathaniel Brandon

In 1957, a group of monks in Thailand decided to move a ten-and-a-half-foot tall clay statue of Buddha to a new temple. As workmen attempted to lift the statue with a crane, the clay cracked, and one of the monks noticed something shining from deep within. He chipped at the statue with a chisel and beneath eight inches of clay, he discovered another Buddha made of solid gold. Weighing over five thousand pounds, it has since been estimated to be worth nearly two hundred million dollars.

Historians speculate that hundreds of years ago, Thai monks had disguised the golden Buddha with clay to protect it from harm by invading Burmese soldiers. Apparently those monks were killed, and the true nature of the inner Buddha remained hidden for centuries.

Like the golden Buddha, each of us is a treasure of enormous value. Like the monks, we too may have felt our treasure threatened years ago. So we disguised our real self beneath our own version of clay — automatic patterns of behaviors, thoughts, and feelings. These habits seemed to protect us from danger. Soon, however, we began to believe that we are our patterns; we forgot that we are a golden treasure of extraordinary value.

Self-worth, then, isn't something that we need to add to our lives. We were born with all of the self-worth we need. What we need to do is to chip away our false self and find the treasure hidden beneath our disguise. To discover our birthright of high self-esteem, we must remember who we are.

Self-worth is the core belief that I AM VALUABLE. It is the unwavering trust that I am a worthwhile person. I may want to change certain things about myself, but I am worthy just the way I am.

We don't need to create self-worth; we simply need to find it again. Underneath all of the protective patterns that we created for safety and control is the acceptable, capable, admirable, lovable person we have always been, the spirit of the innocent child we once were but later hid.

A student named Mary Jane wrote a hilarious essay about all of the outrageous stunts she had done to be named head rabbit for her fifth grade spring festival. As she read her story to the class, everyone howled with laughter. Afterwards, someone asked, "Why was it so important for you to be the head rabbit?"

Mary Jane paused. "Well, that's obvious. The head rabbit got to wear the best costume." Then a serious look came over her face. "The truth is, I thought that maybe people would like me better if I was the head rabbit." She paused again. "Actually, I guess I hoped that, if they liked me better, then *I* would like me better."

John Bradshaw says that the opposite of self-worth is *others'*-worth. When we begin to judge our own value based on what others think of us, we are in for a rough journey.

A friend of mine who is now a medical doctor told me about a traumatic moment he experienced during a sophomore creative writing class. He had written a short story that he liked very much. When his teacher read it to the class, he felt great pride. After reading the story, the teacher announced, "Obviously this is a terrible short story. I wanted you all to see what *not* to do." My friend was crushed. It took him years, he said, to realize that even if his writing had been "terrible," *he* was not terrible. He said, "I wish I'd known back then that I'm okay no matter what a teacher or anyone else thinks of my writing . . . or of me."

As long as we see other people's judgments merely as feedback, we're fine. Then it's simply information. When it's helpful, we can use the information to get back on course. When it's unhelpful, we can simply dismiss it. Other people's opinions of us often say more about who *they* are than who *we* are.

As soon as we see other people's judgments as defining our self-worth, we're in deep trouble. But this mistake is exactly what many of us do. We take other people's opinions and internalize them as our own beliefs about who we are. After a while, those other people don't even have to be around. Our Inner Critic has tape recorded their criticisms and replays them over and over in our minds until the thoughts take on the illusion of reality.

Many students experience test anxiety. If they had a strong sense of self-worth, they wouldn't. Instead, here's what would happen: Before the test they'd do their very best to prepare, during the test they'd demonstrate all they knew, and after the test they'd simply view their results as feedback. The test would merely inform them whether or not they're on course. Then they'd know what choices to make next.

But if you doubt your self-worth, any test in college or in life threatens to confirm your worst suspicions about yourself. If you fail the test, your Inner Critic has license to attack: *You're going to fail this course. You'll probably flunk out of college. You'll never get the job you want. Your life is ruined. You're a worthless failure!* Recall how damaging self-criticism is when it's permanent, pervasive, and personal. What this self-criticism damages is our sense of self-worth.

Rediscovering your self

Instead of our false self, what we are looking for is an experience of our TRUE SELF . . . the experience of total self-acceptance, unlimited self-confidence, immeasurable self-respect, unconditional self-love, and unbounded self-worth. In other words, high self-esteem.

If, like me, you are looking for directions to your authentic Self, let me suggest some core beliefs that seem important.

Here is what my Self is not. I am not my automatic behaviors, thoughts, or emotions. I am not my body, my possessions, my successes, my mistakes, or my failures. I am not my grades, my relationships, or my job. I am not my Scripts. I am not my self-defeating patterns nor my limiting beliefs. I am not my Inner Critic nor my Inner Defender. These are parts of my false self. These are parts of the clay armor that I put on years ago for protection.

Here is what my Self may be: I may be the consciousness that makes my choices when I am not reacting automatically. I may be my own Inner Guide.

How can we see through our Scripts to who we really are? How can we become conscious of the Self we have forgotten? How can we remember who we are? Here are some ways:

Keep a Journal.   I hope you have already discovered the power of using a journal to explore both your outer and inner worlds. Probably at some point while writing, ideas popped out that you didn't even know were in you. Experiences like these offer clues to who we really are. Follow them where they lead. Some of them will take you deep inside to your real Self.

Forgive Yourself.   Let go of the judgments that you hold against your actions, your thoughts, and your feelings. Especially free yourself of judgments you hold against your Self. When you say *I am* . . . be aware of any judgments that follow. Never give yourself a label you don't want to carry for the rest of your life. When you judge yourself as unacceptable, incapable, contemptible, unlovable, or worthless, these limiting beliefs keep you from being your true self. Free

[T]here is something in our mind that is more than the sum of the individual neurons that make up the brain. This something is the self, the brain's awareness of its own form of organizing information.

Mihaly Csikszentmihalyi

A single meditation can change people because it has allowed them to release part of the false self for good.

Dr. Deepak Chopra

yourself from your self-judgments with self-forgiveness. *I forgive myself for judging myself as . . .*

Meditate.   Use extended relaxation sessions in a special way. Invite your mind to let go of each new thought that enters. Keep peeling away one thought after another. Imagine peeling an onion. Allow yourself to go deeper and deeper into your Self. Seek to witness your Self uncontaminated by your automatic thoughts and fears. Observe yourself stripped of what you do and what you have. Just be.

Heed Your Inner Guide.   Become conscious of your complex inner dialogue. Recognize the voice of your Inner Critic as it seeks to make you perfect by criticizing everything you do, think, or feel. Recognize also the voice of your Inner Defender as it tries to protect you by excusing you and blaming others for all that goes wrong in your life. Comfort these voices from your childhood, knowing that all they wish to do is protect you from pain. Then turn to your Inner Guide for directions. Trust that this aspect knows your perfect destinations. Believe that it has the ability to help you learn from each time you stray off course, and the wisdom to keep getting you back on course to your goals and dreams.

Who we are looking for is who is looking.

St. Francis of Assisi

When you rediscover your own self-worth, you will have the key ingredient for creating a rich, personally fulfilling life.

Journal #41

In this journal entry, you'll have an opportunity to rediscover your self-worth. This exploration is one more important step in creating higher self-esteem, your foundation for inner and outer success.

1. On a blank journal page, draw a circle. Within the circle draw your true Self. This depiction needs to make sense only to you. Use colors as appropriate. Put nothing else on this page.

2. On the next page in your journal, write an in-depth description of the Self that you have drawn in the circle. Consider the shapes, lines, and colors that you have used. Observe the true Self that is represented there. Stop seeing the disguise of your Scripts, and begin seeing the golden "you" inside. Stop listening to your Inner Critic and your Inner Defender, and begin listening to your Inner Guide. Think of Creator questions about your Self and let your Inner Guide answer them. Use the four E's (Examples, Explanation, Experiences, Evidence) to support and develop your abstract ideas about your SELF.

Relax, think, write.

Chapter 10
■■■■■■■■■■

Staying on Course to
Your Success ■■■■■■■■■■■■■■■■■■■

■ ■ ■ ■ 42. Planning Your Next Steps

We have come a long way on our journey.

First, we established the influence of **CHOICES** to determine the outcomes of our lives. We saw that with our choices we are the Creators of our lives and that as we become more conscious, we can make increasingly wiser choices. Wiser choices better allow us to create the futures we desire. The foundation of our success, therefore, is **ACCEPTING PERSONAL RESPONSIBILITY** — the ability to respond so that we accomplish our desires without interfering with the opportunity for others to do the same. Although in reality we are not responsible for everything that occurs in our lives, holding this belief causes us to find and act upon options that otherwise we might never see. Accepting personal responsibility, therefore, maximizes the control we have over the outcomes of our lives.

> *You are the only one who can ever determine whether you are successful or not. . . . When it comes right down to it, the grades you give yourself are the grades that count.*
> Shad Helmstetter

Next, we explored the motivating energy of **DISCOVERING A MEANINGFUL PURPOSE.** We saw that choosing our goals and dreams creates a powerful magnet that draws us into our ideal future. The more specifically we can visualize our future life, the more likely it is that we will make it a reality. Although we cannot expect to create everything we want — destiny and chance do play a part in our lives — by committing to clear goals and dreams, we generate positive energy for moving ahead toward our ideal futures.

Then, we considered the power of **TAKING PURPOSEFUL ACTIONS.** We saw that dreams become reality only when we effectively manage our efforts. We defined our conscious action rules, rules that would lay the foundation for our later examination of unconscious scripts. We saw that there is no such thing as time management; all we can manage is ourselves, and we discussed effective tools for focusing our time and energy on our goals and dreams.

Following this, we examined the value of **DEVELOPING MUTUALLY SUPPORTIVE RELATIONSHIPS.** In this chapter, we saw how people mature from dependence to independence and finally to interdependence. Interdependent people create support networks of people to whom they give and receive assistance. By developing effective listening and communication skills, interdependent people strengthen relationships, assisting them to achieve more with their lives while enjoying the journey.

At this point, we began to look inward for the creation of our success. We saw that most people are off course in at least some parts of their lives and that the cause is often buried somewhere deep in their unconscious. To begin our exploration of **SUCCEEDING FROM THE INSIDE OUT,** we considered how we are often unknowingly controlled by our outdated Scripts. We examined our lives to find our self-defeating patterns of behavior, thought, and emotion. With those as clues, we looked for the limiting core beliefs that we invented in childhood to decrease our pain and increase our pleasure. Once we identified these limiting parts of our Scripts, we began making choices to rewrite those that get us off course today as adults. With our knowledge of the unconscious forces in our lives, we began an exploration in the next three chapters of how our Scripts affect our thinking, feeling, and being.

In Chapter 7, we looked at ways for **MAXIMIZING YOUR LEARNING.** We noted how our Scripts often hinder the amazing learning ability with which we were born, and we considered how we could regain the learning ability of a child. We also looked at how we might make course corrections by considering every experience to be life's way of teaching us valuable lessons for success. In particular, we appreciated three of the University of Life's most effective teachers — mistakes, failures, and obstacles. Then we considered how we might rewrite our Scripts to improve our ability to think and learn more effectively.

Coming near the end of our journey, we reflected on the important part that emotions play in our lives and acknowledged that no outer world success is meaningful if we are unhappy inside. Therefore, we considered ways for **CREATING A POSITIVE EXPERIENCE OF LIFE,** putting much of our emphasis on wisely choosing the content of our consciousness. We saw that we are just as responsible for what we create in our inner world as we are for what we create in our outer world. We learned to honor our emotions, using them as a compass to keep us on course. Once more, we worked on rewriting our limiting Scripts, this time seeking to create more emotional balance and happiness in our lives.

Finally, we visited the deepest core of our experience — our true selves. There, we discussed the essential nature of **BELIEVING IN YOURSELF.** Without the core belief that we are worthy, our Scripts will sabotage all of our efforts for success. So we looked at how to develop greater self-acceptance, self-confidence, self-respect, and self-love. We ended our journey to the center of ourselves by discussing ways that we can rewrite our limiting Scripts and thus realize that we are, indeed, worthy of creating and living a rich, personally fulfilling life.

There are admirable potentialities in every human being. Believe in your strength and your youth. Learn to repeat endlessly to yourself, "It all depends on me."

André Gide

Let him that would move the world first move himself.

Socrates

Choices and changes

All that we are is the sum of the choices we have made in the past. All that we will become is the sum of the choices that we will make from this moment on.

Your life is a work of art, and you are the artist. Whatever you wish to have, do, or be, you have the possibility to create . . . if you believe you can . . . and if you are willing to do whatever it takes. Your future can be as rich and wonderful as you conceive it. Your greatest limitations are within you — not outside you — and that means that you will probably have to change before the world changes to accommodate your dreams.

Change is not easy, but it is possible for Creators. We are not chained to the patterns that we have been living. At any moment, we can dissolve the imaginary chains of our Scripts, walk away from our self-imposed limitations, and create a new life.

Although our travels together are coming to an end, your journey has really just begun. Look out there to your future. What do you want? What are you willing to do to get it? Make a plan and go for it.

Realize that you will probably get off course. But know that you have the strategies — both outer and inner — to get back on course. Before you head out again toward your dream, take a moment to assess your tools. Review the table of contents of this book. Look over the chapter-openers, which compare the choices of successful and struggling people. Skim the pages to remind yourself of the many strategies you have learned.

On the next page is another copy of the questionnaire that you took at the beginning of this book. Take it again. (Don't look back at your previous answers yet.) Then compare your first scores with your present scores, and consider the changes that have taken place within you. Acknowledge yourself for your courage to change. Look, also, at the changes that you still need to make if you are to continue creating a rich, personally fulfilling life.

You have much of what you need to achieve your dreams. The rest you can learn on your journey. Be bold! Begin today!

Each of us has the right and the responsibility to assess the roads which lie ahead, and those over which we have traveled, and if the future road looms ominous or unpromising, and the roads back uninviting, then we need to gather our resolve and, carrying only the necessary baggage, step off that road into another direction.

Maya Angelou

We have made thee neither of heaven nor of earth,
Neither mortal nor immortal,
So that with freedom of choice and with honor,
As though the maker and molder of thyself,
Thou mayest fashion thyself in whatever shape thou shalt prefer.
Giovanni Pico Della Mirandola
God's speech to Adam in
On the Dignity of Man

Self-assessment

Read the seventy statements below and score each one according to how true or false you believe it is about you. To get an accurate picture of yourself, consider what is currently true about you (not what you want to be true).

Assign each statement a number from zero to ten, as follows:

totally false 0 1 2 3 4 5 6 7 8 9 10 totally true

1.____ I live day to day, without much of a plan for the future.
2.____ I use my time extremely well.
3.____ I prefer working on projects with other people.
4.____ When I think about performing an upcoming challenge (such as a college test), I picture myself doing poorly.
5.____ I lack confidence about learning something new.
6.____ I make wise choices that help me get what I really want in life.
7.____ I'm comfortable expressing my emotions.
8.____ I have important things in my life that I've put off completing for too long.
9.____ I accept myself just as I am, even with my faults and weaknesses.
10.____ I know very few people on whom I can really count for help.
11.____ I have a written list of specific, long-term goals.
12.____ I finish what I start.
13.____ I have learned important lessons from the obstacles in my life.
14.____ Rather than complain, blame others, or make excuses, I look to solve my problems.
15.____ When I encounter a problem, I ask for help.
16.____ I'm not sure what I want to accomplish in the next three to six months.
17.____ I forget to do important things in my life.
18.____ Whether I'm happy or not depends mostly on me.
19.____ When fun activities come up, I often postpone school assignments until later.
20.____ I feel very committed to what I am doing with my life right now.
21.____ The quality of my life is mostly the result of the choices I've made.
22.____ While other people are talking to me, I often think about what I'll say next.
23.____ I find little value in the feedback I get from teachers.
24.____ I often feel bored or anxious.
25.____ I have a network of people in my life whom I can count on for help.
26.____ I have learned valuable lessons from my failures.
27.____ I often think about my positive qualities.
28.____ I feel very uncommitted to what I'm doing in my life right now.
29.____ I make poor choices that keep me from getting what I really want in life.
30.____ I like myself better when I'm a success.
31.____ I waste a lot of time.
32.____ I break promises that I make to myself or to others.
33.____ I don't make the same mistake twice.
34.____ I seldom express my true feelings.
35.____ The quality of my life is mostly the result of things beyond my control.
36.____ I could do better work on my school assignments if I wanted to.
37.____ I'll accept myself more as soon as I get rid of my faults and weaknesses.

totally false O 1 2 3 4 5 6 7 8 9 10 totally true

38.____ I have a written list of specific goals that I want to accomplish in the next three to six months.
39.____ I often feel happy and fully alive.
40.____ I hold back from telling others what I'm really thinking.
41.____ Whether I'm happy or not depends mostly on what's happened to me lately.
42.____ I'm very aware of why I've made the important choices I have in my life.
43.____ I write lists of the important tasks I need to do each day.
44.____ When I realize I'm not going to be able to achieve a goal that I want, I let it go and move on.
45.____ The feedback I get from most teachers has value for me.
46.____ I have no long-term goals that excite me.
47.____ I prefer working on projects by myself.
48.____ I feel that I'm not as worthwhile as some other people I know.
49.____ I'm confident that I will accomplish my greatest goals and dreams.
50.____ I tend to complain, blame others, or make excuses.
51.____ I do my very best work on school assignments.
52.____ I have trouble finishing what I start.
53.____ I often think about my negative qualities.
54.____ People consider me to be a good listener.
55.____ I tend to hang onto things (people, jobs, dreams) long after they've stopped being good for me.
56.____ I'm not sure I'm capable of achieving my most important goals and dreams.
57.____ My failures have brought me much pain and little value.
58.____ I keep promises that I make to myself or others.
59.____ When I look at important choices I've made, I wonder why I made them.
60.____ I like myself even when I've failed.
61.____ I try to solve my problems by myself.
62.____ I have a written plan that states exactly what I intend to accomplish during my life.
63.____ I tend to repeat my mistakes.
64.____ I forgive people who do or say things I don't like.
65.____ When I think about performing an upcoming challenge (such as a college test), I picture myself doing well.
66.____ When I have important school assignments to do, I postpone fun activities until later.
67.____ I'm good at telling people what I'm thinking in a way that lets them really understand me.
68.____ I believe that I can learn anything I need or want to know.
69.____ Obstacles to my success are a frustration and nothing more.
70.____ I think that I'm just as worthwhile as other people I know.

Transfer your scores to the scoring sheets on page 216. For each of the seven areas, total your scores in columns A and B. Then total your final scores as shown in the sample.

Self-assessment Scoring Sheet

sample		score #1	
A	**B**	**A**	**B**
6. _3_	19. _8_	6._____	19._____
14. _6_	29. _6_	14._____	29._____
21. _4_	35. _5_	21._____	35._____
42. _4_	50. _6_	42._____	50._____
66. _8_	59. _8_	66._____	59._____
	_25_ + 50 – _33_ = _58_		___ + 50 – ___ = ___

score #2		score #3	
A	**B**	**A**	**B**
11._____	1._____	2._____	4._____
20._____	16._____	12._____	17._____
27._____	28._____	43._____	31._____
38._____	46._____	51._____	36._____
62._____	53._____	65._____	52._____
	___ + 50 – ___ = ___		___ + 50 – ___ = ___

score #4		score #5	
A	**B**	**A**	**B**
3._____	10._____	13._____	5._____
15._____	22._____	26._____	23._____
25._____	40._____	33._____	57._____
54._____	47._____	45._____	63._____
67._____	61._____	68._____	69._____
	___ + 50 – ___ = ___		___ + 50 – ___ = ___

score #6		score #7	
A	**B**	**A**	**B**
7._____	8._____	9._____	30._____
18._____	24._____	49._____	32._____
39._____	34._____	58._____	37._____
44._____	41._____	60._____	48._____
64._____	55._____	70._____	56._____
	___ + 50 – ___ = ___		___ + 50 – ___ = ___

Carry these scores to the corresponding boxes in the chart on page 217.

CHOICES OF SUCCESSFUL STUDENTS

Your score	Successful students . . .	Struggling students . . .
score **#1** **#2** —— ——	1. . . .accept **personal responsibility** for creating the quality of their lives.	1. . . .see themselves as victims, believing for the most part that what happens to them is out of their control.
score **#1** **#2** —— ——	2. . . .discover a motivating **purpose,** characterized by personally meaningful goals and dreams.	2. . . .have difficulty choosing a purpose, often experiencing depression and/or resentment about the meaninglessness of their lives.
score **#1** **#2** —— ——	3. . . .consistently plan and take effective **actions** in pursuing their goals and dreams.	3. . . .seldom identify the specific actions needed to accomplish a task. And when they do, they tend to procrastinate.
score **#1** **#2** —— ——	4. . . .build **mutually supportive relationships** that assist them in pursuing their goals and dreams.	4. . . .are solitary, not requesting, even rejecting offers of assistance from legitimate resources.
score **#1** **#2** —— ——	5. . . .**maximize learning** by finding valuable lessons in nearly every experience they have.	5. . . .tend to resist learning new ideas and skills, often viewing learning as drudgery rather than play.
score **#1** **#2** —— ——	6. . . .actively create a **positive experience of life** characterized by optimism, happiness, and peace of mind.	6. . . .experience life negatively, focusing much of their attention on what is disappointing and painful.
score **#1** **#2** —— ——	7. . . .**believe in themselves,** feeling capable, lovable and unconditionally worthy as human beings.	7. . . .doubt their personal value, feeling inadequate to accomplish meaningful tasks and unworthy to be loved by others or by themselves.

A score of less than fifty suggests that, for this choice, you have the beliefs and behaviors of a struggling student. A score between fifty and eighty indicates that your beliefs and behaviors in this realm will sometimes get you off course. A score of more than eighty suggests that you have developed supportive beliefs and behaviors that will help to keep you on course.

Now you can see where you have changed and where you still need to change. In your journal you will have an opportunity to evaluate your results and plan your next steps for creating a great life.

Journal #42

In this journal entry, you'll have an opportunity to plan your next steps toward success in college and in life. This step is a second assessment of your present strengths and weaknesses and is done by comparing your recent questionnaire scores with your first scores. In this way, you'll discover the changes that you have already made in your behaviors, thoughts, emotions, and beliefs . . . and the additional changes you may want to make to stay on course to a rich, personally fulfilling life.

1. Comparing the results from the two self-assessment questionnaires, write a paragraph (or more) exploring the area(s) in which you feel you have changed for the better.

Before writing, remember to list Creator questions that you will answer in your discussion. During your writing, remember to use the four E's to support the opinions and ideas that you express.

2. Further comparing the results from the two self-assessment questionnaires, write a paragraph (or more) exploring the area(s) in which you want to continue changing for the better.

Remember the saying, "If you keep doing what you've been doing, you'll keep getting what you've been getting." With this thought in mind, identify the specific changes you'd like to make in yourself in the months and years to come.

As you write, remember the five suggestions mentioned in the introduction for creating a meaningful journal: 1) Be spontaneous. 2) Write for yourself. 3) Be honest. 4) Be creative. 5) Dive deep. Especially dive deep!

3. Write one last paragraph (or more) in which you sum up the most important discoveries that you have made about yourself while keeping your journal so far.

Before writing, take a few moments to relax using the method that works best for you. As always, you will get much more value from this journal entry and from your life if you take time to relax and collect your thoughts. Then gear yourself up to create a great life!

Relax, think, and write.

He who has begun has half done.
Dare to be wise; begin!
Horace

Bibliography

Adams, Kathleen. *Journal to the Self: Twenty-Two Paths to Personal Growth.* Warner Books, 1990.

Anderson, Walter. *Courage is a Three Letter Word.* Random House, 1986.

Angelou, Maya. *Wouldn't Take Nothing for My Journey Now.* Random House Canada, 1993.

Bradshaw, John. *Creating Love.* Bantam, 1992.

★ ——. *Homecoming.* Bantam Books, 1990.

★ Brandon, Nathaniel. *How to Raise Your Self Esteem.* Bantam, 1988.

Burns, David, M.D. *Feeling Good.* William Morrow & Company, 1980.

Buzan, Tony. *Make the Most of Your Mind.* Simon and Schuster, 1977.

Capacchionc, Lucia. *The Creative Journal.* Northcastle, 1989.

Carnegie, Dale. *How to Win Friends and Influence People.* Pocket Books, 1936.

Chapman, Joyce. *Live Your Dream.* Newcastle, 1990.

Chopra, Deepak, M.D. *Unconditional Life.* Bantam, 1991.

★ Covey, Stephen R. *7 Habits of Highly Effective People.* Simon & Schuster, 1989. Excerpts used with permission of Covey Leadership Center, Inc. 3507 N. University Ave. P.O. Box 19008, Provo, Utah, 84604-4479. Phone: (800) 331-7716.

★ Csikszentmihalyi, Mihaly. *Flow: The Psychology of Optimal Experience.* Harper & Row, 1990.

——. *The Evolving Self.* HarperCollins, 1993.

deBono, Edward. *deBono's Thinking Course.* Facts on File, 1982.

Dewey, John. *Experience & Education.* Collier Books, 1938.

Dyer, Wayne. *You'll See It When you Believe It.* Morrow, 1989.

Ferrucci, Piero. *What We May Be.* J.P. Tarcher, 1982.

★ Frankl, Viktor E., M.D. *Man's Search for Meaning.* Washington Square Press, 1959.

Garfield, Charles. *Peak Performers.* Avon Books, 1986.

Gawain, Shakti. *Creative Visualization.* Bantam Books, 1979.

★ Glasser, William. *Reality Therapy.* Harper and Row, 1965.

Gordon, Thomas, M.D. *Parent Effectiveness Training.* NAL Penguin, 1970.

Griessman, B. Eugene. *The Achievement Factors.* Dodd, Mead & Company, 1987.

Harmon, Willis & Howard Rheingold. *Higher Creativity.* J.P. Tarcher, 1984.

Harris, Thomas. *I'm OK, You're OK.* Harper and Row, 1967.

Hendricks, Gay & Kathlyn Hendricks. *Conscious Loving.* Bantam, 1990.

Hendricks, Gay & Russell Wills. *The Centering Book.* Prentice Hall, 1989.

★ Helmstetter, Shad. *Choices.* Simon and Schuster, 1989.

Hill, Napoleon. *Think and Grow Rich.* Fawcett Crest, 1960.

James, Muriel & Dorothy Jongeward. *Born to Win.* Addison-Wesley Publishing, 1978.

Jampolsky, Gerald, M.D. *Teach Only Love.* Bantam, 1983.

John-Roger & Peter McWilliams. *Life 101.* Prelude Press, 1991.

★ Keyes Jr., Ken. *Handbook to Higher Consciousness.* Living Love Publishing, 1975.

Lao Tzu. *Tao Te Ching*. (trans. Vitor H. Mair) Bantam, 1990.

Lerner, Harriet Goldhor. *The Dance of Intimacy*. Harper and Row, 1989.

Maltz, Maxwell. *Magic Power of Self-Image Psychology*. Prentice Hall, 1964.

Mandino, Og. *A Better Way to Live*. Bantam Books, 1990.

Mazlow, Abraham H. *Toward a Psychology of Being*. Van Nostrand Reinhold, 1968.

McCall, Nathan. *Makes Me Wanna Holler*. Random House, 1994.

McQuade, Walter & Ann Aikman. *Stress*. Bantam, 1974.

Merrill, A. Roger. *Connections: Quadrant II Time Management*. Publishers Press, 1987.

Metcalf, C. W. & Roma Felible. *Lighten Up*. Addison Wesley, 1992.

Moore, Thomas. *Care of the Soul*. HarperCollins, 1992.

Ornstein, Robert. *Multimind*. Houghton Mifflin, 1986.

Ostrander, Sheila & Lynn Schroeder. *Superlearning*. Dell, 1979.

Peck, M. Scott, M.D. *A Different Drum*. Simon and Schuster, 1987.

———. *Further Along the Road Less Traveled*. Simon and Schuster, 1993.

★ ———. *The Road Less Traveled*. Simon and Schuster, 1978.

Postman, Neil & Charles Weingartner. *Teaching as a Subversive Activity*. Dell, 1969.

Progroff, Ira. *At a Journal Workshop*. Dialogue House Library, 1975.

Restak, Richard, M.D. *The Mind*. Bantam Books, 1988.

Riley, Pat. *The Winner Within*. G.P. Putnam's Sons, 1993.

Ringer, Robert J. *Million Dollar Habits*. Wynwood Press, 1990.

Robbins, Anthony. *Awaken the Giant Within*. Simon and Schuster, 1991.

Rogers, Carl. *Freedom to Learn*. Charles E. Merrill, 1969.

———. *On Becoming a Person*. Houghton Mifflin, 1969.

★ Satir, Virginia. *The New Peoplemaking*. Science and Behavior Books, 1988.

Schutz, Will. *Profound Simplicity*. Bantam Books, 1979.

★ Seligman, Martin. *Learned Optimism*. Alfred A. Knopf, 1991.

———. *What You Can Change & What You Can't*. Alfred A. Knopf, 1994.

Sher, Barbara & Annie Gottleib. *Wishcraft: How to Get What You Really Want*. Ballantine, 1986.

Siegel, Bernie S., M.D. *How to Live Between Office Visits*. HarperCollins, 1993.

———. *Love, Medicine & Miracles*. Harper and Row, 1986.

Silva, Jose & Philip Miele. *The Silva Mind Control Method*. Simon & Schuster, 1977.

★ Smith, Hyrum W. *The 10 Natural Laws of Successful Time and Life Management*. Warner Books, 1994.

★ Steiner, Claude M. *Scripts People Live*. Bantam Books, 1974.

Stone, Hal & Sidra Stone. *Embracing Your Inner Critic*. HarperCollins, 1993.

Tannen, Deborah. *You Just Don't Understand*. Ballantine, 1990.

vonOech, Roger. *A Whack on the Side of the Head*. Warner Books, 1983.

Waitley, Denis. *Seeds of Greatness*. Pocket Books, 1983.

———. *Psychology of Winning*. Nightingale-Conant, 1988.

Young, Jeffrey E. & Janet S. Klosko. *Reinventing Your Life*. Dutton, 1993.

Zilbergeld, Bernie and Arnold A. Lazarus. *Mind Power*. Ballantine Books, 1987.

★ HIGHLY RECOMMENDED

Index